D1469138

IN THE FOOTSTEPS
OF THE MASTERS

Desmond M. Tutu
and Abel T. Muzorewa

Dickson A. Mungazi

PRAEGER

Westport, Connecticut
London

Library of Congress Cataloging-in-Publication Data

Mungazi, Dickson A.
    In the footsteps of the masters : Desmond M. Tutu and Abel T. Muzorewa / Dickson
A. Mungazi.
        p. cm.
    Includes bibliographical references and index.
    ISBN 0–275–96680–1 (alk. paper)
    1. Tutu, Desmond, 1931– . 2. Church and state—South Africa—History—20th
century. 3. South Africa—Politics and government—20th century. 4. Muzorewa,
Abel Tendekayi, 1925– . 5. Church and state—Zimbabwe—History—20th century.
6. Zimbabwe—Politics and government—20th century. I. Title.
BR1450.M85 2000
968'.0009'9—dc21   99–043106

British Library Cataloguing in Publication Data is available.

Library of Congress Catalog Card Number: 99–043106
ISBN: 0–275–96680–1

First published in 2000

Praeger Publishers, 88 Post Road West, Westport, CT 06881
An imprint of Greenwood Publishing Group, Inc.
www.praeger.com

Printed in the United States of America

The paper used in this book complies with the
Permanent Paper Standard issued by the National
Information Standards Organization (Z39.48–1984).

10 9 8 7 6 5 4 3 2 1

*To the memory of Bishop E. Trevor Huddleston and
to Bishop Ralph E. Dodge, two religious leaders whose dedication
to the development of Africans extended far beyond the ordinary.*

Until Blacks assert their humanity and their personhood, there is not the remotest chance for reconciliation in South Africa. True reconciliation can only happen between persons who assert their own personhood and those who acknowledge and respect that of others.

—Desmond M. Tutu, 1982

I am sorry to think that at the very time when scientists and theologians are coming to a common understanding of the basic nature of man, the rulers of Rhodesia are still believers in the false doctrine of racial superiority and inferiority.

—Abel T. Muzorewa, 1978

Contents

Illustrations

MAPS

PHOTOS *(photo essay follows p. 107)*

Preface

THE PURPOSE OF THE STUDY

In 1964, African political leaders in South Africa and Zimbabwe began to exert concerted efforts to end the colonial conditions that Ian D. Smith and Hendrik F. Verwoerd represented. In Zimbabwe such men as Ndabaningi Sithole, Joshua Nkomo, and Robert Mugabe exercised political leadership in spearheading African struggle for the transformation of Zimbabwe. In South Africa Nelson Mandela, Walter Sisulu, Oliver Tambo, Tabo Mbeki, and Govan Mbeki played a major role in its transformation. That Smith and Verwoerd tried to maintain white minority governments suggests the conclusion that as each man took office, Smith in 1964 and Verwoerd in 1958, he was not aware that the days of colonial rule were numbered. In South Africa there were three other political leaders after Verwoerd: John B. Vorster, Pieter W. Botha, and Frederik W. de Klerk. In Zimbabwe Smith was the last colonial leader.

The purpose of this study is to discuss the roles that Bishop Desmond M. Tutu and Bishop Abel. T. Muzorewa played in the transformation of South Africa and Zimbabwe, respectively. In taking this initiative the study furnishes evidence to substantiate the following conclusions: As religious leaders Tutu and Muzorewa felt called upon to sustain the legacies established by Bishop Trevor Huddleston in South Africa from 1943 to 1956 and Bishop Ralph E. Dodge in Zimbabwe from 1956 to 1964. As soon as Muzorewa was elected bishop of the United Methodist Church in August 1968 and as soon as Tutu was elected bishop of the Anglican

Church in May 1986, conditions demanded each man to initiate a fundamental transformation of their respective countries from the colonial status they had endured from the 19th century. Both men saw the need to involve Africans in the political process as a matter of absolute necessity to ensure a better future for all. In carrying out their crusades, both men were influenced by the work of their predecessors. These two men were, therefore, following the footsteps of the masters, Father Huddleston (later Bishop) in South Africa and Bishop Dodge in Zimbabwe. In March 1979 Ian D. Smith, then leader of the Rhodesia Front government that ruled Zimbabwe, was forced to relinquish political power by forces that he could not control and Muzorewa succeeded him as interim prime minister. In April 1994 Frederik W. de Klerk was also forced to do the same in South Africa and was succeeded by Nelson Mandela.

The irony of the political behavior of Smith and de Klerk is that Muzorewa, the man Smith kept under house arrest for five years, succeeded him for six months in 1979 pending elections in 1980. In South Africa Nelson Mandela, the man the system of apartheid sent to political prison for 27 years, succeeded de Klerk in April 1994. In this manner the last vestiges of colonialism in Africa were therefore eliminated and the transformation of southern Africa became complete. In playing his role Tutu, unlike Muzorewa, did not seek political office. There is another critical factor that influenced Tutu and Muzorewa to be involved in seeking the transformation of their respective countries. In both countries African political leaders were in prison for extended periods of time. As religious leaders both men enjoyed limited freedom of thought and action that enabled them to do what they felt they had to do in the national political arena.

QUESTIONS TO BE ANSWERED

In presenting the evidence to substantiate the conclusions reached in this study, efforts are made to answer the following questions: What conditions prevailed in South Africa and Zimbabwe at the time to form elements of a situation that Tutu and Muzorewa concluded were important for them to be involved in? In both countries, who are individuals who laid the foundations of action that formed the basis of those of Tutu and Muzorewa? What were the circumstances that compelled Smith and de Klerk to behave in the way they did as leaders of Zimbabwe and South Africa, respectively? What objectives did Tutu and Muzorewa set for Africans in their struggles for the transformation of both countries? What problems did Tutu and Muzorewa encounter in their efforts to seek that? What have these African governments done to resolve these problems?

THE EVIDENCE PRESENTED

The focus of the study is to show evidence that Tutu and Muzorewa, as religious leaders in their respective countries, rose to the occasion to provide leadership that was needed to initiate the process of the transformation of South Africa and Zimbabawe. At the time that these two religious leaders played their leadership roles, African nationalist leaders were in political prison. In presenting this evidence, the study shows that both men were subjected to considerable harassment from the existing governments of their countries. But their determination and that of the two last colonial leaders they confronted created an environment that produced inevitable conflict. As elsewhere in southern Africa, such as in Mozambique and Angola, Africans could not be persuaded to give up their struggle for fundamental change in their countries.

The determination that Tutu and Muzorewa implanted in Africans in seeking the end of the colonial conditions translated into a new level of confidence in identifying new goals and objectives. This confidence could not emerge from the climate of colonial conditions that inhibited both their aspirations and determination. The evidence used to substantiate the conclusions reached in the study was obtained during several research trips to South Africa and Zimbabwe from 1994 to 1998. This evidence consists of original materials and documents that the author was able to secure from the National Archives of Zimbabwe and from the South African embassy in Los Angeles, as well as the Library of Parliament in Cape Town. The author was also privileged to have interviews with various individuals in both countries.

CONCLUSIONS AND IMPLICATIONS

This study reaches the following conclusions: The thrust for the transformation of South Africa and Zimbabwe was undertaken by the Africans themselves, because they understood the negative impact of colonial conditions that inhibited their ability to make progress and that they could no longer allow to continue. Both Tutu and Muzorewa played decisive roles in this development. These conditions included the denial of equal participation in the political process and economic opportunity. By the very nature of their roles in seeking the transformation of Zimbabwe and South Africa, Tutu and Muzorewa were left with no choice but to confront the two men who represented the colonial establishment, Smith and de Klerk, who were unable to recognize the imperative nature of change that had taken place all over the world.

The roles that Tutu and Muzorewa played in the transformation of South Africa and Zimbabwe demanded nothing less than a national endeavor to create the climate needed to develop a new society. Once this transformation became a new reality, the new African majority governments were faced with new challenges to national development. The need for educational reform, the trust for economic development, efforts to maintain democratic principles, protection of the environment in the wake of population explosion, and solving problems of ethnic conflict are among those challenges. The new African governments in southern Africa have to recognize that educational reform must combine with social, economic, and political factors to create essential elements of the thrust for national development. South Africa and Zimbabwe, like other countries of southern Africa, are experiencing enormous economic and political problems that can be resolved by introducing change in the political systems based on educational reform.

The reality that South Africa and Zimbabwe have not been able to face is that failure to initiate successful educational reform translates into failure to initiate successful national developmental programs. In this kind of environment, the nations of southern Africa continue to endure the scourge of conflict and the agony of underdevelopment. The efforts that Tutu and Muzorewa made in seeking a transformation of their countries' Africans demonstrated among Africans of that time a new sense of self. In turn Africans must make similar efforts to ensure the development of their countries. The change of government from colonial dictatorships to African dictatorships in some countries of Africa is a development that both South Africa and Zimbabwe must avoid at all costs. The manipulation of elections, the lack of proper constitutional framework of government, corruption by government officials, and intolerance of different view points on national issues all combine to create the psychology of the colonial systems of government that Smith and de Klerk represented. Any government would continue to do this at its own peril. This is the lesson for South Africa and Zimbabwe today.

Acknowledgments

In the process of conducting a study that discusses the political action of two religious leaders of two countries in a highly accurate manner and logical fashion, in a critical region, one needs to exercise great care in obtaining materials that enable one to interpret the events and the actions they took to shape the developments of which they were part. It is for this reason that the author wishes to express his profound gratitude and appreciation to the South African Embassy and Information Office in Los Angeles for allowing him access to important materials on Bishop Desmond M. Tutu and the events of which he was part during the time Africans were struggling for independence. He also wishes to thank the National Archives of Zimbabwe and the Information Office for access to some important materials they hold on Bishop Abel T. Muzorewa, Ian D. Smith, and the Rhodesia Front (RF) government that Smith led from 1964 to 1979. From these materials the author obtained useful insights into the role that Bishop Muzorewa and Bishop Tutu played in the transformation of Zimbabwe and South Africa during the leadership of Ian D. Smith and Frederick W. de Klerk, respectively.

The author would also like to record his gratitude to Ian Smith, Bishop Abel Muzorewa, and Rev. Ndabaningi Sithole, founding member of the African National Council and former vice-president of ZANU, for granting him interviews in 1983 from which he obtained sharpened insights about the impact of the RF's policy. The author is also indebted to many other individuals who participated in the interviews in Zimbabwe in 1983, 1989, and 1997, but fully understands their reluctance to be identified. However, a partial listing of these individuals is made in the bibliography.

The author particularly wishes to express his appreciation to the Zimbabwe Ministry of Education and Culture for allowing him access to the original documents and materials he needed as part of the data he required to produce the study. He also wishes to thank Betty Russell and George Howington, computer specialists in the Center for Excellence in Education at Northern Arizona University, for their assistance in programming the computer so that the manuscript could be produced more efficiently. In a similar fashion, he wishes to thank the faculty at Northern Arizona University for support and encouragement. The author wishes to thank the members of the National Social Science Association for criticism of parts of the manuscript given while he was presenting papers at national conferences. The author particularly wishes to thank Bishop Trevor Huddleston and his secretary, Mrs. Jill Thompson, and Bishop Ralph E. Dodge, for furnishing him the materials he requested. Finally, the author wishes to extend his special appreciation to Charlene Wingo, his secretary, for helping type parts of the manuscript; to Linda Gregonis, indexer and proofreader; and to Katie Chase, copyeditor and project coordinator.

Introduction

TUTU AND MUZOREWA IN HISTORICAL PERSPECTIVE

At 8:10 a.m. on a very cold day on December 12, 1997, a taxicab pulled in the driveway of the author's home on North Beaver Street, Flagstaff, Arizona, and the author quickly jumped into the backseat for a 15–minute ride to Northern Arizona University. The previous evening the author had called the cab company to ask to pick him up exactly at 7:45 a.m. because his own car was under repair in a local repair shop. The cab was therefore 25 minutes late. Sensing the frustration that the author was going through due to the delay, the driver tried something to ease that frustration. He apologized profusely for coming late, saying, among other things, that the dispatcher had asked him to pick up and deliver one passenger before he picked up the author.

As the cab pulled away the driver began to make disjointed statements and asked disconnected questions in a manner that did not allow the author to respond. He noted that the author spoke with a distinctive British African accent, and wanted to know if he was originally from Britain or Africa and how long he had been teaching at Northern Arizona University, and where he was educated. Finally the driver wanted to know if the author knew Dr. Dickson A. Mungazi, who, he said, was a prominent Regents Professor and author of quite a number of books on Africa and the United States. He added that these books had aroused his interest in Africa and that his favorites were *The Mind of Black Africa*

(1996) and *Gathering Under the Mango Tree: Values in Traditional Culture in Africa* (1996).

The cab driver wanted to know if the author ever had an opportunity to read these books. He expressed a wish to meet the author of these books soon so he could learn from him more about Bishop Desmond Tutu. The driver then concluded, "Dr. Mungazi has appeared on local TV and radio to explain some of the problems in Africa." The driver concluded, "If Dr. Mungazi has written a number of books on Africa, then he certainly must know something about Bishop Tutu. I worry about Bishop Tutu because I think that he is a leftist. I hope that our Secretary of State, Madeleine Albright, who is visiting South Africa right now, will help Bishop Tutu see the error of his political philosophy. I know that he was appointed by President Nelson Mandela to chair a commission to investigate past abuses by the previous government, but who knows for what purpose? Under Bishop Tutu that investigation can easily turn into a witch hunt. That is my fear."

At that moment the cab pulled in front of the building where the author was going, and he pulled from his pocket the $4.00 the meter showed for the ride and gave it to the driver with a gratuity of $1.00. The driver was quite thankful, but unfortunately, he did not have an opportunity to learn the identity of his passenger before he pulled away. He must have been thinking about his next passanger and so did not have time to reflect on the implications of what he had just said, that he feared that Bishop Tutu was a leftist.

As the author walked to his office he began to wonder if this negative impression of Bishop Tutu was as widespread a phenomenon in the United States as the cab driver seemed to indicate. He began to recall that in 1986, during a tour of the United States to explain why apartheid was wrong, Bishop Tutu received some negative response from some American audiences to his message. Following Bishop Tutu's appearance on the *Donahue Show* on January 7, 1986, Rev. Jerry Falwell, for example, used quite strong language to offer a negative portrait of Bishop Tutu. The reader has an opportunity to form his own opinion by reading this book.

The book also discusses some individuals who provided political leadership in both colonial Zimbabwe beginning in 1925, the year Muzorewa was born, and in South Africa beginning in 1931, the year Tutu was born. It is the legacy of the leadership of Bishops Ralph Dodge and Trevor Huddleston that both Tutu and Muzorewa felt called upon to uphold as a matter of religious and social principle. In doing so both men seemed to put the interests of the dispossessed Africans ahead of their own interests. Both men recognized that the conditions under which they served were totally different from those under which Dodge and Huddleston served.

The title of this study indicates the critical nature of the understanding that both Tutu and Muzorewa exercised in launching their crusade for the political transformation of South Africa and Zimbabwe. They were following the footsteps of two great masters. The approach in this study does not suggest that Tutu and Muzorewa were the only religious leaders to launch such a crusade, because there were, indeed, many other religious leaders in both countries who played critical roles in bringing about political change in both countries.

In Zimbabwe there were such people as Father Richard Randolph and Bishop Donal R. Lamont, both of the Catholic Church; and Bishop Kenneth Skelton and the Right Rev. Paul Burrough, both of the Anglican Church. These leaders fought against the infamous Land Tenure Act of 1969 because they felt it was an affront on human dignity, just as religious leaders felt they had to do in seeking an end to apartheid in South Africa. In South Africa Rev. Allan Boesak and Rev. C. Beyers Naude, both of the Dutch Reformed Church, joined Tutu in fighting against apartheid for the same reason that religious leaders in Zimbabwe fought against the Land Tenure Act. The Land Tenure Act and various laws passed under the Rhodesia Front fully entrenched apartheid as it was applied in South Africa. The Rhodesia Front called it "seperate development" to conceal its real intent. Over the years the intent and effect of the laws passed in both countries were identical. That intent was to reduce Africans to the status of mere existence. Tutu and Muzorewa felt that their religious principles and convictions would not allow them to remain silent in the face of this great threat to the future of Africans.

HUDDLESTON AND DODGE: THE LEGACY OF THE MASTERS

The central argument of this study is that as successors to Bishops Huddleston and Dodge, Tutu and Muzorewa found themselves in unique positions that compelled them to do what they felt they had to do to remain faithful, loyal, and true to the religious traditions they found in place and which had been part of their own lives and leaders of their respective church organizations. It is not possible to discuss the roles that Tutu and Muzorewa played without discussing the work of their predecessors. Both Huddleston and Dodge were giants in the cause of defining, fighting for, and defending the sovereignty of the human being as the ultimate manifestation of creation. Their dedication to the development of Africans extended far beyond the ordinary. They believed in the biblical definition of the human being as created in the image of God Himself.

Therefore, Dodge and Huddleston concluded that all people, regardless of their station in life, have dignity and grace that cannot be debased by any form of human action. One has only to read Dodge's *The Unpopular Missionary* (1964) and Huddleston's *Naught for Your Comfort* (1956) to understand and appreciate their commitments to their causes. Given the conditions that were created by the colonial systems, it is easy to see why Huddleston and Dodge committed themselves to this course of action and this kind of service. It is not surprising that both Tutu and Muzorewa also became authors themselves. Muzorewa's autobiography, *Rise Up and Walk* (1978), and Tutu's several books, especially *The Rainbow People of God* (1995), testify to their own commitments to the legacies they had inherited from the two masters whose work was inspirational to their own endeavors. Therefore, in a sense, to discuss the efforts that Tutu and Muzorewa made to bring about the transformation of South Africa and Zimbabwe is to discuss in retrospect the efforts that Huddleston and Dodge made.

Born in Bedford, Britain, on June 15, 1913, E. Trevor Huddleston was educated at Lancing College and Christ Church, Oxford, from which he received his B.A. degree in 1934. He then attended Wells Theological College and became a priest in 1937. In 1939 he joined the Community of Resurrection, a monastic community within the Church of England. In 1941 he took the vows of poverty, chastity, and obedience, three theological tenets that were destined to determine his future.

In 1943 Huddleston was sent to be in charge of the Community of Resurrection in Sophiatown, South Africa. Immediately he became active in the struggle against apartheid. In doing so he formed close relationships with African leaders who included Oliver Tambo, Walter Sesule, and Nelson Mandela. It was not surprising that having remained an active opponent of apartheid all these years, Huddleston was present at the inauguration of Nelson Mandela as the first African president of South Africa on May 10, 1994. Such is the character of a master whose footsteps Tutu felt challenged to follow. Was he equal to it? When he died on April 20, 1998, Bishop Huddleston had been recognized across the world as an unassailable crusader of human dignity. This author mourns the passing of a truly great man who saw God in his service to his fellow human beings, a man who operated by a set of principles that reflected a true meaning of the human being as a child of God, a constant reference that Bishop Tutu used in his crusade against apartheid.

In the same way Bishop Ralph E. Dodge's background and work had a tremendous impact on Bishop Abel Muzorewa's future and the challenge he accepted as leader of the Methodist Church in 1968. Born in Terrel, Iowa, in January 1907, Dodge grew up under the stress of poverty and hard work. In 1931 he graduated from Taylor University with a B.A degree. He then enrolled at Boston University from which he received an M.A. in 1933 and an S.T.B. in 1934. Soon after completing his theological studies from Boston University, Dodge married his college classmate, Eunice Elvira Davis. He enrolled in a Ph.D. program in the Kennedy School of Missions of the Hartford Seminary Foundation receiving his degree in May 1943. In 1936 Dodge's interest in Africa took him and his young family to Angola, a country that was slowly dying because of the policy that the Portuguese colonial government was pursuing.

There Antonio Salazar was implementing the policy of *Estado Novo* in a manner that was systematically subjecting Africans to conditions that were far less than human. Like Huddleston later on, Dodge came face to face with the hard realties that he felt had to be confronted if Africans were to have a future different from the past. When he was elected bishop in 1956, Dodge immediately moved his administrative headquarters to Harare (then called Salisbury) in colonial Zimbabwe. There the drama of conflict between church and state was set in powerful tones and unprecedented ways.

On March 11, 1999, as the author was putting finishing touches to the revision of this study, he reached Bishop Dodge on the phone in his home in Florida and asked him for his thoughts about those days. He was as excited about Africa as he was in 1934. At the age of 92 his voice was as clear as the author has known it over the years. His enthusiasm about the future of Africa was not diminished in any way. His perception of what Africa can become was as sharp as ever. This is a distinguished characteristic of a real master, a visionary in a true sense of the word. Such individuals are rare in a world of doubt, conflict, and confusion. Indeed, the author also pays tribute to this unique religious leader, a gallant soldier who has lifted high the banner calling for human justice. Here are two men who have left legacies that are difficult to match.

One reaches two conclusions about the legacies that Huddleston and Dodge left for Tutu and Muzorewa. The first conclusion is that anyone who tries to follow in the footsteps of a master must be prepared to accept risks and possible failure. St. Peter and Sancho Panza, for example, readily acknowledged this reality. The second conclusion is that Huddleston and Dodge arrived in South Africa and Zimbabwe, respectively, in the same way that Sir Lancelot arrived at Camelot, to study and re-create it. These two men were no ordinary human beings. Their missions and accomplishments could be defined only by the very essence of their beings, which were solidly founded on Christian principles that were part of their own lives. How else could they see society other than from a perspective of Christian principles?

TUTU AND MUZOREWA IN COMPARATIVE PERSPECTIVE

There are striking differences and similarities that one sees in discussing the roles that Tutu and Muzorewa played in the political transformation of South Africa and Zimbabwe in response to the political behavior of John Vorster, Pieter W. Botha, and F. W. de Klerk in South Africa and of Godfrey Huggins, Edgar Whitehead, and Ian Smith in Zimbabwe. Both Tutu and Muzorewa were baptized in the Methodist Church. But when one of Tutu's family members attended an Anglican school, the entire Tutu family converted to the Anglican Church. Tutu himself soon found that the shift from the Methodist Church was not a question of merely seeking a better opportunity for education for members of his family, but one of belief and faith. At the age of 13 he would come under the influence of Father E. Trevor Huddleston, who would help shape his future and work.

Therefore, to discuss Tutu's and Muzorewa's roles in the political transformation of South Africa and Zimbabwe is also to discuss the two white leaders they confronted, de Klerk and Smith. Muzorewa was raised by Methodist parents. His father had an ambition for all his children to go to school and become Christians. When the stress of circumstances forced him, he went to South Africa in search of better opportunity to earn income to support his children. Muzorewa learned from his father the importance of hard work and commitment in search of a better life for himself and his family. The conditions that caused the Second World War also created in him a determination to overcome adversity. At that time Europeans had very low opinions of Africans, using them to advance their own economic, political, and social interests.

Smith and de Klerk inherited the 19th-century belief among colonial officials that the only function Africans could fulfill in society was to serve as laborers. Smith was born in 1919, grew up in Zimbabwe, and has lived there all his life within this inhibiting environment. Early in his life he accepted Africans only as a source of cheap labor. For someone who came to know Africans all his life, Smith should have exercised a proper leadership role in developing a positive attitude toward them. Unfortunately he was unable to overcome the prejudice that had been part of his upbringing.

This failure created major problems for both Smith and the settlers who saw him as their leader. Muzorewa's father wanted something better for his children. As a result he developed a positive relationship between his sense of self and his aspiration for better life for the future. He was not going to allow the notion of servant-master relationships, so common among Europeans of that time, to control his ambition. By the time Smith was elected to the colonial parliament in Zimbabwe in 1946, he was fully convinced that Africans were inferior.

For Smith there was nothing to suggest that they could overcome the genetic inferiority, to which he believed nature sentenced them, to become more fully human. This is a philosophy that church leaders rejected without reservation. Smith's heroes were Cecil John Rhodes, Leander

Starr Jameson, John Milton, Godfrey Huggins, and Roy Welensky. All these men were known for their negative views of Africans. It was not possible to expect Smith to adopt an attitude different from what they did.

That all these men held extremely low opinions of the Africans was an outcome of Victorian practice. Smith adopted their attitude, just as Muzorewa adopted the attitude of previous Methodist bishops that included Joseph C. Hartzell, Eben S. Johnson, John M. Springer, Newell S. Booth, and Ralph E. Dodge. Smith believed that if earlier colonial leaders were able to control Africans, he, too, would be able to do so. He would be disappointed. As a fighter pilot in the British Royal Air Force in the Second World War, Smith learned the cruelty of war and gained an ability to survive under hostile conditions.

For years following the end of the war in 1945, Smith was an active member of the Dominion Party, which rapidly adopted a hostile and negative attitude toward Africans, especially during the Federation of Rhodesia and Nyasaland from 1953 to 1963. As soon as he assumed the office of prime minister in April 1964, Smith came face to face with the intelligence of Africans. He and Abel Muzorewa would cross paths many times in their respective efforts to shape the kind of Zimbabwe they believed should emerge as a result of human intelligence and action.

At the end of the war in 1945, the Liberal Party, which was led by Roy Stockil, adopted a set of policies that were compatible with those of the British Labour Party, led at that time by Clement Attlee. During the ill-fated Federation of Rhodesia and Nyasaland, Smith appeared to support the policy of the ruling United Federal Party led by Godfrey Huggins. But he became disillusioned with the policy of partnership between Africans and whites, even though Huggins defined that policy as the kind of relationship that exists between the horse (the Africans) and the rider (the whites). Smith then became active in supporting the Dominion Party and took advantage of the membership of Isaac Samuriwo, a conservative African, to claim that Africans supported the policy of the Dominion Party.

As soon as Smith assumed the office of prime minister, he led colonial Zimbabwe into one of the most bitter conflicts in Africa, resulting in his own political demise, the end of the colonial government that he represented, and the beginning of the African government that he had pledged would never come in his lifetime. Smith had no choice but to accept Muzorewa as interim prime minister of a country he promised would always remain under white control. Muzorewa was brought into the political arena by events of the time. Most African political leaders were in prison. In 1971, Smith, after trying in 1966 and 1968 to reach agreement with Britain, made one final attempt to have his own way prevail. Africans, believing that Smith was likely to get away with it, invited Bishop Muzorewa to spearhead opposition to the terms of the agreement that Smith had reached with the British government. Indeed, feeling a sense of duty and obligation to his people, Muzorewa rose to the occasion to provide the leadership that was needed to give Africans a sense of hope for the future. In 1972 the British government announced that the people of Zimbabwe as a whole had rejected the terms of the agreement. Muzorewa became an instant national figure, changing the political landscape of Zimbabwe permanently.

In South Africa similar events were taking place. F. W. de Klerk was born in Johannesburg in March 1936 into a prominent Afrikaner political family. His father, Jon "Oom" de Klerk, thoroughly groomed his son in the dynamics of politics, especially remembering to keep Africans in their proper place. For the entire period of white rule in South Africa, beginning with Jan van Riebeeck in 1652 to the end of F. W. de Klerk's term of office in April 1994, the major focus of politics was race relationships. Jon de Klerk served in several cabinet positions, including that of minister of education, the same cabinet position that Frederik held in the administration of Pieter W. Botha beginning in 1978. His uncle, J. G. Strijdom, served as prime minister of South Africa from 1952 until his sudden death in 1958. De Klerk's older brother, Willem, served as editor of *Die Burge*, the influential Afrikaans daily newspaper based in Johannesburg.

Neither Smith nor de Klerk considered Africans a threat to their power until it was too late. Both Tutu and Muzorewa were thoroughly groomed in the various aspects of a new theology, based on the teaching of their faiths, that the church was there to serve the needs of human beings in all aspects of life: religious, spiritual, social, political, and economic. The concept of separation between church and state, a cardinal principle of political operation in some Western nations, such as the United States, did not exist in the Third World, including Africa. There, theology of liberation was far more inclusive to mean liberation from spiritual deficit, economic want, and political oppression. The leaders of the church in general were expected to demonstrate ability to meet all these needs because the human being manifested dimensions that made him complete. Both Huddleston and Dodge fully embraced these dimensions of theology of liberation.

In South Africa, theology of liberation had as profound application as it had in Zimbabwe. As soon as he assumed the office of prime minister to succeed Hendrik F. Verwoerd who was assassinated in 1966, John Vorster, a hard-core Afrikaner, came face to face with a rising star in the struggle for justice, Desmond M. Tutu. Tutu received his master's degree in theology from King's College in Britain in that year. At first Vorster refused to take Tutu seriously simply because he was African, and an African was not supposed to suggest to a white man in position of power that he was pursuing a wrong policy. In May 1976 Tutu wrote a letter to Vorster warning him that unless his administration changed the policy he was pursuing in African education, there was bound to be trouble very soon.

Vorster ignored the warning at his own peril. A few weeks later Soweto exploded in a sound that was heard around the world, raising the ire of the international community about the policy of apartheid. Tutu became an instant national and international figure, just as Muzorewa had become through his opposition to the terms of the agreement between Smith and Britain on independence.

Both Smith and de Klerk felt that the destiny of their respective countries rested on their shoulders. So did Tutu and Muzorewa. Smith operated by the view he inherited from his predecessors that it would take Africans at least a thousand years to acquire the elements of European civilization he believed they needed to make a transition from their primitive culture. De Klerk did not set a time limit, but he believed that Africans were incapable of running a government by democratic means.

Tutu and Muzorewa were there to prove them wrong. But as soon as he assumed the office of president, de Klerk encountered the "Damascus Road" experience (a political conversion), which helped him see himself, his country, and Africans in an entirely different manner from what he did in the past. This Damascus Road experience came partly from Tutu's initiative. Muzorewa would have no such luck with Smith, not becacuse he was not as good a political preacher as Tutu, but because Smith was too much of an agnostic. Within a relatively short period of time, de Klerk became the St. Paul of South Africa, preaching the gospel of social justice and equality as the only means to future security of the Afrikaners. This was the message that Tutu had been preaching since 1966 and was waiting to hear from the Afrikaners themselves.

Both Tutu and Muzorewa recognized that de Klerk and Smith manifested characteristics of political behavior that lay outside ordinary political thought processes. For example, Smith so believed in African inferiority that his political behavior, combined with the policy that his administration designed, led the country to a devastating civil war that resulted in his political fall and the end of the colonial system that he represented. Muzorewa and other African political leaders could not understand his obsession with the inferiority of Africans and the superiority of whites. The war lasted from 1966 to 1979. But Smith, unlike de Klerk, was still angry in December 1979 when Britain concluded a conference convened to work out a constitution that would end the colonial system. De Klerk spared South Africa the agony of the kind of conflict that Zimbabwe experienced under Smith by deciding to negotiate the transfer of power to the African majority.

This decision was implemented by the elections that were held in April

1994 from which Nelson Mandela, the man apartheid considered dangerous and kept in prison for 27 years, emerged the new president. Indeed, de Klerk, unlike Smith, had learned some hard lessons about the determination of Africans to bring the colonial system to an end. Tutu, unlike Muzorewa, accepted de Klerk's gesture of goodwill and even an apology for years of apartheid. Smith would offer no such apology. How was Muzorewa going to deal with problems created by Smith under this environment? This study offers some answers to the question.

TUTU, MUZOREWA, AND NATIONAL DEVELOPMENT

What has been discussed above forms the elements that combine to create a national social climate that brings happiness and security to the citizens. Tutu and Muzorewa argued that national development has its basis in this climate. They concluded that conditions that existed under Smith in Zimbabwe and under the Nationalist Party in South Africa from 1948 to 1990 did not permit Africans to exercise these freedoms. Africans in both countries were faced with a painful choice: to accept the conditions imposed by the colonial systems and deny themselves an opportunity for development, or to struggle for change and face the reprisal of the governments. Recognizing the dangers involved in their decisions and actions, Tutu and Muzorewa were ready to face those dangers. The struggle was on.

Since Ghana gained political independence in 1957, Africans everywhere on the continent were in a restive mood. They were no longer willing to accept political activity that was considered exclusively to belong to whites. But the more the Africans demanded change, the more the colonial officials resisted. This situation created a major conflict between the Africans and the colonial governments. This would suggest to Tutu and Muzorewa that Smith and de Klerk based their political philosophy and behavior on what their predecessors had done. Tutu and Muzorewa accepted the challenge to change this behavior by seeking an end to it.

Tutu's concerted efforts finally led to the release of Nelson Mandela on February 10, 1990, from life imprisonment, sent there following his conviction in 1964 on charges of attempting to overthrow the government of South Africa. The release was a dramatic turn of tragic events that began to unfold with the victory of the Nationalist Party led by Daniel F. Malan in the elections of 1948. Can one define Mandela's release as an element of national development without making an effort to dismantle apartheid? Tutu concluded that the answer is no because apartheid did not allow the components of basic human freedoms to combine and operate in the manner that would translate subsequent events into a thrust for national development. This, then, provides the answer the second question: How did the Africans react to colonial conditions that de Klerk and Smith represented?

Given the conditions arising out of 1964, the year that Smith assumed power and Mandela went to prison, the Africans could no longer accept political domination by the colonial governments. This refusal set the stage for the unprecedented conflict to emerge between the Africans and the colonial governments that Smith and de Klerk represented. The imprisonment of African political leaders in both countries did not kill the spirit of nationalism that began to emerge at the conclusion of the war in 1945. This is exactly what brought Tutu and Muzorewa to the political scenes of their countries.

The enactment of the infamous Bantu Education Act in South Africa in 1953 and the new educational policy Smith introduced in Zimbabwe in 1966 were events that set South Africa and Zimbabwe on deadly national conflicts. Both Tutu and Muzorewa reacted strongly to these legislations. When Malan retired from active politics in 1958, he was succeeded by de Klerk's uncle, J. G. Strijdom. Strijdom was succeeded by Hendrik F. Verwoerd, a man of uncompromising belief in the supremacy of apartheid, the superiority of Afrikaners, and the assumed inferiority of Africans. As the director of Bantu Administration in the Malan government, Verwoerd became the principal architect of apartheid as he systematically formulated new policies from it and then applied them to reduce the Africans to the level of bare existence.

To accomplish this objective, Verwoerd used provisions of the Bantu Education Act to elevate Afrikaners to the pedestal of absolute political supremacy enshrined in their assumed invincibility and infallibility. Under Verwoerd the meaning of political power reached a new level of significance. Neither Tutu nor Muzorewa would accept this line of thinking.

Verwoerd's assassination in 1966 brought John Vorster to the seat of power, from where he directed apartheid and fortified it to new unprecedented heights. The decision of his government to enforce new provisions of the Bantu Education Act created a national climate that led to the explosion that was heard around the world from Soweto in June 1976. The confession made on January 28, 1997, by five former police officers that they killed Steve Biko in September 1977 added a painful episode to the activities of those who were prepared to go to any length to defend apartheid. Facing a barrage of outcries and criticism from the international community, Vorster decided to resign in 1978 on grounds of poor health, rather than face the reality that apartheid was setting South Africa on a course of self-destruction. If he had listened to Tutu's advice then, it is possible that he would have avoided the tragedy that followed. Indeed, apartheid was rolling and roaring with a vengeance. Although it showed cracks in its wall, Vorster felt that he had no choice but to defend it at all cost.

Vorster's successor, Pieter Botha, approached the problems created by apartheid in southern Africa, not just in South Africa, with a new determination to ignore the protest from the international community and to make apartheid the sacred shrine that both Afrikaners and Africans must worship with total supplication. The intensification of the armed struggle, spearheaded by the African National Congress (ANC), along with a series of bomb explosions throughout South Africa, killing many and injuring many more, created a dangerous situation raising questions as to whether Botha was able to defend apartheid in the manner that previous defenders of it had done.

It is not surprising that Tutu's response to de Klerk's call was his own call to initiate change in the political system on the basis of nothing less than dismantling apartheid in order to transform the character of South African society. Tutu advised de Klerk and his fellow Afrikaners to realize that while maintaining a political status quo could not be done forever, it was an equally elusive task to initiate change in the social structure without accepting the challenge of political transformation. This is why he suggested a dialogue between de Klerk and the ANC. Therefore, Tutu saw the immediate challenge to de Klerk as a response to the call to end apartheid in order to change the political system so that a thrust for national development could be made free from efforts to continue to defend it.

ORGANIZATION OF THE STUDY

This study is organized into eight chapters. Chapter 1 presents the legacy that Father Trevor Huddleston left behind in the kind of work he did in South Africa from 1943 to 1956. Huddleston was an uncompromising foe of apartheid. He saw it in the same way that Tutu later did: an evil system that robbed the Africans of their sense of self-pride. Chapter 2 presents the dynamics of Bishop Ralph Dodge's conviction that as long as Africans in Zimbabwe were dominated by colonial conditions educationally, politically, and economically, they would never be able to develop their full potential. He held the view that the church had a responsibility to help bring about the end of the colonial system because it was standing in the way of development for Africans. Chapter 3 examines Tutu, the man and his mission. It presents the elements that formed that mission and the strategy that he designed to carry it out.

In the same way Chapter 4 presents Muzorewa, the man and his mission. The colonization of Zimbabwe, events that influenced his future, and later his involvement in the political transformation of Zimbabwe combine to form the political environment that he needed to define the parameters of that mission. Chapter 5 discusses Tutu's role in the transformation of South Africa, taking into account his vision for South Africa and the problems he encountered in seeking that transformation. Chapter 6 discusses Muzorewa's role in the transformation of Zimbabwe. His involvement in the Geneva Conference of 1976, the internal agreement of 1978, and the elections of 1980 complete his role. Although he was successful in the elections of 1979, Muzorewa lost the elections of 1980 to Robert Mugabe. But for six months he served as interim prime minister when Zimbabwe was at a political crossroads.

Chapter 7 summarizes the main arguments presented in the study, draws some conclusions, and discusses some implications for both South Africa and Zimbabwe following their transformations. As soon as Nelson Mandela was elected in April 1994, he assigned Tutu an entirely new role: as chairman of an important commission to investigate abuses by the Nationalist government. The Truth and Reconciliation Commission was a highly visible exercise intended to discover the extent of that abuse in order to heal the nation. Although Muzorewa and two members of his ANC were elected to a 100-seat Parliament in February 1980, tension between him and Mugabe soon became apparent because of Muzorewa's role in the internal agreement of 1978, which the international community refused to recognize because it excluded other political parties. Now retired from the leadership of the Methodist Church, Muzorewa is still active in the politics of Zimbabwe.

The conclusion (Chapter 8) is reached in this study that just as Tutu and Muzorewa followed the footsteps of the masters, Huddleston and Dodge, in their search for the transformation of South Africa and Zimbabwe, they operated under the principles of democratic behavior. Although both men sometimes utilized methods that were controversial in seeking to achieve their goals, they were motivated by the desire to see their people free from colonial domination. Therefore, South Africa and Zimbabwe cannot afford to betray the thrust that these two men made in seeking the transformation of their respective countries. Zimbabwe has toyed with the prospects of a one-party state, the introduction of which would undercut the very essence of a great society that Dodge tried to create in order to ensure the development of the people. Having witnessed the tragedy of a one-party government in Zaire and Malawi, countries of southern Africa must at all times endeavor to preserve multidemocratic systems of government that some people like Dodge, Huddleston, Tutu, and Muzorewa worked hard to bring about.

CONCLUSION AND IMPLICATIONS

It can be seen that the real tragedy of the conflict that emerged in South Africa and Zimbabwe lay in the inability and unwillingness of the Nationalist and the RF governments to see things from the perspective of conditions of 1966, not those of 1896, when Cecil John Rhodes, Leander Starr Jameson, Earl Grey, and William Milton were at the height of their political powers. These factors include the general political turmoil that characterized political events in Africa following the granting of independence to Ghana in 1957; the breakup of the Federation of Rhodesia and Nyasaland in 1963, with its severe implications for political conflict; the mass arrests and the formulation of the Freedom Charter in South Africa, both in 1955; and the events that led to the unilateral declaration of independence in Zimbabwe in 1965. But when these events combined with what the Africans considered a lack of equal opportunity, the political process itself became a far more important factor than any other issue because it became the ultimate and, thus, the most important, cause of conflict.

When one considers how opportunity was crucial to socioeconomic and political opportunity, one can readily see that the educational process became a major factor that contributed to unhappiness among the Africans. The more the Africans expressed that unhappiness, the more the Nationalist and RF governments suppressed them, and the more these governments suppressed them, the more the Africans resisted them. This is how a major conflict was gathering momentum between the two sides.

Nations of southern Africa must remember that as critically important as they are, national development and independence must be initiated within the environment of fundamental change that must take place in the political system. This means that the political system has to change to embrace the general concept of change itself. The elections held in Namibia in November 1989, to pave way for independence scheduled for March 21, 1990; the change of socioeconomic system in Mozambique announced by President Joaquim Chissano in August 1989; the efforts made toward a negotiated settlement between the warring parties in Angola; and de Klerk's peace overtures toward the ANC and other formerly outlawed political parties—all combine to create a climate of regional peace so desperately needed to place southern Africa on the road to a new society and prosperity.

This task is an enormous undertaking. But it is a task that must be accomplished because while the risk of failure is there, the consequences of not trying are devastating. The relationship between social change and national development are two pillars of stability that the nations of southern Africa need to ensure the success of national programs. For that cooperation to come about, South Africa first had to recognize that apartheid had to go so that a new nonracial society would be created. Smith's and de Klerk's defenses of the systems they inherited must provide lessons for the governments of Africa. This is now the challenge before southern Africa as a region. This study, therefore, is a story not just of two religious leaders, it is a story of the struggle of a people, a story of conflict between religious idealism and political expediency, a conflict between two cultures, between the powerful and the powerless, between what was and what could be, and between African sense of self-worth and colonial definition of it.

Map 1
South Africa

Some Facts about South Africa of Tutu's Time, 1991

Date of colonization	1835
Colonizing nation	Great Britain
Date of independence	May 31, 1910
President of the country	F. W. de Klerk, until 1994 when he was succeeded by Nelson Mandela following first free elections
Area	472,359,000 square miles
Population	39,550,00 million Africans 73.0% Black* 18.0% White* 9.0% Coloreds and Indians*
Annual population growth rate	3.1%
Literacy	99% white 50% Black 60% Coloreds and Indians
Annual expenditure for education	$48.00 for Africans $5.3 million for whites $220,100 for Coloreds and Indians
Leading towns	Cape Town (legislative capital), Pretoria (administrative capital, Bloemfontein (judicial capital), Durban (chief seaport), Johannesburg (industrial center), Port Elizabeth, East London
Leading industries	Textiles, mining (diamonds, gold), agriculture (maize, cotton, coffee, dairy, meat, skins, hides)
Form of government	Dictatorship by a white minority until 1994, when free elections were held for the first time

*These three—Whites, Africans, and Coloreds and Indians—were the racial classifications under the policy of apartheid in South Africa until 1994.

Map 2
Zimbabwe

Some Facts about Zimbabwe of Muzorewa's Time, 1991

Date of colonization	September 1890
Colonizing nation	Great Britain
Date of independence	April 18, 1980
President of the country	Robert G. Mugabe since 1980
Area	150,333 square miles
Population	7.1 million Africans 123,000 whites
Annual population growth rate	3.1%
Literacy	60.0% Africans 99.0% whites
Annual (expenditure for education) (in 1997)	$3.5 million for whites $1.7 million for Africans
Leading towns	Harare (capital), Bulawayo, Mutare, Gweru, Kadoma
Leading industries	Mining, agriculture, textiles
Form of government	Parliamentary democracy since 1980; 100 members elected by districts

17

1

The Role of the Church in South Africa and the Legacy of Trevor Huddleston

> The Church is facing the challenge of the extent which it must meet now and which it cannot meet effectively with official pronouncements alone.
>
> —Father Trevor Huddleston, 1956

CHURCH AND POLITICS IN SOUTH AFRICA

The extraordinary role that Desmond Mpilo Tutu played in the transformation of South Africa is part of a legacy left behind by Bishop E. Trevor Huddleston, an unusual and highly dedicated Anglican priest whose views and role in South Africa were similar to those of Mother Teresa of the Missionary Charities in Calcutta, India, where she dedicated her entire life to serving the poor. Huddleston arrived in South Africa in 1943 at a time when South Africa was going through a period of critical developments that were destined to alter its course for the next 50 years.

On March 26, 1943, *Die Burger*, an Afrikaans newspaper, suggested for the first time that the government of South Africa must develop a racial policy known as apartheid to keep the races apart.[1] On January 25, 1944, Daniel F. Malan, a member of the Nationalist Party, explained that the purpose of the new policy was to ensure the safety of the white race and of Christian civilization by the honest maintenance of the principles of apartheid and guardianship.[2]

This statement, made by a man who had resigned in 1915 as an ordained minister of the Nederduits Gereformeerde Kirk (NGK, a sect of the Dutch Reformed Church) to go into politics, was troubling to Christians who were not members of the three versions of the Dutch Reformed Church. In his political action Malan did not know that he was setting a dangerous precedent for the future of South Africa. Since 1859 the church in general felt that it had a major responsibility to promote the development of all people by its educational programs. It placed its sensitivity on the need to promote political harmony by advocating a position that would enable whites and Africans to see their future in the context of good relationships that developed between them. However, Malan, coming from the constitution of 1908 and the advent of independence in 1910, did not think that such an approach to the development of South Africa was practical, because he shared the view among the Afrikaners that Africans were an inferior race. Throughout its history in Africa the Christian church based its operational principles on its response to the needs of the people as the major focus of its work. However, the three versions of the Dutch Reformed Church based their operational principles on the Calvinist theology of predestination.[3]

In 1859 NGK broke away from the main Dutch Reformed Church because its members could not accept the theology that all people, including Africans, were equal before God. Throughout his life Malan operated by the theological belief that Africans were inferior to whites. NGK then began to develop its own theology to address the question of race. It adopted a new theological perspective on Calvinist theology of predestination to mean that only Africans could not be saved.[4] Malan contributed to this theology until the political crisis that followed independence began to cast a long shadow on NGK's position on race.[5]

The hostility that emerged between the British and the Boers beginning with Napoleon's continental policy in 1789 finally led to the Boer War of 1899. By the time of the end of that war in 1901 it had also generated hostility between members of the Anglican Church and those of the NGK. Members of the two religious organizations saw their roles differently. Those of NGK saw their function as seeking to preserve the position of the Afrikaners as a chosen people. Those of the Anglican Church saw their function as seeking to protect Africans from oppression. As South Africa began to settle down after the end of the Boer War in preparation for independence, the Anglican Church and NGK braced for a new level of conflict caused by serious differences in theology directly related to the political position of Africans. One might say that the Reformation in Europe of the 16th century now resurfaced in South Africa in powerful dimensions.

From its inception in South Africa the Anglican Church made an effort to relate its theology to the needs of all people, both white and African.

When Daniel Malan's administration enacted the Group Areas Act in 1950, Father Trevor Huddleston had been working among the Africans for six years. The new law made it hard for him and the church to discharge their responsibilities to their parishioners. In opposing the new law, Huddleston knew that the Nationalist government regarded his action as part of the British hostility toward Afrikaners. From the beginning of the Nationalist administration led by Malan in 1948, relationships between the Anglican Church and the NGK began to deteriorate rapidly.

Another critical and fundamental cause of conflict between the NGK and the Anglican Church was that Afrikaners promoted their brand of nationalism and political power soon after they won elections in 1948, by introducing the notorious policy of apartheid, which they based on their interpretation of Calvin's theology in order to justify their desire to preserve their political supremacy. The enactment of the Group Areas Act was part of the strategy to achieve that goal. When members of the Anglican Church protested against the human suffering caused by the application of the Group Areas Act, Malan and his Nationalist government regarded the protest as evidence of British anti-Afrikaner hostility.

Leo Marquard suggested that Father Michael Scott and Father Trevor Huddleston could be dismissed "as the modern equivalents of nineteenth century missionaries who blackened the name of the Afrikaner."[6] Marquard concluded that officially those members of NGK who felt that their church was using their own interpretation of Christianity to suit their apartheid policy decided to remain silent, rather than express the opinion that would limit the effectiveness of both government and the church in supporting it.

One must seek to understand the behavior of the Dutch Reformed Church and its role in the politics of South Africa from a broader perspective. When the Second World War broke out in September 1939, it was very difficult to secure Afrikaner chaplains for the armed forces in spite of the fact that 60 percent of the troops were Afrikaners.[7] The reason for this situation is that the Nationalist Party was opposed to the participation in the war by South Africa because its members argued that Germany was acting in self-defense. They saw Adolf Hitler and his Nazi Party as victims of British aggression, especially after Winston S. Churchill succeeded Neville Chamberlain as British prime minister in 1940. To the members of the Anglican Church this conclusion was offensive. How did members of the Dutch Reformed Church explain the holocaust? Many of them argued that the holocaust did not happen in the way many observers said it did. Members of the Dutch Reformed Church argued that the holocaust was the invention of those who were jealous of success that the Third Reich had achieved. Obviously this distortion of the actual facts went a long way in damaging relationships between members of the two church organizations.

When the Bantu Education Act became law in 1953, the Dutch Reformed Council fully endorsed it. But the difference of theology between the Dutch Reformed Church and the Anglican Church became more serious as a political response to a series of laws that began to come into place in 1950. The Dutch Reformed Church took the position that the Nationalist Party was pursuing a correct policy of apartheid. The Anglican Church opposed the policy. Because of this difference of theology, the two church organizations drifted further apart to the point where there was nothing that they would agree on. In time the Nationalist government regarded the Anglican Church as an adversary.[8] The old hostilities that were part of causes of the Boer War began to resurface between the Anglican Church on the one hand and the Dutch Reformed Church and the Nationalist government on the other hand. These hostilities would last until April 1994, when the apartheid government came to an end.

In 1953, having decided that cooperation with other Protestant churches was not possible, the Dutch Reformed Church attempted to restructure itself to reflect the reality that it was the only religious organization to give active support to apartheid. In doing so the Dutch Reformed Church was alienating itself from other religious organizations, not only in South Africa, but also throughout the world. However, at its 22nd annual meeting held in May 1951, the central executive committee of the NGK debated the question of its relations with the Nationalist government. After discussing the issue, the delegates affirmed the right of NGK to express its opinion on political issues, especially its support of apartheid. The council based this resolution on historical interpretation of Calvinist theology.

In response the Anglican Church rejected the Calvinist theology that the Federal Council of NGK used as a basis of its opinion of the government, arguing that any government that does not reflect the principle of equality in the treatment of its people is a dictatorship and that the people have both the right and the duty to replace it. The Anglican Church also rejected the NGK theology that the people cannot expect equal treatment from the government because some people are white, others are black. The Anglican Church took the position that although the government may be sanctioned by God, the form it may assume to discharge its responsibility is actually the work of man himself. Therefore man, not God, must be held accountable for the conduct of the government.[9]

The Anglican Church also took the position that society must not be satisfied with anything that the state does in treating its people differently, because all people are equal children of God. The church concluded that because God does not discriminate His children on any basis, any government that discriminates is not sanctioned by God. Therefore Christians must assume the right to replace a government that is not operating in accordance with the principle of equality. But the Federal Council of NGK rejected this theology, arguing that its application to South Africa would lead to social disintegration. The federation also argued that the greatest problem of trying to apply the principles of social equality to South Africa lay in the ideas of the revolutionary philosophy of Jean-Jacques Rousseau, who argued in his *Social Contract* (1762) that might never made right and that citizens have a duty to obey only legitimate laws made by the powers that the people themselves choose. In presenting its argument, the NGK Federal Council rejected Rousseau's central tenet that society must treat its people equally, and therefore every person is sovereign in the eyes of God.

Rousseau reiterated these views in *Emile* (1872),[10] and went on to argue that the government must at all times become the servant of the people, not the instrument of oppressing them. In this setting the government must derive its authority from the express will of the people. Its members must remember that the people have the right to remove it as soon they are satisfied that it no longer represents their interests. Meeting in Johannesburg in May 1951, the NGK Federal Council concluded that the ideas Rousseau expressed were nothing more than myth. However, all the arguments the NGK rejected are elements that are universally accepted as a basis of good government. Rousseau argued that the power that rulers exercise must originate with the people and that there is no such thing as divine rulers. This is the only point that caused conflict between Rousseau and the Catholic Church of his day. However, he concluded that the only good government is the one that respects democratic principles, and that all people have equal rights to participate in its election so that it governs them well.

The Federal Council also argued that although the Africans did not have the right to vote, they had rights that were protected by the state. Under apartheid it is very hard to see what these rights are. The NGK ignored the fact that people who were denied the right to vote, which is universally associated with citizenship, had nothing else to help them assert their rights as people. The federation also argued that the right to vote must belong only to those who were able to exercise it properly. This is the argument that Ian D. Smith used from 1964 to 1979 to deny the African majority in Zimbabwe their right to vote.[11]

Neither Smith nor the Nationalist government was able to define how one could use the vote properly. However, this argument was not new. Cecil John Rhodes used it in 1896 to deny Africans the right to vote. He was quite blunt in arguing that as to the question of voting his government was saying that Africans were, in a sense, citizens, but not altogether citizens because, he argued, they were still children.[12]

As far as NGK's theology was concerned, the importance of adopting Calvinism lay in what R. H. Townley explained as its purpose, saying it was a creed that sought not merely to purify the individual but also to reconstruct church and state to revive society by penetrating every department of life, public and private, with the influence of religion. He concluded that in the struggle between liberty and authority, Calvinism sacrificed liberty with enthusiasm.[13] This sacrifice included the right to vote for Africans. The Federal Council argued that Calvinist theology of predestination also applied to social and political conditions that included the right to vote. This means the Africans were excluded from the electoral process by the action of divine intervention as a dimension of predestination. Africans could do nothing to ensure their political salvation. God's works would not ensure it. The best they could do was to depend on the grace of the Afrikaners to receive the benefits of civilization as an outcome of the action of a chosen people.

A brief study of the history of NGK shows that it originated from the 17th century mother church in Holland and arrived in South Africa with Jan van Riebeeck in 1652. From that time to 1804, NGK was under the total control of the state in the same way that Henry VIII controlled the Church of England in Britain during the Reformation. In 1843 it was forced to break ties with Holland because the second British occupation of the Cape in 1806 created conditions that demanded adjustment to a new situation. From 1804 to 1843 the NGK made many demands on the state for internal autonomy.[14]

From that period to 1962, NGK went through considerable transformation both in theology and structure. As members of NGK moved from the Cape to the Transvaal, they began to develop a new theology different from the original NGK theology that was part of its operation at the Cape. This is why in 1962 Rev. C. Beyers Naude, a moderator of NGK in the Transvaal, and a group of spirited individuals began to question the original NGK theology of predestination and political philosophy. Naude and his associates founded a monthly publication known as *Pro Veritate*, which published articles in both English and Afrikaans. In 1975 Naude rejected the NGK theology in its entirety and joined other Afrikaners who were increasingly becoming critical of the NGK position on social issues, especially the place of Africans.

Naude took pride in the fact that he was an Afrikaner, born in a deeply religious Afrikaner family whose members were extremely conservative politically. His father had fought in the Boer War on the side of the Boers. Naude pursued his education in the belief that it was his mission to acquire knowledge in order to know how to preserve the position of Afrikaners. Following completion of his studies, Naude spent four years in theological seminary. He served as a member of elite congregations in various parts of South Africa until 1949, when he was called to be chaplain of the Dutch Reformed Church at the University of Pretoria.[15] Here Naude came face to face with the realization that apartheid was wrong, that it was the responsibility of all Christians to rise up to the occasion to demand fundamental change that would bring it to an end because he concluded that it was an affront to human dignity. Naude had a message for Christians all over the world, with special reference to apartheid,

Stretch out your hand and discover those communities, areas and countries where there is suffering, injustice, or a system of oppression. Discover to what degree there are similar patterns of life and suffering being enacted and being experienced in your own country. Don't close your eyes to the injustice of your own country by trying to solve the injustices of another country. That is an evasion of Christian responsibility.[16]

Beginning in 1949, a number of leading Afrikaner theologians seemed to have second thoughts about the evolution of apartheid as the work of God. Professor B. B. Keet of the Theological Seminary at Stellenbosch University and Dr. Benjamin Marais of the Theological Seminary at the University of Pretoria wrote letters to the official Afrikaner church organizations to discuss the shallowness of the argument that apartheid had its basis in the Bible.[17] In 1959 an ecumenical conference was convened in Johannesburg to discuss the church's response to apartheid. The conference adopted a resolution condemning apartheid, putting the NGK in an embarrassing position. The Sharpeville massacre of 1960 invoked a reaction of the World Council of Churches to condemn apartheid in all its aspects. That the NGK refrained from taking similar action put it in a further embarrassing situation, causing some of its members to reexamine their membership in organizations that refused to condemn the violence perpetrated by the state.

However, some hard-core NGK members felt they had a responsibility to defend their church. In order to convey their message they used practices that Joseph R. McCarthy used in 1950 in the United States to generate publicity for his anti-Communist campaign. Among the leaders of this movement was Rev. J. D. Vorster, brother of J. B. Vorster, who was then minister of justice and who served as prime minister of South Africa from 1966 to 1978.

Because Rev. Vorster had connections in high places, he exerted considerable influence on the action that the NGK took in response to the opposition to its support of apartheid. In 1965 Rev. Vorster organized a series of conferences on what he claimed to be the danger of Communism and liberal political views that were being expressed by various elements within the religious organizations of South Africa. Rev. Vorster thought these individuals had lost proper perspective of their role in society and needed to return to original theology to be meaningful in the critical struggle that was soon to come.

The action that Rev. Vorster took to portray opponents of apartheid as agents of the Communist world inspired and invoked the reaction of other church leaders. For example, soon after he was elected archbishop of Cape Town in 1957, Dr. Joost de Blank announced that he would not allow racial discrimination in any church under his charge because the policy of separating people on the basis of race was contrary to the Christian principle of the brotherhood of man and the fatherhood of God.

De Blank was reacting to the Native Laws Amendment Bill that Rev. Vorster fully endorsed, but which was considered to pose a serious threat to the principle of religious freedom by making it illegal for Africans to attend church functions with whites. De Blank's predecessor, Archbishop Clayton, sent a letter only hours before his death to the prime minister, J. G. Strijdom, on behalf of the Anglican bishops, saying that while they recognized the seriousness of disobeying the laws of the land, they felt that they were bound to express their position that they would not obey the law if the proposed bill became law.[18] Instead of generating national support for apartheid, Rev. Vorster succeeded in generating more controversy and even more opposition to apartheid. The fact that he was brother of a very unpopular government official did not help matters at all.

SOPHIATOWN: THE CRUCIBLE OF CONFLICT AND HOPE

In 1947 the Nationalist Party issued a document for the benefit of party members. The document stated that the policy of the party was to encourage total apartheid as the ultimate goal of a natural process policy to promote the welfare of South Africa and the happiness and well-being of its citizens. The document concluded by saying that realizing that such a task could best be accomplished by preserving and safeguarding the white race, the Nationalist Party professed this as the fundamental guiding principle of its policy.[19]

To Huddleston, a young Anglican priest who was trained to embrace a Christian principle that all people are equal before God and in society regardless of their race, station, or role in it, this policy was disturbing. How was he going to discharge his responsibility under conditions that were prohibitive? How should he respond to this challenge to human spirit? When he arrived in South Africa the Nationalist Party manifested a hostile attitude toward Britain because its members believed that Winston Churchill pursued a hostile policy toward Germany.

To understand Huddleston's work one needs to understand the social and political environment in which he worked. Sophiatown was an early mining camp that was founded during the days of gold speculation in the late 19th century. Located four miles west of Johannesburg, the name Sophiatown came from Sophia, the name of the wife of a speculator named Tobiansky, who had bought a stretch of land in the area with the purpose of establishing a residential suburb for white residents. But after pegging out the plots and mapping out the streets Tobiansky ran into trouble with the newly created town council about sewage disposal. Unable to sell more plots to white buyers, Tobianisky decided to sell the rest of the plots to Africans. This was before the Land Act of 1913 made that kind of transaction illegal.[20]

As soon as the Nationalist Party was elected in 1948, it began to apply various forms of the policy of apartheid. Under provisions of the Group Areas Act of 1950, Sophiatown was classified a "black spot" in a white residential area. Sooner or later the Africans would have to move or Sophiatown would have to be demolished. What made Sophiatown unique was the concept of free landhold rights. Although under apartheid the Nationalist government could end these rights at any time, the fact that at the inception of Sophiatown Africans could buy plots and build their own homes means that they had considerable independence to exercise in deciding where they would live.

According to the Nationalist government, that form of independence gave Africans political power as well. Under apartheid this would not be allowed. However, the standard of homes that Africans built in Sophiatown fell below the level of homes in the white suburbs. Therefore, using its own conventional criteria the Nationalist government also classified Sophiatown as a slum. This deprived the residents of rights that were associated with property owners. The Nationalist government also concluded that the streets of Sophiatown were dirty, and that over time the homes acquired the appearance of a shantytown: high-density population, poor sanitary facilities, inadequate garbage disposal arrangements, and poor lighting. The Nationalist government concluded that these inadequacies combined to create conditions that converted Sophiatown into a sprawling ghetto.

There is no question that the Nationalist government was steadily moving in to deliver a fatal blow on Sophiatown. Soon after the Group Areas Act was passed, the Nationalist government decided that Sophiatown would have to go because it was home to both Africans and whites. Although both whites and blacks were allowed to buy plots in Sophiatown, the Nationalist government used provisions of the Urban Areas Act of 1923 to question its existence as a multiracial community. The concept of multiracial residential areas simply did not fit well into the philosophy and structure of apartheid. The Nationalist government decided that South Africa was not going to be an experimental ground for some vague notion about the benefits of multiracial living.

If given the opportunity, Sophiatown would provide a model for the development of a new neighborhood spirit so crucial to national development. The Nationalist government had no opposition to the principle of ownership by white buyers, but it had serious difficulty accepting that concept for African buyers; it was not envisaged in the evolution of the policy of apartheid because it would recognize a measure of authority, independence, and political power for them. When these were exercised they would force change of the country's political system. This is what the Nationalist government feared most in the development that was taking place in Sophiatown. This is why it prohibited Africans from exercising basic elements of human freedom. For these reasons Sophiatown remained on the edge of both development and underdevelopment. Its fate would be determined by the formulation of policy under various forms of apartheid.

Although its uncertain future inhibited the ability of its residents to initiate plans for its development, Sophiatown demonstrated a livelihood unique in South Africa. It inspired a hope that impressed anyone who lived there. This was the place where Alan Paton set his scenes in *Cry, the Beloved Country*, where Kumalo came to look for his son, Absolom. Sophiatown was also the home of Father Trevor Huddleston, the charismatic and legendary priest whom Africans adored and admired beyond the ordinary. As a member among them, Huddleston worked hard to give Africans all over South Africa, not just those in Sophiatown, a new sense of hope under conditions made difficult by the application of apartheid.

Sophiatown was also the place where Desmond M. Tutu grew up and attended church services at the Church of Christ the King located on the hill, and where Father Huddleston was its priest. Alan Paton described both Sophiatown and Huddleston in metaphorical terms, saying that John Kumalo said it with meaning, with cruel and pitiless meaning. Kumalo stood bereft, and the young white man clinched into the car. Kumalo looked to him for guidance, but the young man shrugged his shoulders, saying "Do what you wish, it is not my work to get lawyers. But if you wish to go back to Sophiatown. I shall take you."[21]

There is no question that when Paton described Father Vincent, he had Father Huddleston in mind, saying

It was a pleasant evening at the Mission House. Father Vincent, the rosy-cheeked priest, was there and they talked about the place where Kumalo lived and worked and the white man in his turn spoke about his own country, about the hedges and the fields, and Westminister Abbey, and the great cathedrals up and down the land.[22]

Sophiatown was also the home of playwright Athol Fugard, whose sharpness of mind and perception of social issues made him unique, powerful, and feared by the Nationalist government. It was also the home of a new generation of Africans: urban people uprooted and re-moved from tribal conditions, an emerging working class whose sense of self and future was different from their social and cultural values of the past. Sophiatown was also the home of professional Africans, the homeless, the aspiring politicians, and the destitute.

Sophiatown was home to literary artists, the starting musicians, and the shebeen queens (members of the oldest profession), and of the *tsotsi* (gangsters). They all came to Sophiatown to discover a new world of the diverse group of people who lived there. They all came to Sophiatown to create new conditions of life that had not existed in the past. Indeed Sophiatown was the crucible of conflict and hope. Sophiatown attracted the liberal businessman willing to try new methods of entrepreneurship needed to take risks. It was also a place that attracted conservative African religious leaders who decided to surrender their sense of destiny to the control of the white man.

Before the apartheid policy began in 1948, Sophiatown had attracted some liberal whites who believed that the best way to ensure the future of South Africa was by having whites and Africans live together in the same neighborhoods. If the government had allowed this experiment to continue, it was quite possible that South Africa would have discovered a formula for solution to its growing racial problems. Allister Sparks concluded that by 1955 Sophiatown "was offering a glimpse of what the new industrialized South Africa might become."[23] However, the Nationalist government regarded the experiment that Sophiatown represented in interracial living as a threat to its philosophy of Afrikaner superiority and the epitome of all social evils that the policy of apartheid was designed to solve. It took the Nationalist government 36 years to realize that the policy of apartheid was a recipe for national disaster.

There were other aspects of Sophiatown that made it a unique example of an effort to create crucial conditions that would have led to initiation of national policy and programs to solve the problems of South Africa. As industry in Johannesburg burgeoned, Sophiatown became the home of people who had a vision of a country for the future. Their common belief in the need to eliminate all considerations of race brought its residents together to discuss issues related to problems of development of their community, rather than the rhetoric of the policy of race. For the residents of Sophiatown, race was not an issue, it had no place in their efforts to build a neighborhood that reflected their goals and objectives of trying to have a society embedded in the priceless values of its people. Nelson Mandela describes the hope and the vision that Sophiatown represented:

Several families might all be crowded into a single shanty house. Up to forty people could share a single water tap. Despite the poverty, Sophiatown had a special character. For Africans it was the Left Bank of Paris, the Greenwich Village in New York, the home of writers, artists, doctors, and lawyers. It was home to Dr. Xuma[24] and Berliners and the Americans who adopted the names of American movie stars like John Wayne, Humphrey Bogart. Sophiatown boasted the only swimming pool for African children in Johannesburg.[25]

This situation was part of the crucible of conflict and hope that Sophiatown represented.

The pressure the government was experiencing from its supporters to do something to resolve the anomaly of Sophiatown in order to implement its policy of apartheid compelled Daniel F. Malan and his government to consider the issue seriously. A major question of that consideration was: Could the policy of apartheid be fully implemented while Sophiatown was allowed to develop as a multiracial community? The knowledge among the 60,000 residents of Sophiatown that the government was considering this question inevitably led to loss of confidence in its future. For the next four years, from 1950 to 1954, they were told periodically that they would not be compensated for any building costs or improvement costs of their homes.[26] At the same time they were not informed of when the government might take action against the multiracial character of Sophiatown. The uncertainty led many to neglect their homes. Others tried to sell their homes and move out. Some put up their homes for rent without realizing any financial return. Sophiatown, a community that once gave hope to South Africa as an example of a prosperous society, was dying a slow and painful death caused by the application of a vicious policy of apartheid.

In Chapter 7 of *Naught for Your Comfort*, Huddleston describes how Sophiatown originated and how it could serve as a model to seeking solutions to the problems of race in South Africa. He wrote, "Sophiatown has never become a slum. There are no tenements, there is nothing really old, there are no dark cellars."[27] Huddleston went on to argue that the Nationalist government was undercutting an experiment in human understanding and cooperation, at a time when it needed the support of all segments of the South African community to demonstrate statesmanship in seeking to overcome its overwhelming fear of multiracial cooperation. He concluded that the real problem in South Africa was the government itself. If it would allow Sophiatown to continue, then the entire country would soon find a solution to the problems that the Afrikaners were creating. The best that the government could do was to let Sophiatown be.

Suddenly and without any warning, in 1954, the year that Malan retired and was succeeded by another hard-core Afrikaner, J. G. Strijdom, who served until his unexpected death in 1958, the government sent a team of bulldozers and leveled Sophiatown to the ground. The reason the government used to destroy Sophiatown was that it had deteriorated rapidly to a point where it posed health hazards to the residents. Could anyone really believe that a government that was not interested in the multiracial character of a community could suddenly become interested in their health? The government could not fool anyone. After destroying Sophiatown the government provided trucks to move African residents to a sprawling township known as Soweto, and offered white residents the opportunity to settle in communities surrounding Sophiatown.

The rubble that came from Sophiatown was carefully cleared and the entire area was fumigated to eliminate any possible contamination,[28] as if to suggest the conclusion that Sophiatown had been contaminated by its multiracial character. In 1995 F. W. de Klerk, then the leader of the Nationalist Party, apologized to South Africa and the world for the agony that his government caused the people of South Africa by the application of the policy of apartheid since 1948. However, soon after the demise of Sophiatown, the government passed a law requiring that there must be a buffer strip of land not less than one hundred yards wide to be erected between any African residential area and the system that served it.

Allister Sparks concluded that this strip was necessary in order to separate civilization from barbarism and van Riebeeck's white descendants from the black people of Africa. He suggests that it was the modern version of the bitter almond hedge (representing a bitter-sweet memory).[29] For all practical purposes, Sophiatown now existed only in the minds of those who were part of it. The bulldozers that leveled it actually set the example of social self-destruction that the apartheid system gave itself power to inflict until 1994, when it finally came to an end. The destruction of Sophiatown became the crucible of conflict in South Africa for nearly 40 years. The destruction was therefore a symbol of self-destruction that apartheid represented in all its forms.

TREVOR HUDDLESTON: THE LEGACY OF THE MASTER

There is no question that the destruction of Sophiatown inflicted more than damage to a physical place. It also delivered a severe social and psychological harm to a nation in search of its soul. The Nationalist leaders had no idea of the extent of the harm their action was causing, both to themselves and to the people they claimed to lead. From the time that Sophiatown was destroyed to de Klerk's realization in 1990 that apartheid was a national scourge, some 3 million people were forced to endure trauma in this fashion. Thriving communities were shattered and forced to relocate in places that were less profitable or productive. Many people who had made Sophiatown home were forced to lose their perception of both themselves and their society. For Strijdom, a man who showed no emotion of any kind, who was distant and cold, the destruction of Sophiatown marked a phase in the history of South Africa that convinced him of the absoluteness of the policy of apartheid, the infallibility of the Afrikaner philosophy of the inferiority of Africans, and the invincibility of the Nationalist Party. He went to his grave in 1958 totally unaware that he had created a monster that was to devour the Afrikaners themselves and their helpless victims, the people of South Africa.

Above all Huddleston had come to regard Sophiatown as a shrine indispensable for the development of human brotherhood as a vital condition of cooperation and national progress. He administered to the needs of the people, whether or not they were members of the Anglican Church. In his effort to meet the needs of all people, Huddleston saw Sophiatown as his parish and its residents saw him as their vicar who went out to serve them as the only mission of his life. In the course of his carrying out that mission, Huddleston became the St. Francis of Assisi of South Africa. He held back nothing as he gave everything that he had to serve the needs of all people. Huddleston would not want to live anywhere else in South Africa. His mission was in Sophiatown. As soon as he arrived in South Africa, Huddleston knew exactly what he sought to accomplish by living among the African people.

Huddleston explained why he saw Africans and Sophiatown from this perspective, saying that, apart from the need to arouse the Christian conscience in the world, there was in his heart, from that moment, in clear and unmistakable form, the desire to identify himself with the African people in their struggle for human rights and personal freedom.[30] The Nationalist government knew it and took every occasion to sabotage his efforts. Writing his autobiography, *Long Walk to Freedom*, in 1994, Nelson Mandela paid tribute to Huddleston as one of the greatest people who have ever lived in South Africa.[31] Mandela concluded that Huddleston had a vision of Sophiatown of the future and liked to compare it with an Italian community located on a hill, a biblical expression that suggested that Sophiatown was a light on a hill in the darkness that apartheid was creating for South Africa.

What made Huddleston the kind of religious leader and person that he was? The answer is not easy to give. A simplistic response might suggest that his total faith in the people, his belief in the positive attributes of human experience, his commitment to live a life of total dedication to religious principles, and his pledge to the vows of his order, the Community of Resurrection, became the basis of a life that had meaning to him only as he dedicated it to the service of others. Beyond the practice of religious faith, beyond his dedication to the service of others, beyond his involvement in the activities of Sophiatown to make it a better place for all, Huddleston was motivated by his belief in equality of all people.

Fairness and justice, as Huddleston saw them, were indispensable conditions of a new South Africa and the pillars that sustained its livelihood. However, he knew that the Nationalist Party did not operate by these principles and would not do unless it was compelled by conditions it did not control. He also knew that whatever he did to persuade the Nationalist government to change its policy was like a fly trying to force an African elephant to move, or the palace guard to argue with the king, or Sancho Panza trying to convince Don Quixote that what he regarded as giants to be charged were actually windmills.

However, Huddleston was one of those individuals who operated under the belief that any society that failed to uphold principles of equality, fairness, and justice has nothing else to build itself on because it had lost the essence of its very existence. Huddleston saw evidence of this situation as soon as he arrived in South Africa in 1943. Allister Sparks concluded that in spite of the decay that apartheid forced on Sophiatown, Huddleston saw it and other townships as characterized by vitality, happiness, and hope.[32] Only a member of a community who sees it in this positive light can play a dynamic role in seeking its improvement. One would have to say also that this is what motivated the Nationalist government to bring it to an end.

In 1954, 11 years after Huddleston arrived in South Africa, there were 2 million whites and 15 million Africans in South Africa. These Africans were condemned to lifestyles that were crippled and completely distorted by frustration and contempt of those who treated them as less than human. Africans could not vote, they could not own property. The Nationalist government erased Sophiatown to take away that sense of ownership so that Africans could not claim the right to vote. Hilda Bernstein concluded that the action the government took in this direction was a deliberate act of adopting oppressive measures to subdue a people and reduce it to conditions of servitude.[33] Soon after he arrived in South Africa, Huddleston saw this form of oppression and decided to confront it in his own way. In doing so he was under no illusion of the consequences of his decision and action.

In 1953, when it was known that the government had decided to demolish Sophiatown, the African National Congress (ANC) decided to mobilize the people to resist. By June of that year the local branch of the ANC and the local ratepayers association were helping people become aware of the need to resist the destruction of their community. These organizations decided to convene a public meeting to be held in Odin Cinema to discuss opposition to the decision of the government to erase Sophiatown. More than 1,200 people attended as well as dozens of heavily armed policemen, as is always the case in a police state. Only a few days before the meeting, the banning orders served on Nelson Mandela and Walter Sisulu had just expired, so they could organize and attend meetings.

Just as the meeting was about to start, a police officer saw Sisulu and Mandela outside the cinema talking to Huddleston. The officer immediately informed Sisulu and Mandela that as banned individuals they could not attend this meeting. The police officer ignored Huddleston. He then ordered his lieutenants to arrest them. At that point Huddleston shouted to the police officer, "No, you must arrest me instead."[34] Huddleston argued that if Sisulu and Mandela were guilty of an offense, he, too, should be considered guilty because he was engaged in conversation with them and it would not be fair for them to go to prison from an act of which he was a part. Huddleston knew that the South African police did not exercise ordinary reason and rationale that are part of a democratic society. His effort was therefore directed at trying to inject these basic elements in the operations of an institution that had lost them over an extended period of time.

In the scene that unfolded between Sisulu, Mandela, Huddleston, and the police officer a national confrontational situation was created. Did the police want to risk the development of a situation that would clearly lead to a national crisis from which publicity would be generated against it? Believing that this incident gave him an opportunity to express his total opposition to apartheid, Huddleston continued to plead with the police officer to either let Sisulu and Mandela go or to arrest him as well because he had been part of the planned meeting. The police officer ordered Huddleston to go away, but he refused because he saw that justice was not being served. The incident once more proved to Huddleston that, indeed, South Africa was ruled by a government that did not understand the importance of justice for all its people. As the police officers tried to move Huddleston away, Mandela pleaded with them to check to see if both he and Sisulu were still banned. It turned out that the police officer was wrong in his assumption that they were still banned.[35]

Realizing the possibility that the action of arresting Sisulu and Mandela might trigger confrontation, the police allowed them and Huddleston to participate in the meeting. The organizers concluded that the meeting was so successful that they decided to hold meetings every Sunday evening in the part of Sophiatown that was known as Freedom Square. Soon a slogan was adopted, stating in Zulu, *Sophiatown likhaya lami, asihambi* (Sophiatown is our home, we are not moving)."[36]

Leading speakers at these meetings included ANC officials, representatives of local councils, tenants, stand holders, and Huddleston, who often ignored police warnings to confine his activity to church matters.

He considered his involvement in this kind of activity an important church matter. The police did not know that as a priest Huddleston was trained to preach the gospel of the total human being as part of the emerging theology of liberation. This theology demanded that the physical conditions that affected the human being had a direct relationship to his spiritual welfare and that his political, social, and economic security were necessary to ensure his religious and spiritual growth and development.

Therefore, Huddleston was not about to listen to advice from the police to limit his activity to church matters. In addition to this stand, Huddleston became involved in other activities that were related to the intensifying opposition to apartheid. For example, he took part in opposing the Suppression of Communism Act of 1950, the chief instrument with which the Nationalist government suppressed Africans. He also participated in the defiance of unjust laws campaign that was initiated in 1952.

HUDDLESTON'S ROLE IN THE FREEDOM CHARTER

In June 1955 Huddleston participated in formulating ideas for the famous Freedom Charter.[37] For that role he was awarded the ANC's highest honor, Isitwalandwe, at Klipton,[38] the site of the charter itself. Nelson Mandela concluded that among the individuals that the government feared most in the formulation of the charter were executive members of the ANC, Professor Z. K. Matthews, and Father Trevor Huddleston.[39] The Freedom Charter was one of the best documents ever produced in South Africa by South Africans. Huddleston took tremendous pride in becoming part of its production. The Freedom Charter was adopted at the Congress of the People, which was held in Klipton, near Johannesburg, June 25–26, 1955. The charter addressed the following national issues:

1. That South Africa belonged to all who lived there, black and white, and that no government can justly claim authority unless it was based on the will of all the people.
2. That all South Africans had been robbed of their birthright to land, liberty, and peace by a form of government that was founded on injustice and inequality.
3. That South Africa would never be prosperous or free until all citizens lived in brotherhood, enjoying equal rights and opportunities.
4. That only a democratic state, which was based on the will of all the people, could secure for all its people equal opportunity without distinction of color, race, sex, or creed.

The charter concluded by saying that the people of South Africa, black and white together, adopted the charter and pledged themselves to strive together, sparing neither strength nor courage, until the democratic changes it envisaged had been won.

The Congress was convened by the African National Congress,[40] together with the South African Indian Congress, the South African Colored People's Organization, and the Congress of Democrats, an organization of whites who supported the liberation movement. It was attended by 2,888 delegates from throughout South Africa, and was perhaps the most representative gathering ever held in South Africa. But with an increasing number of countries gaining independence in Africa, and with the assistance given by the Organization of African Unity, ANC intensified its struggle, forcing the Nationalist government to rescind its ban in 1990. Although the government considered the Charter an illegal document, it circulated widely throughout South Africa and the outside world.

The charter became a manifesto of the four sponsoring organizations' struggle for freedom. A year later, 156 leaders of these organizations were arrested and charged with high treason for opposing apartheid. Indeed, the colonial culture of violence in South Africa was reaching alarming proportions. However, the leaders were subsequently acquitted of all charges after a trial that lasted more than four years. But Strijdom and his government would not take defeat so easily in its own courts. It banned ANC and the Congress of Democrats because it considered them the greatest threat to apartheid. The other two organizations were effectively prevented from engaging in political activity of any kind.

SUMMARY AND CONCLUSION

This chapter has presented a discussion of three critical aspects of the problems created by apartheid in South Africa. The first is the role the church played in political activity, especially the difference of opinion between the NGK and the Anglican Church. The second aspect is the crucible that Sophiatown became in the conflict between the forces of apartheid and those opposed to it. However, Sophiatown also became the crucible of hope for solutions to problems that apartheid was creating. It must be remembered that whatever else apartheid was expected to accomplish, its major function was to create enormous problems that lasted for years. The third aspect is the role that Father Trevor Huddleston played in opposing apartheid as a condition of the transformation of South Africa.[41]

During the 12 years that he worked in South Africa and beyond, Huddleston never lost his fierce opposition to apartheid. During a reception held in his honor at Regina Mundi Cathedral in Soweto in July 1991,

Huddleston fumed, "Apartheid was not a political mistake, it was a fundamentally evil system."[42] The recognition of this legacy is what Desmond M. Tutu took into account as he picked up the baton from Huddleston and carried his part of the race against apartheid.

NOTES

1. Brian Bunting, "Origins of Apartheid," in Alec La Guma (ed.), *Apartheid: A Collection of Writings on South Africa by South Africans* (New York: International Publishers, 1971), p. 23.

2. Ibid., p. 24.

3. Leo Marquard, *The People and Policies of South Africa* (London: Oxford University Press, 1969), p. 221.

4. Ibid., p. 222.

5. When the author was in high school in 1957, he heard a story told about Malan and how he became a preacher in NGK. It was said that before he became a minister he became very sick and went into a coma. After he recovered he began to preach about the beauty of heaven. At a news conference soon after, he was asked if he saw Africans in heaven. Malan looked surprised at the question and responded, "No, I did not go to the kitchen, that is where Natives stay."

6. Marquard, *The People and Policies of South Africa*, p. 231.

7. Ibid., p. 224.

8. Ibid., p. 226.

9. Ibid., p. 227.

10. History notes that the Catholic Church condemned this book because it was considerd too revolutionary, forcing Rousseau to seek refuge in Britain where he was protected for expressing his views of society.

11. For details see Dickson A. Mungazi, *The Last Defenders of the Laager: Ian D. Smith and F. W. de Klerk* (Westport, CT: Praeger Publishers, 1998).

12. Stanlake Samkange, *What Rhodes Really Said About Africans* (Harare: Harare Publishing House, 1982), p. 27.

13. Quoted in Marquard, *The People and Policies of South Africa*, p. 229.

14. Robert Buis, *Religious Beliefs and White Prejudice* (Johannesburg: Raven Press, 1975), p. 9.

15. Jim Wallis and Joyce Holleyday (eds.), *Crucible of Fire: The Church Confronts Apartheid* (Maryknoll, NY: Orbis Books, 1989), p. 104.

16. Ibid., p. 114.

17. Marquard, *The People and Policies of South Africa*, p. 231.

18. Ibid., p. 235.

19. Bunting, "Origins of Apartheid," p. 25.

20. Allister Sparks, *The Mind of South Africa* (New York: Alfred A. Knopf, 1989), p. 188.

21. Alan Paton, *Cry, the Beloved Country* (New York: Charles Scribner's Sons, 1948), p. 102.

22. Ibid., p. 71.

23. Sparks, *The Mind of South Africa*, p. 188.

24. A. B. Xuma served as president of the ANC from 1940 to 1949. A dedicated

nationalist, Xuma believed in a multiracial concept for South Africa. This is why he decided to live in Sophiatown.

25. Nelson Mandela, *Long Walk to Freedom: The Autobiography of Nelson Mandela* (Boston: Little, Brown, 1994), p. 134.

26. Ibid., p. 135.

27. Trevor Huddleston, *Naught for Your Comfort* (New York: Doubleday, 1956), p. 121.

28. Sparks, *The Mind of South Africa*, p. 187.

29. Ibid., p. 189.

30. Huddleston, *Naught for Your Comfort*, p. 72.

31. Mandela, *Long Walk to Freedom*, p. 133.

32. Sparks, *The Mind of South Africa*, p. 228.

33. Hilda Bernstein, "Schools for Servitude," in Alex La Guma (ed.), *Apartheid: A Collection of Writings on South Africa by South Africans* (New York: International Publishers, 1971), p. 45.

34. Mandela, *Long Walk to Freedom*, p. 135.

35. Ibid., p. 135.

36. Ibid.

37. Since its release on June 26, 1955, the Freedom Charter became a public document. The author received a copy from the UN Anti-Apartheid Committee.

38. Anti-Apartheid Movement, *Trevor Huddleston, CR: 80th Birthday Tribute* (London: Anti-Apartheid Movement, 1994).

39. Mandela, *Long Walk to Freedom*, p. 163.

40. The African National Congress, which was founded in 1912, was outlawed in 1964, and its leaders, including Nelson Mandela, were arrested, tried, and convicted under provisions of laws passed under apartheid. Mandela and his associates spent 27 years in prison. They were released in February 1990 to begin talks with the South African government on the future of the country.

41. For various considerations of that transformation, see Dickson A. Mungazi and L. Kay Walker, *Educational Reform and the Transformation of Southern Africa* (Westport, CT: Praeger Publishers, 1997).

42. Allister Sparks, *Tomorrow Is Another Country: The Inside Story of South Africa's Road to Change* (Chicago: University of Chicago Press, 1995), p. 92.

2

The Role of the Church in Zimbabwe and the Legacy of Ralph E. Dodge

He who is dominated by another spiritually, economically, academically, or politically, will never develop his full potential
—Bishop Ralph E. Dodge, 1963

ORIGINS OF THE METHODIST CHURCH IN ZIMBABWE

Part of the purpose of this study is to discuss the role that Methodist Bishop Abel T. Muzorewa played from 1971 to 1979 in the political transformation of Zimbabwe from colonial rule to an African majority government. In order to discuss that role, it is important to review the origins of the Methodist Church in Zimbabwe and the legacy left behind by its leaders, from Bishop Joseph C. Hartzell beginning in 1896 to the end of Bishop Ralph E. Dodge's term of office in 1968. The period that Muzorewa served as bishop of the Methodist Church, from 1968 to 1993, was part of great traditions of Methodist leaders who had left a legacy he was called upon to uphold.

In this regard the challenge that Ralph Edward Dodge responded to in assuming his duties as a Episcopal leader of the Methodist Church in Zimbabwe in 1956 and the record of his accomplishments from then up to the time that the right-wing Rhodesia Front (RF) Party deported him in July 1964, was also part of the Methodist heritage that he felt called upon to preserve.[1] When Bishop Joseph Crane Hartzell[2] was elected

Bishop of the Methodist Episcopal Church and assigned to Africa in May 1896, he fully understood the magnitude of the challenge he was about to accept. This was to lay a foundation upon which the Methodist Church would build institutions designed to serve the needs of the Africans.

Although Hartzell, a devout Methodist clergyman from Ohio, was overwhelmed by the episcopal responsibility that he was invited to assume, he readily recognized that the Methodist Church should introduce the Africans to Christianity as a new religious and cultural dimension giving them new hope for the future. He approached his task with a prophetic sense of the urgency of its importance. Hartzell served at a time when Africa was being subjected to colonial conquest and imperial domination, making it hard to measure the results of his efforts.[3] This is why by the time that he retired in 1916, Hartzell recognized the limits of his accomplishments. He was moved to write in 1918: "Africa has suffered from many evils. Slave trade and exploitation by the white man have through many years preyed upon the life of Africa and have left its population reduced and uncertain about the future."[4]

In suggesting that the major task of the Methodist Church was "the introduction of education, Christian marriage, the sanctity of life, and the creation of a Christian African civilization,"[5] Hartzell was warning that the consequences of any other course of action would be severe, both for the Methodist Church itself and for the Africans. This was the foundation upon which his successor, Bishop Eben S. Johnson, who served from 1916 to 1936, was able to build Methodist institutions whose purpose was the full development of the Africans, educationally, religiously, and socially as part of its mission. Those were the elements that Hartzell believed constituted his definition of the sanctity of human life, which was the main focus of his own mission.

By the time Bishop John M. Springer succeeded Johnson in 1936, the Methodist Church had fully understood and accepted the importance of that mission. Springer's contribution to the total Methodist mission in Africa was his effort to widen the base that his predecessors had established so that the Methodist Church assumed a new direction. When he retired in 1944, the work of the Methodist Church could be measured in terms of its accomplishments. In 1923 alone, for example, the Methodist Church spent $55,750 on improving education, health, and social services in Africa.[6] In addition to this financial commitment, the Methodist Church aroused in Africans a new level of thinking and a collective consciousness that educational endeavors would make it possible for them to progress in the future and so enable them to make a visible contribution to the development of the country. The effort by the Methodist Church increasing this new level of awareness stands out as one of its major accomplishments in Zimbabwe and other countries in Africa.

When he retired, Springer was succeeded by Bishop Newell S. Booth, who served until 1956, the year that Ralph Dodge succeeded him. Faced with many arduous tasks and formidable problems, the Methodist Church leaders from Hartzell to Booth fulfilled their obligations and carried out their mission in a manner that demonstrated their commitment to the advancement of the African as a condition of being fully human. However, the negative attitude of the colonial governments to any form of advancement of the Africans themselves made their work particularly difficult.

But believing in both the importance of their assignment and what they clearly saw to be the potential of the African to function effectively in the future and in the context of the white man's culture, they all pursued their objectives with vigor and dedication. Even though conditions of the times demanded otherwise, their sensitivity to African opposition of anything that represented the white man's culture would later prove to be the hallmark of Methodist Church commitment to the African struggle for selfhood. Slowly but steadily, the Methodist Church and the Africans began to build a viable basis of mutual respect. This is the kind of atmosphere that Dodge found when he arrived to succeed Booth in 1956. The commitment of his predecessors to a great cause provided him with the strength he needed to face new challenges and new commitments.[7]

THE ADMINISTRATION OF CHARLES P. COGHLAN

When Muzorewa was two years old in 1927, three events that took place in colonial Zimbabwe would determine his future in profound ways. The first event was the death of Charles P. Coghlan, prime minister of colonial Zimbabwe since 1923 (he served from October 1, 1923, to September 1, 1927). Coghlan was born in South Africa, where he was educated and studied law. He came to colonial Zimbabwe at the beginning of the 20th century and decided to try his hand in politics. He was first elected to the legislature in 1908 and supported the view that the country should attain the status of responsible government. The term "responsible government" was used by the British to indicate a political status considered to be higher than that of direct rule from Whitehall. It had no other significance except for the colonial government to claim that it had the power to determine its own internal affairs with little interference from Britain. In 1965, Ian Smith used this status to claim independence under his administration.[8]

Coghlan was part of a delegation to London to negotiate with the British government, led at the time by James Ramsay MacDonald, the liberal leader of the Labour Party. That both MacDonald and Coghlan shared liberal views about the future of British colonial Africa reflected the conditions of the times. MacDonald served as secretary to the Labour Party for 11 years beginning in 1900. As leader of the Labour Party, MacDonald opposed Britain's entry into the First World War.

Both MacDonald and Coghlan felt that the government must assume a major leadership responsibility in assisting its citizens in their struggle for development. Coming out of the Victorian era, MacDonald embraced a social creed that compelled him to recognize the social and economic problems that the British masses were facing. For MacDonald and Coghlan, building and defending the colonial political system took different dimensions from those advocated by other leaders of the British colonial empire.

In colonial Zimbabwe Coghlan was trying to ease the economic burden thrust on the people by the exploitive feature of colonial policy. This is why the two men developed an unusual understanding of the role of government in seeking improvement in the conditions of the lives of the people. Coghlan's sudden death on September 1, 1927, at the age of 64 brought an entirely different political situation that put his successor Howard Unwin Moffat in an uncomfortable position, not because he was unable to exercise proper political leadership at a critical time, but because Coghlan had such a high reputation as a colonial leader that was difficult to match. Indeed, Moffat tried to build the same type of system as McDonald and Coghlan had tried to build, but the forces of opposition were too strong to permit him to succeed.

The second event that took place in 1927 was the naming of the Hadfield Commission to study and make recommendations on African education. The commission was chaired by F. L. Hadfield, a senior civil servant in Bulawayo. The Hadfield Commission recommended that education for Africans should be under the responsibility of the missionaries under government control. The Hadfield Commission suggested that a partnership between the church and the government was critically important in the process of formulating and implementing a national policy designed to ensure the advancement of Africans. But within the normal operation of governments, the process would mean that the government would formulate the policy and the church would implement it. If this is the kind of partnership the Hadfield Commission had in mind, and it certainly appears that it was, then it did not seem to offer anything substantially different from previous practice.

The conclusion of the Hadfield Commission that "natives are inordinate beer drinkers, grossly immoral and incredibly steeped in superstition and manifest an absence of tribal control"[9] as the basis of its finding suggests a further conclusion that the commission did not have a positive image of Africans and that the missionaries would have a more positive influence on their lives. The missionaries accepted the challenge to enhance their work and increase their influence. By the time Muzorewa arrived at Old Umtali in 1940, he found a much different environment from the one under which Josiah Chimbadzwa and Tenze Mutasa found forty years earlier.

The third event that took place in 1927 that would later have a profound impact on African struggle for development was the creation of the Department of Native Education under the directorship of Harold Jowitt. When the Committee on Native Development of 1925 recommended the establishment of the Department of Native Education separate from the Department of Native Affairs,[10] the colonial government found a temporary solution to the embarrassment it had experienced in the failure of the plan that Herbert Keigwin had outlined in 1920.[11] The Department of Native Education was allocated $9,520 for its installation. Harold Jowitt, a liberal at the level of Coghlan and MacDonald, and far more intellectual than Keigwin, was appointed its first director. Jowitt had 14 years of experience in education for Africans in South Africa. He was assisted by four inspectors.

A relentless negotiator and a cunning diplomat, Jowitt made an approach to his new responsibilities that was a breath of fresh air for church leaders, who felt that under Keigwin their influence was slipping. Jowitt seemed to have healthy relationships with the various segments of the communities involved in African education. In his desire to succeed where he thought Keigwin had failed, Jowitt had become a fragile bridge over troubled water. With respect to the education of Africans, he tried to mediate in the conflict between political philosophy and the reality of human existence, between past policies and a new idealism. He tried to strike a functional balance between politically expedient programs and realistic philosophy, between the African desire for a good academic education as a means of eliminating the old colonial stereotypes and the shackles that bound their minds, and the colonial intent to have them provide cheap labor. He tried to satisfy both the Africans' desire for a good education and the expressed wish of the white entrepreneurs to sustain their economic and political power base through cheap labor, which only the Africans could provide.

Conditions of the times made Jowitt's task much harder than that of any of his associates in the colonial government. He knew that his options were few, and that he had to play his limited number of cards carefully. There was no room for error, and the stakes were high. Believing that it was possible to strike a working balance between these conflicting positions, Jowitt began his task with a clear understanding of the importance of his mission.

In his first annual report submitted in 1928, Jowitt acknowledged the fact that he faced some rather serious and unexpected problems, and went on to discuss some of them, saying,

"The non-existence of data and records regarding the work, the thinking that education for Natives is a stepchild receiving the crumbs from the dinner table of the
accredited educational family, the absence of any qualified officials in Native education, all tend to preclude the development of an adequate system of official records and constitute the fundamental problems in Native education." [12]

There was no question that Jowitt wanted to offer Africans a kind of
education that would help shape their future in a larger national context
than had been done in the past.

CONDITIONS IN ZIMBABWE IN RELATION TO
AFRICA, 1928–1956

By 1928 the education of Africans had been "an appendage of the
European Education Department, the stepchild, invariably receiving the
crumbs from the dinner table of the accredited educational family."[13]
Because the educational process was regarded as the criterion of deter-
mining the Africans' place in colonial society, the colonial government
itself decided to control it effectively so that it would find grounds for
justifying its claim that the African was inferior to the white man. Events
elsewhere in Africa between 1920 and 1936 had an impact on colonial
Zimbabwe that the Methodist Church could not ignore if it were to remain true to its mission and faithful to its calling.

Although some members of the colonial government "felt that the Native has demonstrated that the African in general is teachable," [14] colonial
officials did nothing either to demonstrate this belief or show an interest
in the educational advancement of Africans by providing an opportunity
for them to secure it. This was one reason that compelled the Methodist
Church in colonial Zimbabwe to recognize the increasing environment
of conflict between itself and the colonial government. In 1928, during
the episcopal leadership of Bishop Eben Johnson, Reverend T. A.
O'Farrell stated the rightness of the Methodist policy of providing an
opportunity for education for Africans as part of its understanding of
Hartzell's call for the sanctity of human life, when he decried colonial
opposition, saying that the leaders whom the church was developing
may become pilots of their race in far larger areas of Rhodesia. As this
institutional conflict showed no signs of abating, it began to erode away
the limited achievement that had been made in the 19th century for mutual confidence and cooperation in the development of the country. This
is why, by 1934, the colonial government recognized the increasing tension between the two institutions, saying "for the Missions this is a year
of tensions due to an uncertainty which they have felt regarding the
future of education for Native."[15]

The conditions of life of the Africans began to deteriorate rapidly when

Godfrey Huggins assumed the position of prime minister in 1933. Until he resigned in 1952 to become the prime minister of the Federation of Rhodesia and Nyasaland, Huggins remained a true and loyal believer in the values of the Victorian era; among them that Africans were inferior to the white man socially, intellectually, and in any other way. This is why, in 1952, during a political campaign speech Huggins claimed that the white man's claim of superiority was based on the color of his skin, education, cultural values, civilization, and heredity.[16]

To accentuate the difference of opinion on this important issue, Dodge argued in 1964 that intellect was not an exclusive possession of any one racial group, it existed in all people.[17] It is evident that Huggins was attempting to reaffirm a form of the Victorian myth that had become the preoccupation of colonial officials all along. This was the myth that leaders of the Christian Church could no longer accept. It is no secret that Huggins was also rejecting the missionary call for a clearer policy on the educational development of Africans than the one that was in force. Meeting at Waddilove in February 1946, the Methodist Church passed a resolution that condemned Huggins's policy and called for a new approach. "We believe that a satisfactory educational policy awaits a clearer enunciation of principles regarding the African's place in social, economic and political life so that they reach the full and unrestricted citizenship which we believe is unquestionably their right."[18]

That Huggins did not believe in African advancement through education is demonstrated by the policy he pursued as prime minister of the Federation from 1953 to 1956. That policy was based upon an educational policy that he had formulated in 1939 for white students. That policy meant that his government was going to raise the school-leaving age to 16 to provide secondary education to all white children because they must be given an opportunity to keep their position in life to prevent the creation of a poor white class.[19] Huggins was sending a clear message that Africans must never hope to have equal opportunity for development. This is exactly why he stated on August 26, 1954, that the doctrine of racial segregation was based on his government's belief that there were fundamentally unchangeable differences between the races that could not be reconciled.[20]

As Huggins saw things, the racial differences that he claimed could not be reconciled meant that he totally rejected the concept of racial equality in society. That he chose to deliver a speech on a major policy of his administration before a body of church leaders who disagreed with his Victorian views, suggests that he fully recognized the seriousness of the opposing views that he and they held and that he was desperately attempting to convert at least some of them to his side of the growing conflict. But to his disappointment, this was not to be. The rise of African nationalism beginning with the end of the war in 1945 was a development that was destined to alter permanently the nature of relationships between the colonial government and the Africans. This shattered Cecil John Rhodes's dream of building a British empire throughout Africa and, indeed, the entire world.[21]

DODGE'S DEPORTATION AND ITS CONSEQUENCES

Recognizing the delicate balance that he felt he had to maintain between sustaining the momentum for his crusade for fundamental social change and trying to avoid a confrontation between him and the colonial government, Dodge attempted a Vatican-style diplomacy. But faced with a Machiavellian situation, he was forced to change his strategy in order to continue his crusade. This is essentially why he warned that the church found itself in a dilemma when it recognized that there were certain archaic or unjust laws on the statute books of a country that it could not conscientiously uphold, but that it was not able to alter through the legal process. In that situation the church was in the embarrassing position of trying to maintain and encourage the enforcement of laws that it sincerely felt should not be observed. He concluded that the most common area the church found itself in such a dilemma was to submit to discriminatory legislation.[22]

The second conclusion is that Dodge was of the opinion that all religious leaders must embrace specific action beyond their religious pronouncements in order to arouse a popular passion for meaningful social change. This action may include nonviolent demonstrations that may be necessary to mobilize common constructive emotion, giving cohesion to a popular demand for progressive and meaningful change. But in colonial Africa, as has been demonstrated by events in South Africa since the Soweto uprising of June 16, 1976, nonviolent demonstration implies confrontation with the powers that be. The question is: To what extent were Dodge and other Christian leaders who shared the importance of his crusade prepared to face the consequences of this confrontational strategy?

The third conclusion is that it was the duty of the people to force those who make the laws to remember that they have a right to disobey those that are discriminatory. Civil disobedience and conscientious objection are forms of social action that Christian leaders have historically urged their followers to adopt as a means of fighting injustice. This is why Dodge says, the church must support its members who defied colonial laws which were unfair and discriminatory.[23] The problem that church leaders have faced in this religious belief and teaching is that the government sees it as nothing less than urging the people to break the law.

Therefore, Dodge's interpretation of freedom of conscience and his understanding of the purpose of the colonial law were in direct conflict with the interpretation and purposes of the colonial government itself.

Serious as these differences were, they were not the only events that paved the road to a crisis between Dodge and the colonial government. One fundamental difference between the two sides is the way they saw the African, his place in society, and his intellectual potential. On the one hand, from the time that Cecil John Rhodes characterized the Africans in 1896 as having the brains of children[24] to the time of Ian Smith's view of 1983 that they did not believe in education because they thought it was something that belonged to the white man,[25] the colonial government persistently framed its national policy based upon this Victorian myth. On the other hand Dodge argued that his close association with Africans gave him a very high appreciation of their natural ability. "Make no mistake about it, world leaders will come from Africa."[26]

Dodge's belief in the potential of Africans compelled him to argue that there was a tremendous potential among Africans, but that it would never come to full fruition until the opportunities of training were comparable with those received by other people of the world. He concluded that only then could Africans attain full nationhood to which they were entitled.[27] From these differences of perception, especially regarding the place of Africans in society, it is fairly easy to see how neither the colonial government nor Dodge was prepared to give up the philosophy that was needed to build a foundation for the future.

This church-state conflict also shows something more important. Dodge's conclusion that Africans possessed intellectual potential equal to that possessed by people of any other race was, in effect, a practice of religious belief in the total equality of all people. This is why he expressed his conviction that God has divided His gifts fairly evenly among his various children of all races so that in the end there is no superiority or inferiority associated with any one race.[28] This was the first time since Rev. William Wade Harris openly challenged the colonial educational policy in 1921 that a Christian leader openly challenged it again.

The view of colonial officials that Africans were inferior to the white man was nothing more than part of an unfounded social philosophy and myth that became a colonial political mausoleum as Africans acquired better opportunities for educational development. Therefore, the place of Africans in society became a highly political and emotional issue about which it was not possible to reach a compromise or even an accommodating understanding. The conflict only served to widen the gap between church and state. By the time Dodge arrived in Zimbabwe in 1956, that conflict had acquired major proportions. Those writers who make a blank conclusion without distinguishing the periods that they discuss—

that the missionaries were agents of the colonial government—miss a very important truth. The 20th-century missionaries lived and practiced a religion different from that lived and practiced by Victorian missionaries. Let us now try to furnish some more evidence that supports this view to understand how Dodge sought a transformation of Zimbabwe.

While the road to a showdown between Dodge and the colonial government began to appear in 1959, it took a perilous turn in 1963 and 1964. During the annual conference of the Methodist Church held at Murewa in May 1963, Dodge delivered one of his best episcopal addresses in which he argued that the church indeed had a responsibility to start a social revolution. Comparing the situation in colonial Zimbabwe with that in ancient Palestine, he drew a striking similarity, saying, "it was those in top positions in synagogues, society and government who resisted change. People who lived comfortably did not agitate for change. However, there was a great need for change in Southern Rhodesia because those who possessed power and wealth must be willing to share.[29]

This perspective of the modern church was the first important event that took place in 1963 that became part of the cause of the crisis between the church and the colonial government. The second event was the genuine concern Dodge expressed over the political events that began to unfold in December 1962. The right-wing Rhodesia Front Party, led by Winston J. Field and Ian Smith, assumed power after a bitter election campaign in which race was a major issue. The RF promised the white voters that if it was elected it would elevate the white race to the pinnacle of absolute political power enshrined in the philosophy of racial superiority of the white man and the assumed inferiority of Africans. It also promised to do this by amending the notorious Land Apportionment Act of 1929 to make it more applicable to conditions of 1962.[30] The RF also promised the white voters that if elected it would seek independence from Britain by either legal or illegal means.[31] The RF neither tolerated the church's opposition to its policy nor appreciated its concern.

A political crisis within the RF itself helped to precipitate a crisis between church and state. In April 1964 Field was removed from the office of prime minister in a political coup that was led by Ian Smith (just as F. W. de Klerk did in South Africa in 1989 to remove P. W. Botha from the office of president) because Field had shown some signs of respecting the British demand of African educational advancement and had released African political prisoners who had been arrested under the state of emergency declared by Edgar Whitehead on February 28, 1959. When Smith assumed office on April 24, 1964, the character of the relationships between the church and the RF took a turn for the worse. Smith, a colonial official with traditional views of Africans, cared little for the condition of the people he ruled. His political philosophy, *No black majority government in my lifetime, not in a thousand years*, became an obsession, a religion that he worshipped with total devotion.

Both the RF's victory in the general election of December 1962 and Smith's assumption of the office of prime minister in 1969 were received with measured feelings of dismay by both Africans and church leaders. Three weeks before Smith became prime minister, the Methodist Church held a conference at Murewa. Instead of addressing social issues in his episcopal address, Dodge opted for an alternative. He entertained a motion from the floor, and after a considerable debate mainly on the wording, the conference passed a resolution[32] stating that any unilateral declaration of independence would constitute an act of rebellion and create a grave situation in which the church might find it necessary to advise its members that they were under no moral obligation to carry out the commands of an illegal government.[33]

There are two possible reasons to explain why Dodge entertained the motion that led to this resolution. The first reason is that he had been in the spotlight since he opposed the state of emergency of 1959 and wanted the colonial government to know that other Methodists shared his views. The second reason is that the RF government would have no justification for singling him out for vindictive action. This would protect his position and so enable him to continue his crusade for social change.

Of course, this was a miscalculation because the RF was not guided by this kind of rationale and reasoning. That the resolution ended with a grim warning and appeal for the convening of a constitutional conference that would make provision for a majority government[34] and was signed by the committee secretary, Rev. Robert Hughes, another uncompromising foe of the RF policy, proved to be an ominous sign for Dodge and the Methodist Church.

The cumulative effect of these developments can be measured in terms of a series of rapidly moving events that caught Dodge and Hughes by total surprise and shock. Unwilling to take any criticism of the RF's policy and frustrated by the British persistent demand for the advancement of Africans, Ian Smith found an easy target for his vengeful action. On July 16, 1964, his government served Dodge and Hughes with deportation orders, requesting them to leave the country within 15 days. Dodge's request of July 17 for an extension of 40 days to allow him to complete his assignment as president of the Southern Rhodesia Christian Conference, which terminated with the Biennial Conference September 5–9, and to permit Mrs. Dodge and him to attend the wedding of their daughter Lois on August 15th[35] was denied with the exception that William Harper, the RF minister of Internal Affairs told him, he was willing to authorize the issuance of a temporary permit to enable him to visit Southern Rhodesia on August 14, 15, and 16 for the sole purpose of attending Lois's wedding.[36]

But the letter dated August 13, 1964, written by D. E. Shephard, private secretary to Harper, and addressed to Mrs. E. Griffin, interim secretary to the Methodist Church's board of finance and coordination (BOFAC), demonstrates the serious nature and extent of the conflict that existed between the church's religious principles and the RF's political philosophy, saying that the severe action that had been taken against Bishop Dodge was fully justified. The statement concluded that action was taken after very careful consideration of all the facts and circumstances which showed that it was in the best interests of the country to take such action.[37] Of course, the RF was considering its own political interests.

REACTION TO DODGE'S DEPORTATION

Where then did Dodge's deportation lead the country, and what were some of the consequences of this action? Since Rev. William Wade Harris demanded involvement in the formulation of a national policy in 1921, Dodge was the most popular church leader among the Africans.[38] Because of irreconcilable differences between him and the RF, the RF concluded erroneously that his action threatened national interests. Everyone knew that this argument was indeed a galaxy of absurdities. A study of the reaction, both African and white, furnishes enough evidence to show that indeed the RF feared that Dodge's influence among the Africans would increase their political consciousness.

Let us discuss briefly only a few of the many examples that led to this conclusion.[39] Among the first people who sent Dodge messages of support was Garfield Todd, the man who was removed from the office of prime minister in 1958 for attempting a progressive policy toward the development of Africans and whom Dodge praised in 1959 for expressing opposition to the state of emergency of February of that year. In a telegram Todd wrote, "DEEPLY GRATEFUL FOR CONTRIBUTION YOU HAVE MADE. EXPRESS MY APPRECIATION TO YOUR CHURCH. HOPE NOT LONG UNTIL WE WELCOME YOU BACK WITH HONOR."[40] Neither Dodge nor Todd was aware that his return to independent and free Zimbabwe would have to wait until 1979. Indeed, when Dodge returned in that year, he was welcomed with honor.

Beyond the fact that Todd was supporting Dodge in 1964 in the same way that Dodge had supported him in 1959 was an unquestionable hope and wish that the RF would soon be eliminated from the political scene of Zimbabwe, because its policies were totally out of tune with reality and the conditions of the time. Although Todd and Whitehead had serious political differences, those between Todd and Smith were so grave that the RF placed Todd and his daughter Judith under house arrest for several years beginning in 1966.[41] Could this mean that Smith feared that there was something more than an alliance of religious and political ideology between Dodge and Todd against him? It is difficult to resist the temptation to reach this conclusion. But Todd clearly believed that Dodge's influence among Africans was what the RF feared most.

A day after Todd had sent the telegram to Dodge on, July 18 Joshua Nkomo, the veteran president of ZAPU which Smith outlawed in April, and who was now in detention at Gonakudzingwa, sent a letter of support to Dodge, saying as he added another dimension to the meaning of the deportation that Christ had died on the cross, not because those who were responsible for His crucifixion believed that He was doing wrong, but because he was an unusual leader who was doing new and innovative things.[42] What Nkomo was in effect saying is that Smith and his RF government were ill-advised to think that Dodge's crusade for fundamental social change would suddenly come to an end with his deportation. If anything at all, it was likely to intensify that demand.

Two days later, on July 20, 73 Methodist missionaries signed a letter written in Shona, supporting Dodge and calling on the RF to rescind the decision to deport him, saying that at the conference held at Murewa in 1963 there was a discussion about the rumors that some missionaries had written to the government urging it to deport Bishop Dodge. The missionaries stressed the fact that they publicly pledged their total and unconditional support to Dodge, and that they were appalled by the action that was taken by the government in deporting him. They asked that the decision be rescinded to enable him to carry on his important work.[43] On the same day 58 ministers of the Christian Church Council wrote a letter to Smith himself urging him "with all the urgency to rescind the decision."[44]

The spirit of urgency in calling the RF to rescind the deportation order came from many organizations and individuals who saw severe consequences for the country if it decided to go ahead with it. One such person was the Catholic Bishop Donal R. Lamont. An uncompromising foe of RF racial policy, Lamont came to Zimbabwe as a missionary from Ireland in 1946. He was appointed bishop of Mutare in 1957 and immediately became known as a champion of the oppressed African masses. Lamont wrote a letter to Dodge on July 21, in which he expressed deep sadness to learn of the action that the RF had taken against him.[45] It was ironic that in 1972 Lamont himself would pick up the banner that Dodge had left behind. But on October 1, 1976, he was sentenced to ten years in prison with hard labor for his role in opposing the RF.[46] Lamont was well on his way to becoming a political martyr when, in March 1977, the RF stripped him of his citizenship and deported him. He, too, became a victim of the RF's vindictive action. The RF's intolerance of opposition to its policy had reached an alarming level.

The problems that the RF was creating by deporting Dodge and

Hughes were discussed by other people who wrote letters of support to him. One such letter came from Lazarus Mandizha, an African student from Zimbabwe attending Morningside College, who concluded that the RF's action came from the fact that the country lacked statesman.[47] G. D. Mhlanga, the first black Zimbabwean to receive a college degree, wrote to say that Africans would never forget him when they attained their independence.[48]

These few of the many letters that Dodge received illustrate an important point. If the RF thought that by deporting Dodge and Hughes it was eliminating their influence from the political struggle the Africans were waging, subsequent events proved that this kind of thinking was erroneous. Dodge was more influential outside Zimbabwe than he was inside it. For the next four years he operated from his office in Kitwe, Zambia, from where he directed the activities of the Methodist Church in Zimbabwe without ever slowing down or diminishing the effectiveness of his administration in the struggle for the advancement of the Africans. With a team of dedicated assistants based inside Zimbabwe, led by Rev. Jonah Kawadza, the work of the Methodist Church continued to grow and to discharge its responsibilities in an efficient manner.

The RF's deportation of Dodge leads one to ask some questions that, though without answers, can help in understanding the real reasons why the RF took this action. It is quite clear that the resolution passed by the Methodist Annual Conference held at Old Mutare in 1964 was the final piece of cumulative evidence that the RF needed to conclude that Dodge was actively working to establish a black majority government as a condition of ensuring the future of the church and initiate progress that he felt could not be made under colonial domination. But Dodge himself felt that he was exercising his Christian responsibility when he said that if he was being deported because of what had done and written, then he had no apology to make.[49]

THE ACTION OF A CHURCH IN TRANSITION

As soon as Dodge arrived in Zimbabwe in 1956 to assume his episcopal responsibility, he let it be known that he believed in a nonracial society and he would try to associate myself with all segments of the population in the country.[50] After his deportation he pledged himself anew to this social creed. From this vantage point he concluded that the problems of colonial Zimbabwe were compounded by the inability of the RF to recognize that they were basically moral and political, and that the search for solutions must entail the application of Christian principles of honesty, nonracial respect of all people, and human brotherhood.[51]

Dodge argued that this would eliminate the practice of racial discrimination, prejudice, false pride, all of which were characteristics of successive colonial governments. Is it not possible that because the truth hurts, the RF did not want to be reminded persistently of its weaknesses? But by evading the truth the RF had to face the consequences of its action beginning in April 1966, when the war of independence broke out.

It is quite evident that Dodge was an active participant in several Christian organizations in which he held office and to which he made considerable contributions. The main objectives of these organizations was to end racial discrimination in all its forms. Through working in these organizations, Dodge recognized the strength that comes from unity of purpose and candidly expressed his views about what was wrong, adding "I have made my witness that true Christian piety leads to constructive non-violent action."[52] While he was sorry that his record of service in the country was being ignored, Dodge wondered why a government that claimed to preserve Christian civilization[53] would act in such an arbitrary manner.

This realization came about because the church was an institution in transition. This is why it soon became clear to the Christian community following Dodge's deportation that the political behavior of the RF led to the conclusion that it was impossible to build a nation based on universal human dignity unless it was undergirded by the values that would preserve it.[54] Dodge was quite candid on expressing his view that the policies of the RF represented a national situation that citizens must tolerate. In this regard, Dodge appears to be a modern-day Edmund Burke.[55] The church of Dodge's time could no longer remain silent in a national situation that demanded correction and still maintain its loyalty to its calling and mission. This conflict could not be avoided unless the church failed to recognize the critical nature of this transition.

To do this Dodge urged the church to play an entirely new role, one that was different from the one it had played in the 19th century. He argued that the conditions of the times demanded that the church put itself squarely on the side of the struggling Africans in order to remain true to its mission. He also argued that the church of 1966 was a church in transition, that it had come to recognize that to fulfill its mission, it had to demonstrate its commitment to ending the misery to which the colonial condition imposed on Africans.[56]

A change in the perception of its role enabled the church to see the RF policy not only from perspective of its Christian duty, but also as a demonstration of its sincerity to show its support for the African cause. It did this in the knowledge that the continued denial of equal educational opportunity to the Africans under the RF would prove to be its own demise. This knowledge demanded a complete reversal of the role that the church had played during the days of David Livingstone and Robert Moffat. Indeed, beginning in 1922, the church steadily recognized the error of its 19th-century belief that the colonial government was its ally in an effort to convert the Africans to Christianity.[57] Conditions in the 20th century demanded that the church take new realities into consideration in reevaluating its position.

The conflict that was increasing between the church and the government regarding the education of Africans reached its peak in 1970 as the two institutions, due to incompatibility of their respective policies, continued to drift further apart. Unable to tolerate criticism of its educational policy, the RF lowered a heavy hand on the leaders of the church, including Bishop Muzorewa and Bishop Dodge, both of the United Methodist Church, and Bishop Donal Lamont of the Roman Catholic Church. The deportation of Bishop Dodge and the arrest and trial of Bishop Lamont created an environment of a major institutional conflict.

For church leaders to support the Africans' struggle for political independence as a prerequisite of educational and socioeconomic advancement constituted a central tenet of its religious practice that it could no longer compromise. This is the setting from which all three were arrested and the last two deported for assisting Africans in their struggle for advancement. For the RF to arrest the leaders of the church was proof indeed that the church had gone through a period of transition and had taken the side of the Africans as a matter of religious conviction. This is most evident in what Lamont had to say in an open letter to Ian Smith in 1976, "Have not those who honestly believe that they are fighting for basic human rights of their people a justifiable claim to the church's support?"[58]

For the church to recognize that, indeed, the RF policy sought a systematic oppression of Africans, both mentally and politically,[59] was to acknowledge the reality of its threat, both to its own survival as an institution, and to the development of Africans, who are the object and purpose of its mission. The ideas which David Livingstone and Robert Moffat had expressed during the formative years of Christianity in Africa and of the government were no longer relevant or appropriate to the conditions of 1966. Because the Africans had been weakened by the RF ban of their political parties, the focus of conflict temporarily shifted from a struggle between themselves and the RF to one between the RF and the church. Thus it was that a triangle of badly strained relationships would be crucial to the struggle between the RF and the Africans beginning in 1972.

THE RF'S POLICY AND CHURCH-STATE CONFLICT

To understand the situation clearly, we must find answers to two questions: What were the elements of the RF educational policy that the church opposed? What was the effect of implementing that policy on the relationships between the church and the RF itself? When Charles S. Davies, the RF secretary for African education, blamed the African nationalists for the problems it was experiencing in 1964, he saw nothing wrong with the educational policy of the RF government.

Davies even attempted to justify that policy by arguing that there are inherent differences which would prevent desegregation of the two systems of education.[60] What Davies seems to neglect is that, because the Africans of 1964 were different from those of earlier times, continued segregation in education could not be justified on any grounds. He also neglected to mention that the white students were enjoying free education because the government chose to make it free, and that African education was made neither free nor compulsory, also because it chose not to do so. The repugnance and the justifiable indignation which the RF educational policy aroused among the Africans, combined with the real threat that it posed, compelled the church to break faith with it. There was no other course of action for the church to take.

Church leaders considered the new policy contained in a document entitled *The Dynamic Expansion of African Education*[61] as neither dynamic nor an expansion to suggest the extent of their lack of confidence in whatever policy the RF formulated. We have only enough space here to discuss briefly its major provisions. While stating that full primary schooling would be achieved in stages, beginning with children who were within walking distance from the school, the RF was fully aware that most African schools, both rural and urban, were not within walking distance. What this aspect of its educational policy meant, therefore, is that it was not going to make an effort to support the building of more schools. It is therefore clear that the RF was less than sincere when it stated: "Within the limits of financial resources, measures will be taken to develop secondary schools."[62] Even then, the policy meant that only 12.5 percent of the graduates of the primary schools would enroll in the academic secondary schools. Another 37.5 percent would enroll in industrial and vocational schools under the same conditions that Earl Grey had outlined in 1898 when he introduced the Education Ordinance of 1899.

MUZOREWA AS A PIECE OF THE CRISIS PUZZLE

As the crisis between the RF and the church deepened, it compelled many church organizations to convene special sessions of their conferences or governing bodies to discuss it. Thus, Bishop Abel Muzorewa of the United Methodist Church felt he had a duty to convene a special session of the Methodist governing body known as the Conference to be held June 12–13, 1970, to discuss the crisis. The conference expressed its unreserved opposition to the policy by passing two resolutions:

(1) Now is the time to stand firm against the payment of the 5% by the parents, church, local school committees or council. If, as a result of our opposition, schools are closed, it is the government which is to blame.[63]

(2) We will not as a church pay the 5% of the primary teachers' salaries demanded by the government or collect it from the parents. We affirm our desire to strengthen African education and call upon the government to restore the 5% cut to enable us to continue our primary schools.[64]

To emphasize the fact that he was opposed to the policy, Muzorewa received a standing ovation when he added a personal position, saying "Let it go on record that I will fight as a Christian and by Christian methods of nonviolence. I will sit in the same chair as I have been sitting in the church before, and I will not move from it. They will have to carry me away instead."[65] The RF-church conflict now took a new and dangerous turn.

When the RF decided to hold Bishop Muzorewa responsible for the United Methodist Church's rejection of its policy and singled him out for attack, there was a perilous twist in the unprecedented church-state conflict. M. G. Mills angrily accused him of disloyalty, adding defensively that his ministry was just as concerned with orderly schooling of African children in 1971 as the United Methodist Church, and that he would say this with the greatest respect of Bishop Muzorewa. Mills concluded, "The paragraph about 'blame' puzzles me. Where else can 'blame' lie other than upon the government, or upon me personally, if you like? Not one of us wishes to waste a moment on apportioning blame. I do not recall any part of the Scripture enjoining us to apportion blame."[66] This attitude and language did not help solve the problem of the 5 percent cut policy.

It is not surprising that the relationship between the church and the RF had reached a breaking point and that nothing could be done to restore the mutuality of confidence and respect between the two institutions to ensure that the education of the Africans did not suffer a severe setback. Unable to tolerate the criticism of its policy any longer, the RF suddenly served Bishop Muzorewa a notice to put him under house arrest for the next five years. When Bishop Muzorewa responded that he would rather obey God than man,[67] the RF felt challenged and was compelled to show that it had power to act against him. While the ban was in force, the RF vigorously implemented its policy and so did the greatest damage to the education of the Africans since the enactment of the Education Ordinance of 1899.[68]

In 1983 Bishop Muzorewa put these tragic events into perspective when he told the author that the policy of 5 percent cut in salary grants for the African primary teachers was a definite part of the RF's strategy to ensure that it sustained Rhodes's and Huggins's promise to perpetuate white political power for at least a thousand years. He added that for the RF to put him under house arrest for five years was a vengeful act, an attempt to use him as a piece of the puzzle of a major national crisis that it had created.[69] It would appear that the only way to end the crisis was for the RF to withdraw its policy. Because the RF refused to do this, Africans felt that it was their duty to redesign a new strategy to end the RF itself.

SUMMARY AND CONCLUSION

Two conclusions can be made at this point about the RF educational policy beginning in 1966. The first is that in announcing its new policy on April 20, 1966, the RF demonstrated its lack of interest in the real educational development of the Africans. What resulted, instead, was confusion and chaos that dominated its entire educational program for the remainder of its administration. It was not possible for either the Africans or the church leaders to make any sense or logical interpretation of what the RF was really trying to do, other than to give itself more power to retard the educational programs of the Africans. The church leaders could only conclude that "the Rhodesia Front government was all out to get them."[70] This was an act to confuse both the Africans and the church of its real intentions.

The second observation is that in announcing a series of policy changes from 1966 to 1968, the RF was indeed putting together the elements of an unprecedented institutional conflict. In a relentless pursuit of its educational policy, the RF also wanted the church to know that it was the undisputed authority in the area of policy on African education. At the same time, in resisting the RF educational policy, the church leaders wanted the RF to know that the days of cooperation between the two institutions were numbered, and that the church still could claim traditional authority to operate schools for the Africans in accordance with the religious principles that were essential to its mission.

NOTES

1. Methodist Church, *Official Journal of the Rhodesia Annual Conference* (Old Umtali: Rhodesia Mission Press, 1971), p. 154.

2. Hartzell Secondary School at Old Mutare Methodist Center, which the author attended, is named after him.

3. For detailed discussion of the problems that Victorian missionaries encountered in Africa, see Dickson A. Mungazi, *The Honored Crusade: Ralph E.*

Dodge's Theology of Liberation and Initiative for Social Change in Zimbabwe (Gweru: Mambo Press, 1991). The author obtained the materials used in this study from the Dodge papers at the University of Syracuse Library from 1986 to 1989. These are the main sources used for this chapter.

4. The Methodist Church, *The Christian Advance*, vol. 12, no. 1, July 1918, p. 8.

5. Ibid., p. 9.

6. Ralph E. Diffendorfer (ed.), *The World Service of the Methodist Episcopal Church* (Chicago: Council of Board of Benevolencies, 192), p. 110.

7. Ralph E. Dodge, "Churches and the Color Bar," *The Presbyterian Outlook*, Vol. 146, No. 9 (March 2, 1964), p. 1.

8. Southern Rhodesia, *Commission of Inquiry into Native Education* (F. L. Hadfield, chairman) (Salisbury: Government Printer, 1927), para. 20, p. 7.

9. Ibid., para 21, p. 8.

10. Southern Rhodesia, Committee on Native Education, 1925, p. 58.

11. For a detailed discussion see Dickson A. Mungazi, *Colonial Education for Africans: George Stark's Policy in Zimbabwe* (Westport, CT: Praeger Publishers, 1991), p. 15.

12. Harold Jowitt, *Annual Report of the Director of Native Education, 1928*, p. 1 (Zimbabwe National Archives).

13. Ibid., p. 2.

14. Southern Rhodesia, *Annual Report of the Director of Native Development, 1930*, p. 27.

15. Southern Rhodesia, *Annual Report of the Director of Native Development, 1934*, p. 1.

16. H. M. Bate, *Report from Rhodesia* (London: Melrose, 1953), p. 164.

17. Ralph E. Dodge, *The Unpopular Missionary* (Westwood, NJ: Fleming H. Revell, 1964), p. 86.

18. The Methodist Church, "The Waddilove Manifesto: The Education Policy of the Methodist Church," an unpublished statement of policy, February 8–9, 1946.

19. Godfrey M. Huggins, *The Education Policy in Southern Rhodesia: Some Notes on Certain Features* (Salisbury: Government Printer, 1939), p. 2.

20. Godfrey M. Huggins, "Taking Stock of African Education," an address to Southern Rhodesia Missionary Conference held at Goromonzi Secondary School, August 26, 1954 (Zimbabwe National Archives, Ref. AV/1/GH/8/26/54).

21. David Hapgood, *Africa in Today's World Focus* (Boston: Ginn and Company, 1971), p. 33.

22. Ralph E. Dodge, "The Church and Law and Order," an assay, February 1964, p. 3.

23. Ibid., p. 6.

24. Stanlake Samkange, *What Rhodes Really Said About Africans* (Harare: Harare Publishing House, 1982), p. 30.

25. Ian D. Smith interview with the author, Harare, Zimbabwe, July 20, 1983, in Mungazi, *The Honored Crusade*, p. 80.

26. Ralph E. Dodge, "The African Church Now and in the Future," an essay, August 1966, p. 9. In 1996 Kofi Annan of Ghana was elected secretary-general of the United Nations, making Dodge's prediction come true.

27. Ibid., p. 10.

28. Ibid., p. 86.

29. Ralph E. Dodge, "The Church in Africa, " an Episcopal address in *The Official Journal of the Methodist Church* (Old Mutare: Rhodesia Mission Press, 1963), p. 43.

30. In 1969 the RF fulfilled its promise by enacting the Land Tenure Act, which was more oppressive than the Land Apportionment Act of 1929.

31. The RF kept this promise also. When it found that it was unable to secure independence from Britain on its own terms, the RF unilaterally declared Rhodesia independent.

32. Chapter 5 of Mungazi, *The Honored Crusade*, discusses the circumstances surrounding another Methodist resolution directed at the RF government with severe consequences for both the church and the RF itself.

33. The Methodist Church, "A Warning Against the Declaration of Independence," a press release, May 17, 1964, cited in ibid., p. 91.

34. Ibid.

35. Ralph E. Dodge, in a letter dated July 17, 1964, addressed to William Harper, the RF minister of Internal Affairs, cited in ibid., p. 90.

36. William Harper, the RF minister of Internal Affairs, letter addressed to Dodge, July 22, 1964, in Ibid., p. 91.

37. D. E. Shephard, private secretary to the Minister of Internal Affairs, in a letter dated August 13, 1964, addressed to Mrs. E. Griffin.

38. For evidence leading to this conclusion, see Chapter 10 of Mungazi, *The Honored Crusade*.

39. Ibid., p. 92.

40. Garfield Todd, telegram to Dodge, sent from his home in Shabani, July 17, 1964. See ibid., p. 92. The letters quoted in the rest of this chapter come from these sources. For detailed discussion of Todd's role in the political transformation of Zimbabwe, see Dickson A. Mungazi, *The Last British Liberals in Africa: Michael Blundell and Garfield Todd* (Westport, CT: Praeger Publishers, 1999).

41. For a detailed discussion of the action that the RF took against Todd and his daughter Judith, see Judith Todd, *The Right to Say No: Rhodesia 1972* (Harare: Longman, 1987).

42. Joshua Nkomo, in a letter dated July 18, 1964, addressed to Dodge from Gonakudzingwa Restriction Area where he was kept as a political prisoner, cited in Mungazi, *The Honored Crusade*, p. 93.

43. Letter written on July 20, 1964, by 73 Methodist missionaries pledging their support to Dodge.

44. Christian Church Council, letter dated July 20, 1964, addressed to Ian Smith.

45. Bishop Donal R. Lamont, in a letter dated July 21, 1964, addressed to Dodge.

46. R. Kent Rasmussen, *Historical Dictionary of Rhodesia/Zimbabwe* (London: Scarecrow Press, 1979), p. 145.

47. Lazarus Mandizha, letter dated July 21, 1964, addressed to Dodge.

48. G. D. Mhlanga, letter dated July 27, 1964, addressed to Dodge.

49. Ralph E. Dodge, Statement on Deportation Order, July 19, 1964.

50. Ibid.

51. Ibid.

52. Ibid.

53. Ibid.

54. Ralph E. Dodge, "Zimbabwe, Oh Zimbabwe," farewell address following his deportation delivered at the Methodist Church, Harare, July 31, 1964.

55. Edmund Burke was a British statesman, author, and political thinker. He opposed slavery and worked to eliminate social injustice and evil wherever they existed. Burke warned that social injustice would continue as long as responsible citizens remained silent.

56. Bishop Abel T. Muzorewa, interview with the author, Harare, July 28, 1983.

57. Geoffrey Kapenzi, *The Clash of Cultures: Christian Missionaries and the Shona of Rhodesia* (Washington, DC: University Press of America, 1978), p. 6.

58. Bishop Donal Lamont, *An Open Letter to the Prime Minister*, October 26, 1976. Courtesy of the Old Mutare Methodist Archives.

59. Ibid.

60. Southern Rhodesia, *Annual Report of the Secretary for African Education*, 1964.

61. Rhodesia Front Government, *The Dynamic Expansion in African Education*, Ref. INF/NE/AC/2710, April 20, 1966. Courtesy of the Zimbabwe National Archives.

62. Rhodesia, *Parliamentary Debates*, April 20, 1966.

63. The Methodist Church, "Resolution Condemning the Government Policy of Five Percent Cut in Salary Grants for African Primary Teachers," passed by Special Session of Conference, Old Mutare, June 12–13, 1970 (Old Mutare: Methodist Archives).

64. Ibid.

65. Bishop Abel Muzorewa, address to Special Session of the United Methodist Conference, Old Mutare, June 13, 1970.

66. M.G. Mills, letter to George Fleshman, Methodist Secretary for Education, June 18, 1971.

67. *Rhodesia Herald*, August 15, 1971. In March 1979, Bishop Muzorewa, Rev. Ndabaningi Sithole, Chief Jeremiah Chirau, and Ian D. Smith reached an agreement about the future of Zimbabwe on terms that the international community rejected because they were considered to favor the continuation of white minority rule that the RF represented.

68. Bishop Abel Muzorewa, during an interview with the author, July 28, 1983.

69. Ibid.

70. Ibid.

3

Tutu's South Africa and Muzorewa's Zimbabwe Compared

A human being is a human being only because he belongs to a community.
                                        —Desmond M. Ttutu, 1981

Christianity was a common denominator which brought my parents together.
                                        —Abel T. Muzorewa, 1978

EVENTS THAT INFLUENCED FUTURE RACE RELATIONS IN SOUTH AFRICA

When Desmond Mpilo Tutu was born on October 7, 1931, South Africa had been independent for 21 years. While the attainment of independence on May 31, 1910, gave Afrikaners a sense of freedom from the old political enemy, the British, it aroused in them a new fear that at some point in time Africans would rebel against them as they had done in 1835 under the great Zulu king, Dingaan. In 1910 Afrikaners simply changed their fear of the British to be controlled by the fear of the Africans. From that time to April 1994 Afrikaners would never be free from that fear. This is why they designed and applied the policy of apartheid to ensure that Africans had no chance of exercising any form of political power that would threaten them. This is why politics in South Africa acquired racial dimensions. In fact, race was the major focus of political activity for these 84 years.

The three major political leaders at that time were Afrikaner heroes of the 1899–1902 Boer War: Louis Botha, Jan C. Smuts, and J. B. Hertzog. From the beginning of the Union of South Africa, election contests were based on fear of what Africans might do in response to Afrikaner political domination. This fear controlled the behavior of both government leaders and Afrikaners in general. Louis Botha, who served as prime minister from 1910 to 1919, was the leader of the South Africa Party that advocated reconciliation with the British-speaking community in order to create a stronger association of white people against Africans. But Botha did not want to have any meaningful relationships with Africans themselves.[1]

Botha and his cabinet presented an impressive agenda leading to a remarkable legislative achievement. However, within two years Botha and Hertzog began to have serious differences of opinion regarding reconciliatory gestures toward the British. Botha and Smuts thought it was necessary to put the bitterness of the past behind them in order to mobilize national and human resources for purposes of building the country for the good of all white people. Hertzog argued that the British would exploit this gesture to make maximum political gain over the Afrikaners. In 1908 Hertzog, as minister of education in the Orange River Colony, had angered the British-speaking community and the English-language press by insisting on what he considered equality of the two languages and promoting bilingualism in schools.

But the difference between Botha and Smuts on the one hand and Hertzog on the other hand was much deeper than their respective opinions on reconciliation and bilingualism in schools. It had to do with the position of Africans in South Africa. Botha and Smuts felt that Afrikaners should make genuine efforts to at least recognize the political aspirations of Africans. Hertzog argued that such an effort would be dangerous as they would begin to demand more rights. There was no middle ground between the two positions.[2]

One must remember that discriminatory legislation and practice were an integral part of South Africa and colonial Zimbabwe from the very beginning. For example, in South Africa a series of laws was passed in quick succession. In 1911 the Mines and Works Act was passed to deny African workers industrial competency certificates that would have placed them on the same economic position as white workers. The Land Act of 1913 allocated 87 percent of the land to whites and the remaining 13 percent to Africans.

In addition to this Africans were not allowed to purchase land at all. The Industrial Reconciliation Act of 1913 (amended in 1956) required Africans employed as cheap labor to carry passbooks as a form of identity. The Wages Act of 1925 classified African workers as unskilled labor who were paid low wages. The Color Bar Act of 1926 made it illegal for

Africans to perform skilled labor. The Separate Development Act of 1948 did not allow Africans to live in exclusive neighborhoods. The Native Passes Act of 1952 required Africans to secure permits to enter certain urban areas. The Prohibition of Mixed Marriages Act of 1949 provided severe penalty for Africans who married across the color line. The Bantu Education Act of 1953 provided for separate educational facilities for students of different races.

During the height of colonial rule in Zimbabwe, especially during the last 15 years of the Rhodesia Front government, discriminatory legislation was supreme and vicious in all aspects of national life. The two countries were very similar in practicing discrimination. Both Tutu and Muzorewa suffered under this practice. That is why they thought they had to do something to change the situation. But the task was not easy; it required sacrifice and dedication. It also required a demonstration of high call to duty. But it was a task that both of them felt called upon to fulfill.

In an effort to create a common ground on which to base national programs without controversy, Botha invited Hertzog to join his administration in order to coordinate their efforts to ensure that the Africans had no chance of ever acquiring and exercising political power. However, Hertzog's political adventure had enabled him to coin an expression "Hertzogism" to characterize his extreme position on the question of race and defense of Afrikaner nationalism.[3] He was also accused of promoting racism to disrupt the reconciliatory efforts that Botha and Smuts were making toward the English-speaking community.

While he was reviled by some, Hertzog was also admired by many Afrikaners. He became their leader in the forthcoming struggle between the two positions on reconciliation and the question of race. Hertzog saw these two issues as principal factors that would determine the future of South Africa. Therefore, while he accepted Botha's invitation to join his administration to minimize controversy on two critical issues, Hertzog refused to give up his views on both of them. This refusal created the impression that Botha's administration was handicapped by serious internal dissension and conflict. This impression put Botha in a difficult situation, unsure of what he should do.

Realizing that Hertzog's presence in his government was divisive and disruptive, Botha felt compelled to ask him to leave the administration. In that same year, 1912, only a few months after the founding of the ANC on January 8, Hertzog and his supporters formed the Nationalist Party, which was destined to rule South Africa continuously from 1948 to 1994. Hertzog then challenged Botha's South Africa Party, which he led as prime minister from 1910 to 1919.

In 1914 Mohandas K. Gandhi, who had arrived in South Africa in 1893 to do some legal work, led a campaign of nonviolence against Botha's discriminatory policy of limiting immigration from India while he encouraged it from European countries, especially from the Low Countries (Belgium and the Netherlands) that spoke the same language as the emerging Afrikaans. In Gandhi's reaction to his policy, Botha was faced with a problem that he never thought he would encounter given his relatively liberal position on the question of race.

This situation played into Hertzog's hands. For several years to come the two men were steadily drifting apart with very few issues on which they could agree. The cooperation that they had used as military leaders in the war against the British was now transforming into the Tower of Babel syndrome in the political arena. With the passage of time it was quite clear that the difference of opinion between the two men about the future of the country was getting wider, with each man assuring the other of pursuing a wrong policy.

To make matters worse for Botha, the protest that was led by Gandhi coincided with two serious strikes on the Rand in late 1913 and 1914. Tension between labor and management came to a head as a result of the efforts of white trade unions to classify white mineworkers as skilled labor and all African workers as unskilled labor. A disagreement between the two sides led to a general strike called by the mineworkers' union in 1913. As is often the case in strikes, violence led to bloodshed on a considerable scale.[4] By the time Botha tried to intervene, the damage had already been done. Hertzog seized the opportunity to portray Botha as a weak leader with no understanding of the critical issues facing the young nation. The outcome of the strike was in favor of labor, giving Hertzog reason to suggest that social and economic strife would be the lot of the country under Botha's leadership. The two men waged a vicious campaign against each other paralyzing the normal operations of the country.

Slowly public confidence in Botha began to erode away. In January 1914 the mineworkers' union took advantage of Botha's deteriorating fortune to stage another strike in demand of higher salaries and better conditions of work. This time the strike was directed against the employment of Africans in the mining industry at a salary comparable to that of white workers. This time Smuts, as minister of defense, was better prepared to respond to a national crisis. He called the military units to maintain order. He also banned the leaders of the strike without due process, putting them on a ship in Durban Harbor leaving for Britain.[5]

Slowly Smuts was being seen as a more effective and decisive leader than Botha. When the First War broke out in Europe in August 1914, the British asked South Africa to occupy the German territory of South-West Africa. For all practical purposes Germany was driven out of its colonies in Africa.[6] Botha effectively occupied South-West Africa and took Windhoek, its administrative capital city, in 1915. On his return to South

Africa he faced a general election. But the Afrikaner nationalist feeling went against Botha and placed Hertzog in a more favorable position. Although Botha won the election, he had a reduced majority to work with in Parliament while Hertzog's Nationalist Party increased the number of seats by 27, giving it more power and influence over national programs.[7]

On July 20, 1914, the African National Congress submitted a petition to King George V protesting the enactment of the Land Act of 1913 and general decline of conditions of life under Botha. The ANC also asked the British government to exercise its constitutional responsibility to protect the African population as provided for in the South African Act of 1908 that the British government passed to prepare for independence in 1910. The petition stated its reason for making the request, saying "The petitioners consider themselves and the Native races to be still under the direct rule and control of the Crown through the governor-general, and therefore appeal to the Crown."[8] The petition added that Africans had never accepted the government of South Africa as legitimate in place of the British government, but that they had only accepted the administration of Louis Botha as adviser to the governor-general through the ministers on behalf of the British government.[9] Although the British government took no action on the petition, the publicity it generated went far in promoting understanding in Britain about the deteriorating conditions under which Africans were forced to live. The seeds of conflict between Africans and Afrikaners were sown early in the evolution of the system of apartheid.

Botha's death in 1919 seemed to enhance Hertzog's political fortunes. However, in the elections held in that year the voters decided to return Smuts to power because he was less controversial than Hertzog. Smuts's victory in the elections seemed to seal Hertzog's political future. Smuts served with distinction until he lost the elections to Hertzog in 1924.[10] Hertzog's victory over Smuts was because the Nationalist Party and the Labor Party made an election pact that was too strong for Smuts to overcome. With the assistance that N. C. Havenga gave him, Hertzog set the country on the road to one of the worst forms of racial conflict that ever existed in Africa. The South Africa Party and the Nationalist Party engaged in the battle of wills rarely known in the history of Africa.[11]

From 1924 to 1939, when Hertzog served as prime minister, the economic situation stabilized with the discovery of new gold deposits. Confidence increased as part of the roaring twenties. Havenga, the minister of finance, promised that he would produce a budget with a surplus. In 1925 Hertzog passed legislation to protect local industry.[12] In March 1928, and in accordance with its policy, the administration of Hertzog established the South African Iron and Steel Industry Corporation, in which the government had major interest. As soon as he assumed the leadership of the government, Hertzog introduced an official policy of racial segregation, arguing that this was necessary in order to address issues of national development that were peculiar to the culture of each racial group.

Hertzog then classified the people of South Africa into three racial groups: whites, Indians and Coloreds, and Africans (known officially as Natives until 1975). These were the elements that constituted apartheid. In his autobiography Nelson Mandela attempts to give an account of the political differences between Smuts and Hertzog, saying that while Hertzog led a drive to remove Africans from the common voters' role in the Cape Province, Mandela found Smuts a sympathetic leader toward all people. Mandela also says that he cared more that Smuts had helped found the League of Nations to promote freedom of all people than the fact that he had denied Africans at home their basic freedoms.[13] Mandela concludes that Smuts showed some sensitivity about the position of Africans, while Hertzog had none because he was preoccupied with the notion of Afrikaner superiority.

The declaration of war in Europe in September 1939 brought Smuts and Hertzog on opposite sides of the conflict as they had done in the First World War. Smuts immediately argued that South Africa must support Britain because Germany was under the spell of Adolf Hitler and his Nazi Party, which would spread across the world if they were not stopped. Hertzog argued that Hitler and his party were fighting to end the oppressive measures imposed on Germany by the Treaty of Versailles. Seeing an opportunity to make political capital gains, Daniel F. Malan quickly came to the Smuts-Hertzog feud by taking Hertzog's argument, saying that Hitler and the Nazi Party were acting in self-defense, and that Britain and France were the real aggressors. There is no question that both Hertzog and Malan were venting their anger at Britain for the Boer War.

HUDDLESTON'S RESPONSE TO APARTHEID

Among Huddleston's most important contributions to the struggle for social justice in South Africa is his book, *Naught for Your Comfort* (1956), a serious indictment of the policy of apartheid. In the preface Huddleston stated that the book had been written in the odd hours of a very busy year, and concluded that perhaps this alone may give it value because it had certainly come red hot out of the crucible that was South Africa of the day.[14] Huddleston went on to state the nature of the problems that the Nationalist government was creating for him and explained that he wrote the book only to throw light on one small corner of the world that few people outside South Africa knew much about.

Huddleston said that it was his personal viewpoint and that it did not reflect the position of the Anglican Church or the Community of Resurrection. He said that because he was a South African citizen, he felt he had a responsibility to express his concern about the direction the country was taking in response to the policy of apartheid. He stated his wish that he would like to be considered a citizen of Africa along with Alan Paton.

The title of the book came from G. K. Chesterton,[15] a British essayist, novelist, and poet who wrote *Ballad of the White Horse* in 1927, in which appear the lines:

I tell you naught for your comfort,
Yea, naught for your desire,
Save that the sky grows darker yet,
And the sea rises higher.

In the opening chapter of his book, Huddleston paints a picture of South Africa that reflects the hope of Smuts, who served as prime minister of South Africa from 1919 to 1924 and from 1939 to 1948, and the despair of Alan Paton and Robert Sobukwe,[16] a brilliant African nationalist whose vision of South Africa had been marred by the application of the policy of apartheid. Huddleston places himself in the context of the pain that he experienced in having been asked to leave South Africa and recalls a French expression "Partir, c'est mourir un peu" (To leave is to die a little).[17] For a man who regarded himself as a citizen of a troubled country, for a religious leader who had given 12 years of his life to the cause that demanded nothing less than total devotion, to be asked to leave represented a removal of the major life-giving substance that could not be replaced. There was no greater cause for Huddleston to live for than the struggle for social justice in South Africa. He goes on to contrast the majestic beauty of the Magaliesbuerg Mountains and the luxurious homes that whites owned compared with the shanty homes in which African masses were crowded. He concluded that for these African masses life had become a torment far too painful to endure. He stated that he had no apology in writing this indictment of the apartheid system and its authors.

Right at the beginning of the book Huddleston informs the reader of what he intends to do: to present the evils of apartheid from the perspective of an individual who had come to observe details of its operation on the spot. He warns the reader, "What I shall try to avoid is that most common and persistent goal in all such assessment—the attempt to be impartial. I shall write this book as a partisan for I believe that Christians are committed in the field of human relationships to a partisan approach."[18] Huddleston argued that apartheid was a blatantly partisan and partial system and that there was no point in trying to respond to it in a nonpartisan and impartial way. An attempt to give an impartial response would be a distortion of the actual problems that apartheid created.

There is no doubt that Huddleston was motivated by his belief that because God became man, therefore human life itself is a reflection of the dignity and value that are infinite in their meaning. He also argued that the two elements carry the message that the state exists to serve the needs of the people, not its own purpose as the Nationalist government was doing by implementing the policy of apartheid. Huddleston concluded that there was no virtue in trying to be impartial in discussing a sinister policy that was self-serving in every way. He also concluded that any political system that was based on racial or color prejudice and ruthlessly enforced by the state is an affront to human dignity and an insult to all people.

In summing up his indictment of the apartheid system, Huddleston placed the responsibility for the evils of apartheid on the Afrikaners themselves for supporting it. He argued, however, that the overwhelming majority of South Africans of the white group had no conception whatever of human relationships except the one that was based on racial domination. He went on to state that the only Africans they knew were servants or employees. He concluded that the greatest tragedy of apartheid was the total ignorance of those in responsible positions of government about the way in which young Africans engaged in the thought process.[19]

Huddleston advanced a powerful argument for his view that after 12 years of the closest possible contact with Africans he could claim an authority to speak at first hand about the conditions that affected them. He lived with them every day in Sophiatown. He came to understand their thoughts, their oppression, their anger, and their frustration. With this knowledge of the way apartheid had reduced the Africans to the position of mere existence, Huddleston concluded that candor and honesty in discussing apartheid must serve as a guiding principle.

Utilizing Chesterton's metaphor of daylight growing drearier than darkness,[20] Huddleston describes the political, social, and economic darkness that surrounded the African world under apartheid and the daylight that abounded in the Afrikaner world. He quoted what the archbishop of Cape Town once wrote in a church magazine to describe how the complacency of the government created an erroneous impression that all the people of South Africa were happy. Huddleston agreed with the archbishop that nothing was further from the truth as the African world was surrounded by a veil of darkness. The opportunity to live in Sophiatown helped broaden his understanding of the cruelty of the policy of apartheid. He recognized the reality that one of the unfortunate things that happened to those living in South Africa was the acceptance of a situation that could not be justified on any moral principles.

Huddleston concluded that throughout human history society has been heading for serious conflict when its members allowed injustice of the magnitude to exist in the form that it did in South Africa. Germany experienced it when the people allowed the Nazi Party a free hand in pursuing its policy. He also concluded that unless the Africans decided to do something to change the situation, they would be unable to convert the darkness that was part of their existence into the light of their aspiration. He quotes Msimungu's bitter and yet profound words in Alan Paton's *Cry, the Beloved Country* about the African response to apartheid, "I have one great fear in my heart that when they are turned to loving we shall be turned to hating."[21] Fortunately, when apartheid came to an end in 1994, the Africans did not turn to hating.

Discussing what he identified as a Christian determination, Huddleston asked Christians to promote the development of the Africans as a condition of the development of the Christian community. He concluded that Christians faced a dilemma: if they are in the forefront of development of the Africans they are seen as patronizing them, if they continued to exercise leadership in the struggle to end apartheid they would be considered to want to be in the forefront of the movement. He suggested that Christians demonstrate their commitment to the development of Africans by their actions. He used his own action as an example, stating that apart from his effort to arouse conscience among Christians all over the world, his basic desire was to identify himself completely with the Africans and their plight and to participate in the struggle for human rights and personal freedoms. He expressed this position clearly at a meeting of the African National Congress soon after he arrived in South Africa.

Huddleston knew that for one to identify oneself with a cause required a corresponding action, but it is also this action that can bring danger or reprisal from those who feel threatened by such action. In this setting he was under no illusion that the Nationalist government would take action against him. But the fear of reprisal could not deter him from pursuing the objectives he had identified. In his daily life Huddleston practiced the example that because whites and Africans worshiped in separate church buildings that practice itself constituted the principle of segregation. He urged all Christian organizations to recognize this segregation for what it was: support of the policy of apartheid. He argued that any Christian organization could not faithfully discharge its duty and remain loyal to its principles when it continued to discriminate against one group of people. He concluded, "The Church is facing the challenge of the extent which it must meet now and which it cannot meet effectively with official pronouncements alone."[22]

Huddleston then turned his attention to the discussion of an issue of great concern to all the people of South Africa: the rise of crime among the African population. The Nationalist government capitalized on this phenomenon to conclude that Africans were uncivilized and lacked moral values. However, Huddleston saw the causes of this phenomenon from an entirely different perspective when educated Africans were known as "educated Kaffirs," "cheeky niggers," or "smart skellums." When Afrikaners used these terms to describe the aspiring Africans, their dignity and sense of pride were taken away.

What remained was anger and frustration, and these human emotions led to criminal behavior. Instead of blaming Africans for the rise in crime, Huddleston challenged the Nationalist government to examine its policy and the effect that it was having on human behavior. In the same way Huddleston discussed the effect of the shantytown, the effect of the behavior of the policy, the nature of education Africans received as major factors that contributed to deviant behavior among Africans.

To substantiate his argument that the Nationalist government was educating Africans for servitude, Huddleston quoted Hendrik F. Verwoerd, then minister of Bantu Affairs, as stating in the South African Parliament in 1954 that the school must equip Africans to meet the demands which the economic life of South Africa would impose upon him. Verwoerd concluded by stating that there would be no place for Africans in society above the level of certain forms of labor.[23]

Verwoerd was refuting the report of the Eiselen Commission, which recommended in 1949 that because education for all people was good for the country it must be provided on the basis of equality. By the time the Nationalist government invited Huddleston to leave South Africa, he was recalled by his superiors in Britain in 1956 to receive a new assignment. He felt he had carried his message across. Although apartheid was still operating strongly, Huddleston had aroused a passion to fight against it. He had left footprints that those who came after him followed with remarkable success.

When he left South Africa in 1956, Huddleston continued his campaign against apartheid, taking it to an international stage. The highlights of his activity include the following: he led a mass protest against the visit to Britain of Pieter W. Botha in June 1984. He led a delegation to meet with Margaret Thatcher to protest against Botha's visit. He played a prominent part in organizing 120,000 demonstrators in London in November 1985 to protest Britain's antisanctions stance against South Africa. He participated in Nelson Mandela's "Freedom at 70" campaign held at Hyde Park in London in 1988.

There, both Desmond Tutu and Huddleston participated by addressing the crowd. He addressed dozens of meetings held throughout Britain, including schools, churches, trade unions, and other organizations on the evils of apartheid.[24] By 1990 it was quite obvious that the Nationalist government would no longer be able to overcome the effect of the campaign against apartheid waged relentlessly by both Tutu and Huddleston.

EVENTS THAT INFLUENCED THE FUTURE OF ZIMBABWE

When Methodist Bishop Ralph E. Dodge arrived in Zimbabwe in 1956, there were a number of events that indicated that colonial society was drifting into the shadows of church-state conflict. The retirement of Godfrey Huggins from the office of prime minister of the Federation of Rhodesia and Nyasaland in that year and the erratic behavior of his successor Roy Welensky, the limitations placed on Garfield Todd's new education policy for the Africans, the resurgence of the right-wing Dominion Party, the inauguration of the African National Congress, all were events that made 1956 a unique year. Even the colonial government itself recognized this fact.[25]

Dodge was unique in his perception of the role of the church in colonial Zimbabwe. Since his arrival in Angola in 1936, Dodge and the colonial government would never agree on policy and agenda. He was always revolutionary in both his thinking and action.[26] When it came to the application of principles of justice and fair play, Dodge was no compromiser. That the colonial society disregarded these basic principles in its policy for Africans inevitably led to church-state conflict. This was the kind of environment that marred relationships between Dodge and the Rhodesia Front government as soon as it assumed office in December 1962.

The promise that Winston Churchill made in the Atlantic Charter of August 1941 on behalf of the colonial governments to the Africans, of improved conditions of life as a reward for their service during the war, remained as remote and unfulfilled as it was vaguely made.[27] Racial discrimination in all aspects of national life was increasing dramatically. The economic boom that followed the end of the war was an exclusive right and benefit of whites.[28] There was neither any indication nor any hope that Africans would share in the affluence that had come partly as a result of their toil and suffering during the war. While the standard of living for whites was steadily improving, that of Africans was steadily declining. Africans remained removed from any political participation except in meaningless ways as much as they remained distant from meaningful educational opportunity.

This was the situation that Dodge found as he arrived in Zimbabwe in 1956 and one that he felt the church must not allow to continue if it was to be a true witness to its mission.[29] What really disturbed Dodge is what disturbed other Christian leaders of his time: any social structure that reduced some people to the level of bare existence has a negative impact on Christianity and society itself unless its leaders rise to the occasion and seek an end to it.[30].

The knowledge that the church would be subjected to severe criticism from Africans for remaining silent in the face of great social injustice is what compelled Dodge and later other church leaders to speak against the conditions under which Africans lived.[31] But in doing so, he, as well as other church leaders who chose to criticize the policy of the colonial government, risked the possibility of serious reprisals. There is no doubt that Dodge was prepared to take such a risk because he could not abandon his vision of a completely transformed Zimbabwe.

It is for this reason that in the first chapter of his *The Unpopular Missionary* that Dodge discusses the question, "Does the church perpetuate colonialism?" He recognized that because most missionaries belonged to the same race as the original colonizers and the government in power, the African masses tended to repudiate them and their teachings.[32] Dodge went on to argue that not only must the church help break the colonial grip on the life of Africans, it must also join the African crusade for a social revolution because the colonial condition with its negative character was inadequate to meet the needs of all people.[33]

From this vantage point Dodge concluded that the Africans were also oppressed by a combination of four forces: ignorance, poverty, disease, and denial of political participation. He believed that all were directly related. This is why he argued, "He who is dominated by another spiritually, economically, academically, or politically, will never develop his full potential."[34] In arguing that any effort to end the power of these forces of oppression must be directed at ending the colonial conditions that produce them, Dodge was in effect suggesting that the colonial government itself must be brought to an unconditional end as a final outcome of freedom from domination.[35]

In retrospect, the crisis that was rapidly building up in 1964 was a climax of events that began to take place in 1959. When Edgar Whitehead declared the state of emergency of February 28, 1959, his predecessor, Garfield Todd, opposed it. In supporting Todd, Dodge was aware that he was adding fuel to an already raging political fire. Writing a letter to Todd in March 1959, Dodge praised him for taking a stand against the Whitehead regime, saying that although he had not had the privilege of meeting him, he wished to express his appreciation to the stand which he had taken during the present emergency.[36]

At that time little did Dodge know that he would need Todd's support in 1964. The apparent alliance between Todd and Dodge was noted by Ian Smith, Winston Field, and William Harper, who were then members of the extreme Dominion Party, which was the opposition in Parliament. The alliance also sent a message early in his administration that Dodge intended to provide a leadership that envisaged a total transformation of Zimbabwe. As soon as it became the government, the RF began to watch Dodge very closely.

TUTU'S VISION OF SOUTH AFRICA

Writing in September 1981 a foreword to *Crying in the Wilderness: The Struggle for Justice in South Africa*, Bishop Huddleston said of Tutu: "I have a very special reason for pride in writing the foreword to this collection of Bishop Desmond Tutu's writings. It is wonderful for me to see how he has become the voice of African hope and aspirations at this most dangerous time."[37] Huddleston goes on to add that it was particularly gratifying to watch Tutu develop into a national leader who has a clear vision of his country without apartheid.

Tutu's ability to speak on behalf of his people and to provide effective leadership during a difficult time testify to the degree of his commitment to the transformation of South Africa to make it a home for all people. Huddleston concludes his foreword by saying that it is equally gratifying that Tutu's voice had remained as prophetic as it had been since he first came to national spotlight in 1984. Huddleston suggests that Tutu's vision for South Africa is anchored on his conviction that society without justice has nothing else to build itself on.[38]

In 1984 Huddleston wrote a foreword to Tutu's *Hope and Suffering* in which he said that reading the sermons, addresses, and writings in this book would enable one to discover that hope and suffering intertwine in almost every paragraph. He also said that it was inevitable that this should be so, for Tutu looked out upon his country and spoke to its leaders as a concerned citizen for the welfare of all its people. Huddleston concluded that in the recurring crises and tragedies, Bishop Tutu always looked out in love and compassion.[39] Huddleston went on to add that Tutu was not afraid to proclaim with great urgency the truth about the harmful effect of apartheid as the evil and destructive force that it was. He was also not afraid to challenge the government and its representatives for their callous and sustained assault on human dignity and rights. He concluded that it was for these reasons that Tutu was totally committed to bring about the transformation of South Africa so that peace, cooperation, and harmony would prevail to ensure the development of the country.[40]

Huddleston went on to discuss Tutu's vision and mission in South Africa, saying that in becoming committed to playing his role in the transformation of South Africa Tutu was motivated by what he considered to be the best interests of the country. This is why he was not afraid to risk the consequences of his action and beliefs as he tried to convey so unmistakably his own certainty about the future of the country.[41] Huddleston concluded that Tutu's vision for South Africa was based on his understanding of the biblical expression that where there is no vision the people perish. Mandela added that Tutu's vision, coupled with his courage, constituted the kind of character of a determined fighter against apartheid needed to the extent that his independent mind became a tribute to his courage to face adversity in the struggle for democracy. His relentless campaign led to the first elections in April 1994 in which all people participated.[42]

As individuals closely related to apartheid, both Huddleston and Mandela fully understood the mental anguish that Tutu was experiencing in trying to provide an effective leadership to a people who were oppressed. In launching a crusade against apartheid, Tutu encountered two major problems that only he in his position faced. The first problem was that as a religious leader he saw his country from an entirely different perspective from that of a political leader. He therefore advocated an approach that was political in content and so often got misunderstood by some people. In this context he recognized the fact that some members of the church lost faith in the values the church was trying to develop as its modus operandi.

The second problem was that as the first African leader of a major religious denomination, he needed to show that he was as aggressive as a white leader in seeking to elevate the Anglican Church to the status where it was equal to the position of the government in its influence in the lives of the people. Since the Nationalist government did not show any respect for Tutu because he was black, it did not appear to respect his opposition to apartheid. In return Tutu did not show any respect for the government for forcing an inhumane policy on the people in order to protect the privileged position of Afrikaners. In its turn the Nationalist government did not show any respect for the Anglican Church under the leadership of an African whose religious principles and theology were quite different from those of NGK, to which most of its members belonged. Therefore the conflict between Tutu and the Nationalist government was both political and religious. The combination of these two powerful forces compounded the problems of institutional relationships and elevated them to a point where they were particularly difficult.

This outcome was also the result of the assistance that Tutu received from three major sources. The first source was that the Organization of African Unity was increasingly becoming more determined to recognize apartheid as a cause of continental instability. The second source was the increasing pressure from the international community, including the World Council of Churches and Western governments, whose leaders were more convinced of the need to tighten economic sanctions to force an end to apartheid. The third source of support for Tutu was the increasing activity of the ANC, which left the country completely paralyzed. Therefore, the end of the apartheid system in 1994 was a combination of all these three major forces.

In initiating the campaign to bring apartheid to an end, Tutu was fully aware of the importance of the developments that were taking place in Africa since the end of the war in 1945. The struggle against colonial systems soon acquired continental dimension following Ghana's achievement of independence in 1957. No matter how the colonial governments tried to stop the advent of independence in Africa, their actions merely had a delaying effect.

The struggle for independence could not be stopped. Although the 17 years from 1971 to 1988 are known as a period of the emergence of dictatorships in Africa, Africans never lost sight of their vision of democracy.[43] In South Africa during this period the Nationalist government defended its policy of apartheid, arguing that other African governments were even worse in the treatment of their people than it was through the application of apartheid laws, and that to single it out was unfair. Yes, some governments of Africa were oppressive, such as Idi Amin Dada in Uganda, Kamuzu Hastings Banda of Malawi, and Mobuto Sese Seko of Zaire. But nothing was comparable to the brutality of apartheid. It was unique in every way. No other government in Africa operated by principles by which the Nationalist government was operating under apartheid. It took away from Africans everything that was associated with the human being. Therefore, the application of apartheid laws put the Nationalist government of South Africa in a class of its own when it came to the application of national policy that had a devastating effect on the people. Nowhere else in the world was such a policy ever developed.

In Malawi, Zambia, and Zaire the struggle for democracy led to the end of dictatorships. The movement for multiparty democracy had been rejuvenated. This changed the entire political complexion. The release of Nelson Mandela in February 1990 added an impetus to an already fast-moving set of events. Any African leader who sought to entrench himself in dictatorship did so at his own peril. For example, in 1990 in the west African nation of Benin, Mathieu Kerekou, president since 1972, was forced to submit to a multiparty reform and elections that removed him from office.[44]

Combined with his own mission, Tutu used the trend toward the struggle for democracy in Africa to sharpen his own vision of South Africa. Fundamental to that vision was his theology of liberation, which most religious leaders of the Third World have adopted as intended to address various aspects of human needs—religious, spiritual, economic, social, and political. This line of thinking was relatively new, but once it was adopted, religious leaders used it to deliver a message that was intended to promote the total human being. The old theology that human beings must endure physical suffering on earth—including the lack of necessities to enable the human being to live a full and comfortable life as a condition of better life in the next world—no longer had an appeal to both the religious leaders and the people.

Addressing the needs of people in breadth and depth became Tutu's focus and the vision of his mission. On March 25, 1979, he advanced this vision saying that Africans should all have the freedom to become fully human beings because a human being can be a human being only because he belongs to a community. He suggested that a person is a person because he has relations with other persons and that separation of persons because of biological accidents is reprehensible and blasphemous.[45]

MUZOREWA'S EDUCATIONAL SAFARI AND HIS VISION OF ZIMBABWE

Several events produced Muzorewa and shaped his future. Methodist traditions were thoroughly part of his growing experiences. He was born prematurely under the care of a dedicated Swedish Methodist missionary nurse, Ellen E. Bjorklund, who had arrived at Old Umtali in 1915 and served until her death on November 19, 1930. Bjorklund was the only missionary nurse who had training in taking care of premature babies. When Muzorewa was only a few weeks old his weak, little body encountered a bout with a vicious pneumonia.

Miraculously Muzorewa pulled through with the assistance of everyone, including his parents who were among the first of their respective families to become Christians. Muzorewa himself concluded on this part of his background, saying that Christianity was a common denominator that brought his parents together.[46] The fact that his parents were the first to have a church wedding stressed how the Methodist Church would shape his destiny.

Rev. H. I. James, an early British Methodist missionary, and Rev. Samuel Chieza, an early African Methodist preacher, officiated at the wedding ceremony, creating a background that would later remind Muzorewa of his responsibility to the Methodist Church and the people. Old Umtali Methodist Center was also the birthplace of Enock Chieza, a distinguished musician[47] and educator. Born there in 1914 Enock was the son of Philip Chieza, an early Methodist preacher. To be born at Old Umtali Methodist Center was to inherit the fountain of inspiration that Hartzell created in his vision for its success in the future.

Like children of his day, Muzorewa was in no hurry to go to school.

He started at the age of nine at Chinyadza School in the Rusape district. There he learned as much as he could from his teachers. After the elementary grades he went to Old Umtali Center. At the age of 15 he was considered too young to leave home and go to school by himself. His parents asked Chabarwa Matthew Mataranyika, who was returning to Old Umtali, to travel with him and protect him from teasing by older bully boys who had been there before him.[48] To arrive at Old Umtali Muzorewa and Mataranyika traveled by train from Inyazure or Rusape to Mutare, then walked ten miles over the mountains to Old Umtali. He remembered the first trip that it was exciting for students to board the train that he had seen and heard about for years, but had never ridden before.[49]

Muzorewa remained at Old Umtali for four years, studying from Standard 3 to Standard 6. The curriculum was quite intense, seeking a functional balance between academic study and practical training that included agriculture, building, and carpentry as the colonial government inspector of schools had recommended for Mutambara School in 1925. He enjoyed all the subjects he studied. On one occasion his Standard 3 class prepared to present a dramatic play of the Good Samaritan. He played the part of the man who fell into the hands of robbers. To make the drama as real as possible, the class teacher, Edward Mazaiwana,[50] borrowed a real donkey from the local people so that Muzorewa could ride it as part of the drama. The metaphor that this simple educational experience gave Muzorewa remained with him permanently. It gave him the realization that Africans had fallen into the hands of colonial robbers and that they needed rescue by those in a position to do so. In the midst of an educational safari Muzorewa was afflicted with an illness that almost brought his educational pursuit to an untimely end. But with ready medical care available at Old Umtali, his ailments were soon resolved.

Halfway through his studies Muzorewa went through what he called his second birth—a religious experience that would determine the course of the rest of his life. During the Easter season each year all school activity came to a halt for one week in order to have spiritual renewal services, known as revival week. Some students saw this week as short period of vacation and resented the required attendance at services. Others welcomed it as an opportunity to renew their religious growth and spiritual development. At that time Rev. Josiah Chimbadzwa,[51] the pastor of Old Umtali Center, preached sermons that challenged students and members of the community to relate their lives to Christian experiences. Muzorewa was one of those students who accepted the challenge and came to the conclusion that although he had been brought up in a devout home environment, he made his own commitment to follow Christ as his savior.[52]

In the midst of his success in education and new religious experiences,

Muzorewa encountered a new problem from an unexpected source. For a number of years his father had considered training for the ministry in the Methodist Church. But the difficulty in making the decision was compounded by economic conditions of the time. On the one hand he wanted to build a family home in Chinyadza. On the other hand he wanted to respond to a call to train as a minister. During his third year at Old Umtali, Muzorewa's father decided to accept the invitation from Rev. M. J. Murphree to come to Old Umtali to study theology.

This decision would mean radical change for the entire family. Livestock would have to be sold, agricultural operations would have to be given up. As soon as Muzorewa's father accepted the invitation, Rev. Murphree went on furlough in the United States and his successor as principal of Old Umtali Center did not approve of married theological students because they were more expensive to maintain than single students.

However, determined to go through with his decision, Muzorewa's father refused to give up his decision. But the financial considerations compelled him to recognize the need to reexamine his decision one more time. He just did not have sufficient financial resources to support his wife and eight children by working part time at Murewa Methodist Center. He decided to seek better employment opportunity in South Africa, where many young men went to work in the mines and other forms of industry.

Muzorewa's father worked in Cape Town as a waiter earning 16 pounds sterling per month. This income was much higher than most workers earned in Zimbabwe. The young men from Zimbabwe and other countries of southern Africa, including Mozambique, Nyasaland (Malawi), Botswana, and Northern Rhodesia (Zambia), saved their money and hoped to return home to establish themselves finally. This is what Muzorewa's father hoped to do on his return to Zimbabwe.

However, in 1948 political events in South Africa would put a stop to the practice of Africans from other countries of southern Africa to seek employment in South Africa. This migratory labor system started in 1935, when new gold deposits were discovered in Johannesburg. In 1948 Daniel F. Malan, leader of the Nationalist Party waged a vicious campaign for political power, partly out of fear of the demands the Africans were making for equal political rights and partly out of a desire to allow the Afrikaners to maintain the political status quo.

As soon as Malan won the elections and formed the government, his administration immediately introduced the notorious policy of apartheid. The policy had already been in place unofficially since 1910, but Malan introduced elements of its structure in ways that posed serious implications for all people. As part of implementing provisions of the apartheid policy, Malan ordered Africans from other countries to leave.

Muzorewa's father returned to Zimbabwe to try to establish himself and provide for his family the necessities of life. He moved his family from one area to another until April 1957 when he bought a small piece of land in Zwiyambe, not far from Inyazure. With hard work he managed to raise enough funds to continue sending his children to school. By this time Abel had completed his primary schooling and was employed as a teacher at a monthly salary of one pound and ten shillings.

It soon became clear that teaching at such a low income was not for Muzorewa, but there were few alternative opportunities for young Africans with a level of ambition as he had. One frustration after another eventually led to a discussion with a dedicated Methodist missionary teacher, Edith H. Parks, who taught many Africans, including this author, in both primary and secondary school.[53] Parks recognized a potential that Muzorewa possessed for greater service to his people than he was rendering as a teacher. She encouraged him to consider entering the theological school at Old Umtali Center. After further discussion with Rev. T. A. O'Farrell, superintendent of schools of the district in which Muzorewa was teacher, he edged closer to a decision to enter the ministry.

After serving as an evangelist for a few years, Muzorewa enrolled at Old Umtali Theological Seminary in January 1950 and graduated on December 11, 1952. During his second year he fell in love with Maggie Rutendo Chigodora, who was working for the Murphree family at Old Umtali. Maggie's mother was a devout Christian widow, who had raised four daughters with the help of the Murphree family. Abel and Maggie were married on August 11, 1951, with Rev. Murphree officiating at the ceremony. In accordance with African tradition, Abel's family paid 25 pounds sterling and two head of cattle to Maggie's family. They eventually had five children.

Over the years Maggie proved such an ideal wife, companion, and support for Muzorewa that he dedicated his autobiography to her, saying with a sense of appreciation, "To Maggie Muzorewa, my life partner whose courage and sacrifice made this adventure possible."[54]

From 1950 to 1958 Muzorewa continued his studies privately. In 1959 he had earned enough credits to earn the equivalent of a high school diploma. His constant advisor, Edith H. Parks, began to explore the possibility of pursuing his higher education in the United States. This was a formidable challenge but both Parks and Muzorewa seemed able to meet it. Charles E. Fuller, a Methodist missionary from the United States, managed to raise sufficient funds to enable Muzorewa and his family to have a scholarship. He left in August 1958 to study at Central Methodist College in Fayette, Missouri, where he studied religion and philosophy. His family joined him later. When he graduated in 1962 he enrolled at Scarett College for Christian Workers in Nashville, Tennessee, where he graduated with a master's degree. Muzorewa was ready to return to play his role in the transformation of Zimbabwe.

SUMMARY AND CONCLUSION

By the time that both Tutu and Muzorewa decided to be involved in efforts to bring about change in South Africa and Zimbabwe, the two countries were similar in some important respects. Both countries had severe racial discrimination laws that gave Africans no chance for development unless they were changed. The laws of South Africa were based on the Land Act of 1913. The laws of colonial Zimbabwe were based on the Land Apportionment Act of 1929. These laws placed severe restrictions on Africans in both countries.

In South Africa laws that were passed under apartheid entrenched the system of segregation to the extent that they did not allow Africans to exercise any rights. In colonial Zimbabwe a series of laws was passed to have the same effect. The enactment of the Bantu Education Act in South Africa created social and educational conditions that placed severe limitations on the ability of Africans to do anything on their behalf. In the same way the replacement of the Land Apportionment Act of 1929 by the Land Tenure Act of 1969 in Zimbabwe had an equally disabling effect on Africans as they tried to struggle for development. Tutu and Muzorewa shared the view of other Africans that these laws had to be rescinded if Africans were to have an opportunity for development.

The task of convincing the existing governments to change the laws was an enormous one. Tutu had better success than Muzorewa simply because the conditions there by 1990 were suggesting that apartheid was a thing of the past, while in Zimbabwe of 1971 the Rhodesia Front government thought it was invincible. Tutu and Muzorewa were working under similar conditions that summoned all their determination to confront unjust systems.

Both countries had sent African political leaders to prison for opposing the existing political systems that did not allow Africans participation in any significant ways. In South Africa Nelson Mandela, Walter Sisulu, Govan Mbeki, and other African nationalist leaders had spent years in prison for opposing the Nationalist government. In Zimbabwe Robert Mugabe, Joshua Nkomo, Ndabaningi Sithole, Edgar Tekere, and others were also in prison for opposing the Rhodesia Front government. Both Tutu and Muzorewa decided to lead a campaign against the minority governments of their respective countries in order to keep African consciousness alive. In doing so they both took the risk of being arrested and sent to political prison. Both men felt it was better to take risks than to do nothing. This was their call to action.

NOTES

1. Leo Marquard, *The People and Policies of South Africa* (London: Oxford University Press, 1969) p. 145.

2. Ibid., p. 147.

3. South Africa, *Official Yearbook* (Pretoria: Government Printer, 1982), p. 42.

4. Ibid., p. 44.

5. Ibid., p. 45.

6. These colonies were Tanganyika, South-West Africa (Namibia), Rwanda, Burundi, and Cameroon. Germany had acquired them as a result of the partition of Africa effected at the Berlin conference from December 1884 to February 1885. Germany never reacquired these colonies.

7. South Africa, *Official Yearbook*, p. 46.

8. Thomas Kevin and Gwendolen M. Carter (eds.), *From Protest to Challenge: A Documentary History of African Politics in South Africa, 1852–1964* (Stanford, CA: Stanford University Press, 1972), p. 127.

9. Ibid., p. 127.

10. Smuts served as prime minister of South Africa for two terms, from 1919 to 1924, and from 1939 to 1948. Other leaders were Louis Botha, 1910–1919, J. G. Hertzog, 1924–1939, Daniel F. Malan, 1948–1954, J. G. Strijdom, 1954–1958, Hendrik F. Verwoerd, 1958–1966, J. B. Vorster, 1966–1978, P. W. Botha, 1978–1989, and F. W. de Klerk, 1989–1994. De Klerk was succeeded by Nelson Mandela in April 1994, the first African leader.

11. Nelson Mandela, *Long Walk to Freedom: The Autobiography of Nelson Mandela* (Boston: Little, Brown, 1994), p. 42

12. Ibid., p. 43.

13. Ibid., p. 13.

14. Trevor Huddleston, *Naught for Your Comfort* (New York: Double day, 1956) p. 7.

15. Chesterton has been called the Prince of Paradox. His novels include *The Man Who Was Thursday* (1908), and a crime-fiction series known for its whimsical and wise detective. He is especially known for his witty essays. His studies of Robert Browning and Charles Dickens for the English Men of Letters series provide enlightening criticism.

16. For a tribute to this remarkable African nationalist, see Desmond Tutu, "Robert Mangaliso Sobukwe," in his *Crying in the Wilderness: The Struggle for Justice in South Africa* (Grand Rapids, MI: William B. Eerdmans, 1982), p. 65.

17. Huddleston, *Naught for Your Comfort*, p. 13.

18. Ibid., p. 17.

19. Ibid., p. 19.

20. In his poem, *"The Briscrat"* (1927), Chesterton wrote, "Where the splendor of the daylight grows drearier than the dark."

21. Huddleston, *Naught for Your Comfort*, p. 44.

22. Ibid., p. 76.

23. Ibid., p. 157.

24. Anti-Apartheid Movement, *Trevor Huddleston, CR: 80th Birthday Tribute* (London, Anti-Apartheid Movement, June 14, 1984).

25. Southern Rhodesia, *Annual Report of the Secretary for African Education, 1957*, p. 2.

26. For a detailed discussion of Dodge's philosophy of the role of the church in Africa, see his *The Revolutionary Bishop: An Autobiography* (Pasadena, CA: William Carey Library, 1986).

27. The Atlantic Charter was a seven-point declaration made by President Franklin D. Roosevelt of the United States and Prime Minister Winston Churchill of Britain on August 11, 1941, stating, "We respect the right of all people to choose the government under which they will live and we wish to see sovereign rights and self-government restored to those who have been forcibly deprived of them."

28. Southern Rhodesia, *Commission of Inquiry into Native Education* (Alexander Kerr, Chairman) (Salisbury: Government Printer, 1951), p. 11.

29. Ibid., p. 74.

30. Ibid., p. 75.

31. Dickson A. Mugazi, *The Honored Crusade: Ralph E. Dodge's Theology of Liberation and Initiative for Social Change in Zimbabwe* (Gweru: Mambo Press, 1991), p. 112.

32. Ralph E. Dodge, *The Unpopular Missionary* (Westwood, NJ: Fleming H. Revell, 1964), p. 33.

33. Ibid., p. 34.

34. Ralph E. Dodge, *The Church and Politics* (Old Umtali: Rhodesia Mission Press, 1960), p. 5.

35. Dodge, *The Unpopular Missionary*, p. 35.

36. Ralph E. Dodge, letter dated March 18, 1959, addressed to Garfield Todd, former prime minister of colonial Zimbabwe from 1952 to 1958, Syracuse University Library.

37. Trevor Huddleston, "Foreword," in Tutu, *Crying in the Wilderness*, p. 7.

38. Ibid.

39. Trevor Huddleston, "Foreword," in Desmond M Tutu, *Hope and Suffering* (Grand Rapids, MI: William B. Eerdmans, 1984), p. 9.

40. Ibid., p. 9.

41. Ibid., p. 10.

42. Nelson Mandela, "Foreword," in Desmond Tutu, *The Rainbow People of God* (New York: Bantam Books, 1995), p. xiii.

43. For details see, for example, Dickson A. Mungazi, *The Mind of Black Africa* (Westport, CT: Praeger Publishers, 1996), p. 159.

44. *The Christian Science Monitor*, March 21, 1990, p. 6.

45. Tutu, *Crying in the Wilderness*, p. 99.

46. Abel T. Muzorewa, *Rise Up and Walk: The Autobiography of Bishop Abel Tendekai Muzorewa* (Nashville, TN: Abingdon Press, 1978), p. 3.

47. In 1949 Chieza and Ruth Bartholomew, an educator from Paine College, Georgia, composed the famous "Hartzell Song" that was sung on many school occasions.

48. This ritual was a common practice of initiating new students, known as new comers, to the school. It entailed teasing but no physical abuse like hazing in the United States. The ritual lasted about two weeks.

49. Muzorewa, *Rise Up and Walk*, p. 18.

50. See Dickson A. Mungazi, *The Last Defenders of the Laager: Ian D. Smith and F. W. de Klerk* (Westport, CT: Praeger Publishers, 1998), for reference to this remarkable educator.

51. For details of this Methodist preacher, see Dickson A. Mungazi, *Colonial Policy and Conflict in Zimbabwe: A Study of Cultures in Collision, 1890–1979* (New York: Crane Russak, 1992).

52. Muzorewa, *Rise Up and Walk*, p. 21.

53. Miss Parks arrived in Zimbabwe as a Methodist missionary teacher and was assigned to Nyadiri in 1939. In 1950 she started the secondary school at Old Umtali and at Murewa in 1962. She was a capable teacher with skills and background to teach a variety of subjects that included English, mathematics, and Latin.

54. Muzorewa, *Rise Up and Walk*, p. vii.

4

Desmond M. Tutu: The Man and His Mission

We are committed to black liberation, because thereby we are committed to white liberation. You will never be free until we blacks are free.

—Desmond M. Tutu, 1980

EVENTS THAT SHAPED TUTU'S FUTURE

Beginning in 1931, the year Desmond M. Tutu was born, when he thought he was secure in his political position, J. B. Hertzog began a campaign to elevate Afrikaner nationalism to a new level that he believed would later create a situation to overcome the confrontation that would come from the rise of African nationalism. Allister Sparks captures the dynamics of this cultural and political crossroads between Hertzog and the Africans, saying that James Munnik launched the Afrikaner nationalist revolution like Steve Biko did in his Black Consciousness Movement half a century later, because his people needed to be uplifted before there could be any talk of joining hands with their conquerors and oppressors.[1] Sparks goes on to conclude that the Afrikaners had to take care of their own needs first, before they had themselves rehabilitated in the national environment and tried to determine the nature of their relationships with Africans, a group of people they considered inferior. Hertzog was not a man who could be persuaded to believe that Afrikaners and Africans had anything in common on which to build a country for the future. Sparks's description of Hertzog's efforts to raise Afrikaner nationalism to new heights fits perfectly the description he might have made about the rise of African nationalism even before the end of the war in 1945. Where would these two forms of nationalism lead South Africa? By the time he left office in 1939, Hertzog had placed South Africa on the highway to a national conflict that would end only with the end of the system that he created, apartheid, in April 1994.

Ironically what motivated Hertzog is exactly what motivated the Africans. For nearly 20 years as a politician and 9 as prime minister, Hertzog was fully determined to restore to the Afrikaners their sense of self-pride with all the rights he thought they had lost in their humiliating defeat in the Boer War. He wanted them to demonstrate their superiority over the Africans. At the end of his term of office, Hertzog felt he had accomplished his objectives, and now he could fall away like a spent shell after a decisive battle as Afrikaner nationalism soared to a new level. But in doing so Hertzog had no idea of how African nationalism would first match that of the Afrikaners and then surpass it. Hertzog belonged to an era when he failed to remember that Africans were part of the national political landscape. He saw them as the source of cheap labor, people less than human, but who he believed his government awarded the respect due to human beings. He had no understanding at all of the extent to which the Africans would raise a sense of self to demand fundamental change in all aspects of national life.[2] This reality was for the future generations of Africans to experience.

TUTU'S BACKGROUND AND EDUCATION

This discussion and that at the beginning of Chapter 3 provide the background and a set of events that influenced Desmond M. Tutu's future. There is no question that Hertzog succeeded in creating conditions on which apartheid was built. But he did not have to deal with the consequences of its implementation. When Tutu was born, Hertzog was at the height of political power. The program that his administration created affected both whites and Africans in different ways.

It is quite easy to see that Tutu and other Africans had a high mountain to climb in order to overcome the imposition of apartheid. Tutu was born in the gold mining town of Krugersdorp, Witwatersrand, in the Transvaal, one of the four provinces of South Africa (the other provinces are Natal, the Cape Province, and the Orange Free State). The Transvaal was settled by the Boers who were escaping from British rule at the Cape during the period of the great trek, beginning with the British occupation of the Cape in 1806 and lasting until 1842. One of the most famous Boer War leaders was Paul Kruger, who was born in the Cape Province and fought in the Boer War from 1899 to 1902. A frontiersman, uneducated and simple in his ways, Kruger fiercely resisted the British invasion. His family helped organize the Transvaal. After considerable internal feuding, the British allowed the Transvaal some degree of autonomy in 1883. Kruger served as its president from that time until 1900. However, the discovery of gold brought thousands of *uitlanders* (foreigners), most of them British. In 1895 Leander Starr Jameson led an unsuccessful raid, known to history as the Jameson Raid, on behalf of Cecil John Rhodes, greatly embarrassing and disgracing both men.[3] The raid was partly responsible for the Boer War.

While he exercised political power, Kruger was absolute in his belief in the superiority of Afrikaners and the inferiority of Africans. He constantly urged Africans to train to fulfill the labor needs of the province. With little education himself, Kruger expressed his own philosophy of education, saying that Africans had to be taught that they not hope to achieve social equality with whites. They had to understand that they belonged to an inferior class that must obey and learn.[4] During and after Kruger, the Transvaal attracted the most extreme of the Afrikaners, who extended Kruger's philosophy far beyond the level he had intended. Most Afrikaners who went into politics from the Transvaal adopted more extreme racial policies than those from the other three provinces.[5]

In addition to conditions that imposed difficulties on Africans as a result of national policy, Afrikaners from the Transvaal introduced racial policy that imposed even harder conditions than those imposed by the national government. Tutu was born there under these conditions. His father, Zachariah Tutu, was a successful teacher originally from the Xhosa tribe, the same as Nelson Mandela. His mother, Arletta Tutu, was a simple domestic servant whose ancestry was from the Tswana tribe. Desmond was baptized a Methodist because his father taught in Methodist schools. In this regard he and Bishop Abel T. Muzorewa have something in common. Later, when an older sister enrolled in an Anglican school, the whole Tutu family switched denominations to enable the Tutu children to attend school. The availability of educational opportunity heavily influenced the religious affiliation of the family. This was a common practice among Africans in colonial Africa, especially after the end of the war in 1945 when Africans suddenly realized the importance of education as means of seeking an improvement in the conditions that governed their lives and as a preparation for the future. The practice of religion could not be removed from the educational process.

When Desmond was 12 years old the Tutu family moved to Johannesburg where Zachariah had found a better opportunity as a teacher and Arletta was employed as a cook in an Anglican Church missionary school, where she was treated with respect by the missionaries. When the family returned home at the end of the day they talked at length about the humility of the missionaries and the dignity and respect they extended to Mrs. Tutu. This had a profound impact on young Desmond.

The Anglican missionaries seemed to accept the entire Tutu family as they were because their theology was based on full acceptance of any human beings.[6] This theology would later bring Tutu into conflict with the government of South Africa. At the Anglican school young Desmond was completely impressed by the many examples of kindness and that were part of the manner in which missionaries conducted themselves and did their work. Their dedication to serve human needs as part of their mission demonstrated to the Tutu family the epitome of human goodness as a result of applying Christian principles to human conditions.

It was here that the Tutu family came into contact with a young Anglican priest who had been in the country only a few years. He was sent by the Community of Resurrection based in Britain. His name was Trevor Huddleston. Later he was elevated to the position of bishop long after his tour of duty in South Africa was over. Tutu and Huddleston developed a special relationship that would continue until Huddleston's death in 1998 and would influence their future in profound ways. Unlike the relationship that developed between Bishop Ralph E. Dodge and Bishop Abel T. Muzorewa, which began when Muzorewa was in theological school, Father Huddleston and Desmond Tutu developed a unique relationship early in life. Father Huddleston became a leading antiapartheid advocate as soon as he arrived in South Africa in 1943. A parish priest in Sophiatown, Father Huddleston was on his way to becoming an international celebrity by his dedication to the struggle against apartheid.[7] From his early association with Huddleston, Tutu learned the dynamics of adopting as a fundamental tenet principle of human behavior and action.

In 1985 Tutu recalled how Father Huddleston came to influence his life, saying, "I was standing with my mother one day when this white man in a cassock walked past and doffed his big hat to her. I could not believe it, a white man raising his hat to a simple black laboring woman?"[8] Although this show of respect for humanity was unusual to young Desmond, he immediately learned that respect of all people was an essential component of the function of religious institutions, and for those who are their members.

Young Desmond's reaction to Huddleston's showing respect to his mother is a powerful indicator of the extent that whites used race as a criterion of treating people. As a young person he was so used to associating poor treatment of Africans by whites as normal. This is a sad commentary on the system of apartheid. When Tutu was hospitalized for the treatment of tuberculosis, Father Huddleston visited him every day.

The disease and Father Huddleston's care of Tutu helped to strengthen relationships between them (as did similar circumstances between Mu-zorewa and Dodge). Tutu immediately regarded Huddleston as his men-tor, a man after whom to patent his own life. As a teenager Tutu earned some pocket money selling peanuts at a railway station and by working at a golf course in Johannesburg. This was a common practice among African boys who were trying desperately to supplement their parents' meager income. For these young Africans their efforts were more than just trying to earn some spending money, it was a serious business of trying to survive in a hostile environment.

When Tutu graduated from elementary school he entered a high school in Johannesburg with the intent of studying medicine later on. But his family could not afford the tuition required for medical school. He turned to teaching instead. After attending the Bantu Normal College in Pretoria and following his obtaining a B.A. degree, he taught at Ma-dibene High School in Johannesburg from 1954 to 1955 and Munsieville High School in his home town of Krugersdorp from 1955 to 1957. Tutu and Lear Nomalizo were married on July 2, 1955. Together they have walked the rough road of life, raising a family and confronting apartheid at every turn. They have received support of those who shared their belief in the rightness of their cause and opposition from those who have not.

When the government of J. G. Strijdom introduced the second-rate state-run system of Bantu education in 1957, Tutu and many other Af-rican teachers resigned in protest. Strijdom introduced the measure in response to the Freedom Charter of 1955, leading to the arrest and charge of high treason of 156 individuals in December 1956. When the accused were found not guilty by the Supreme Court, apartheid was exposed for what it was: an oppressive system designed to enshrine the supremacy of the Afrikaners.

Instead the trial of these distinguished South Africans brought shame and disgrace to a government that did not care for the welfare of its own people and to a system that was an instrument of oppression. From this point on the international community knew exactly the extent to which the government of South Africa was acting outside normal ways of a government. Serious questions were now coming from the international community about what should be done to bring this government to an end.[9]

Once he was out of the classroom, Tutu regarded the Anglican Church as a more likely channel of service and saw his transition from teaching to religious ministry as his call to higher service. When he began his theological training under the priests of the Community of Resurrection, Father Huddleston's Anglican religious order, Tutu made a spiritual commitment that has remained part of his life today. He appeared to be heading toward prominence because of that commitment.

Following the completion of his studies for the licentiate in theology at St. Peters' Theological College in Johannesburg in 1960, Tutu was received in the Anglican diocese and was ordained as a priest in 1961. His first assignment was as curate of St. Albion's Church in Benoni and St. Philips's Church in Alberton from 1961 to 1962. At the same time he was earning his bachelor's degree in divinity and a master's degree in theology at King's College in London. He served as a parish priest at St. Albion Church in London, where he remained until 1965, and at St. Mary's in Bletchingley in Surrey from 1965 to 1966. From 1967 to 1969 Tutu was lecturer at the Federal Theological Seminary in Alice in the tribal homeland of Ciskei.

During the next two years he was a lecturer at the national University of Lesotho, known at the time as the University of Botswana, Lesotho, and Swaziland. A former British colony once known as Basutoland, Lesotho achieved independence in October 1966. But it is completely surrounded by South Africa, a cruel irony of the colonial legacy. In 1986 South Africa under P. W. Botha imposed a blockade because Lesotho was giving sanctuary to rebel groups fighting to overthrow the apartheid system. The aim of the blockade was to generate internal political instability. As a result a military coup occurred on January 20, 1986, forcing the rebels to leave the country.[10]

In 1972 Tutu returned to Britain as associate director of the Theological Education Fund, a position in which he administered World Council of Churches scholarship for three years. From his operational base in Bromley, Kent, Tutu traveled extensively in Asia and Africa. He returned to South Africa as the Anglican dean of Johannesburg in 1975. The following year Soweto burst into an unprecedented riot caused by the educational policy of the Botha administration. Tutu was thrust into a national spotlight where he tried to bring a peaceful resolution to a problem that was increasingly deteriorating.

Soon after he was elected bishop of Lesotho, Tutu saw violence brewing among angry youth of Soweto. He enlisted the help of Ntoto Motlana in an effort to channel the rage that the youth of Soweto were expressing over apartheid into peaceful demonstration. On May 6, 1976, Tutu wrote a letter to J. B. Vorster, the prime minister of South Africa, to warn him of the deteriorating situation, which he said could lead to a national catastrophe unless something was done soon to eliminate apartheid.[11] But Vorster dismissed the letter as a political ploy engineered by the Communist opposition. On June 16 Vorster was muted when Soweto exploded into one of the worst outbreaks of violence in the history of South Africa. Over 600 people, most of them Africans, were killed and thousands were injured.[12] Tutu's response to this national tragedy was one of sadness.

What Vorster ignored was a serious situation that began to develop in 1974, when the government decreed that instruction in secondary schools for Africans must be done in Afrikaans, rather than in English. For the next two years African students protested the new policy because they regarded Afrikaans as the language of an oppressive system. They also regarded Afrikaans as a local dialect intended to limit their understanding of the broader world in which they lived. On June 16, 1976. 15,000 students gathered in Soweto to protest the policy. They did not want to learn and teachers did not want to teach in the language of their oppressor.

During the previous two years petitions by parents, letters from leaders of the African community, and diplomatic action by those who believed in peaceful resolution of the problem failed to persuade Vorster to reconsider the notorious policy. Police and military reinforcements were dispatched to Soweto and an ugly situation quickly developed with severe consequences for the country. Nelson Mandela concluded that in this situation the Bantu Education Act of 1963 had come to haunt its authors.[13]

In 1978 Tutu was elected the first African secretary-general of the South African Council of Churches, South Africa's official contact organization with the World Council of Churches, which represented millions of Christians around the world and whose major functions include seeking solutions to problems of social injustice in the world. Because of the policy of apartheid, South Africa became the target of its activity. The South African Council of Churches represented more than 13 million Christians, more than 80 percent of them Africans in a country of 45 million people.[14]

However, conspicuously absent from membership of the South African Council of Churches were the members of the Dutch Reformed Church, 60 percent of the Afrikaner population. Over the years the Nationalist government appealed to the members of the Dutch Reformed Church to stay within the fold and give it the support it needed to implement the apartheid policy, under the assumption that Afrikaners were the chosen group of people. Therefore Tutu's election as leader of the South African Council of Churches did not mean a thing for the loyalty of members of the Dutch Reformed Church. They did not see Tutu as their leader or representative on matters of church policy and theology. In South Africa much of the Council's budget was spent on legal action against apartheid, especially in fees toward defending Africans imprisoned or in detention without trial for offenses arising from violation of many apartheid laws.

With African nationalist parties outlawed, the South African Council of Churches under Tutu's leadership became an important means of African protest. In 1979 Tutu offended the Nationalist government under P. W. Botha on two occasions. The first occasion was the enactment of the new Group Areas Act, an amendment of the original law passed in

1950 authorizing the government to remove Africans from urban areas to desolate and unproductive tribal areas.

After observing the sad conditions that controlled African life in the squatter camps, Tutu outraged Botha's administration by describing conditions in these camps as the government's final solution to the African problems. He argued that the policy of the government was deliberately designed to have the Africans starve to death, not because there was no food, but because it was the policy the government had defined and was now pursuing. Tutu predicted that instead of silencing the Africans the policy would invoke stronger determination among them to intensify the struggle to end oppression.

The second way in which Tutu angered Botha and his administration was his advocacy of the withdrawal of all foreign investment from South Africa. In a television interview aired in Denmark in the fall of that year, Tutu challenged the Danish government to stop buying coal from South Africa as a way of supporting the struggle against apartheid. On his return home his passport was taken away to prohibit him from traveling abroad again.

The practice in South Africa was that whenever one's passport was confiscated, it was usually a sign that one was about to be banned. Undaunted, Tutu took on a new national crusade. He persuaded the parents of mixed ethnic background, known in South Africa as Coloreds, to support a nationwide school boycott because the students were discriminated against under apartheid laws. The government, as usual, reacted by regarding that action as Communist-inspired and the protesters were subjected to arrest under provisions of the Suppression of Communism Act of 1950. But Tutu warned the government that any arrest of protesters would trigger a new riot worse than that of June 16, 1976.[15]

When Tutu's passport was restored in January 1981 he toured European countries and the United States to deliver to the members of the international community one constant message: that if the international community genuinely wanted to see the end of apartheid, then its members must support the struggle against it to ensure peaceful change by political, diplomatic, and economic means. The Nationalist government took Tutu's position as urging the international community to intensify the economic sanctions that had been imposed since the Soweto uprising. This time Tutu was far more effective as an advocate of peaceful change in South Africa than in the past.

The tragic death of Steve Biko in September 1977 under police custody combined with the Soweto uprising of June 1976 placed Tutu in a position of authority in expressing the view among Africans that if apartheid was not ended it would sooner than later lead to a major national catastrophe in South Africa. Wherever he spoke the international community listened intensely. Community and religious leaders, the business community, politicians, and ordinary members all over the world began to consider ways of intensifying economic sanctions. In Washington, D.C., President Ronald Reagan was embarrassed to find that the Congress voted to sustain economic sanctions against South Africa against his veto. Tutu was the man of the hour. His counsel and advice were sought by those who wanted to see a peaceful end of apartheid.

Tutu's passport was once again confiscated on his return to South Africa in April 1981. When Columbia University conferred on Tutu an honorary degree of sacred theology in August 1982, he was denied permission to travel to New York to receive it. Because Columbia University does not grant degrees in absentia, its president, Michael I. Sovern, traveled to Johannesburg to confer the degree. In his remarks Sovern praised Tutu as a fearless advocate of justice, especially peaceful change and reconciliation among the people of a deeply troubled country. Sovern concluded that Tutu's leadership of the struggle to end the oppression of apartheid compelled the admiration of those who wanted to see peaceful change in South Africa.

While this was happening the Nationalist government appointed Mr. Justice Alexander Eloff to investigate the South African Council of Churches, especially how it was collecting and spending funds. The fact that the Council was spending most of its funds defending those accused of breaking apartheid laws served as a motive of the government to launch the investigation. It is also true that the government was desperate in its efforts to find something that would discredit both Tutu and the Council so that they would divert attention from launching a damaging campaign against apartheid to defending themselves. Tutu saw this action as kicks of a dying horse, an oppressive system that was trying to harass the organization that was discharging its responsibility to the people. For the government to suggest that Tutu and the council he led were engaging in questionable methods of raising money was to indicate real questionable methods of maintaining power. In his response Tutu paraphrased Paulo Freire, the Brazilian thinker who advanced a theory that in a relationship between the oppressor and the oppressed, oppression dehumanizes the oppressor as much as the oppressed. Freire concluded that in the end the conflict between the oppressor and the oppressed often ends with the defeat of the oppressor.[16]

Freire's theory evinced itself in April 1994 when the apartheid system finally came to an end, brought to its demise by the determination of the Africans. Tutu was quite consistent in taking this position. Speaking to the students at Witwatersrand University on March 18, 1980, he reiterated this position, saying, "We are committed to black liberation because we are committed to white liberation. You will never be free until we blacks are free. So, join the liberation struggle. Throw off your lethargy and apathy of affluence. Work for a better South Africa for yourselves, ourselves, and for our children."[17] In challenging white students to come forward in the struggle to end apartheid, Tutu was quite aware that in Freire's theory the conflict between the oppressor and the oppressed has significance when the oppressed are motivated by a desire to free themselves by freeing their oppressor. Because the oppressor has no intention of freeing the oppressed, he lacks proper focus in his action except to maintain oppression as part of his fear of real freedom.[18]

It was clear that the Eloff Commission failed to find anything illegal in the activities of the South African Council of Churches and its leader, Tutu. It was as embarrassing to P. W. Botha as the treason trial of 156 prominent South Africans was to J. G. Strijdom in 1957. It would appear that Botha had not learned any important lessons from the past. However, the Commission argued that the Council's opposition to apartheid was causing the government considerable problems both in South Africa and abroad. In its report submitted in February 1984, the Eloff Commission found no evidence to substantiate the government's suspicion that the South African Council of Churches, especially under Tutu's leadership, was an instrument of foreign organizations that were trying to bring Communist revolution to South Africa. The only criticism by the Eloff Commission was that the South African Council of Churches was spending money on political campaigns, rather than on humanitarian causes and the promotion of religion. The Eloff Commission also criticized the Council's financial support of the ANC, but admitted that this was not illegal. This basic finding by a high-level commission raised serious questions about the strategies that the Nationalist government was using to maintain apartheid, not only in South Africa, but also among members of the international community. Botha and his administration stood condemned by the court of public opinion, increasing pressure to bring apartheid to an end. Tutu had no apology for that support, arguing that the ANC was struggling for the freedom of all South Africans in the same way the South African Council of Churches was doing. He argued that both the Council of and the ANC were seeking an end to the policy of apartheid in order to create a truly democratic South Africa where race was not a factor of society.

Father Huddleston added his own reaction to the Eloff Commission, concluding that there was no doubt that its purpose was to discredit and destroy the work that Tutu was doing through the Council, especially its work in caring for the families in need and in working against apartheid.[19] Huddleston argued that because the Council advocated nonviolent methods of bringing about change in South Africa, all people of South Africa should come to its assistance. He also argued that the ultimate benefactor of such an approach would be the Afrikaners themselves. He warned the Nationalist government that as conditions in the world and in Africa would determine, it was not possible for Africans to give up their struggle to end apartheid. It remained a question of what means they will use to bring the oppressive system to an end. The longer the Nationalist government resisted the concept of change, the more increased were the prospects of bringing it to an end by bloodshed.

While these important developments were unfolding, other events began to occur in rapid succession, making the report of the Eloff Commission totally irrelevant to Tutu's activity. In September 1984 he began a three-month sabbatical leave at General Theological Seminary in New York. On October 16, while he was trying to settle in to assume his new responsibilities, Tutu and the rest of the world received the news he never anticipated. The Norwegian Nobel[20] Peace Committee announced that it was selecting Tutu the 1984 recipient of the Nobel Peace prize.[20]

In making this announcement Egil Aarvik, chairman of the Nobel Prize Committee, stated that the Nobel Peace prize had been awarded to a South African once before in 1960. This was to Chief Albert John Luthuli, who was elected president of the ANC and served from 1952 to 1967. But Luthuli was killed at a railway station in Johannesburg in 1961, only a few months after he had received the Nobel Peace prize. His death raised suspicion that the South African government, led at the time by Hendrik F. Verwoerd, was implicated in it. Aarvik said that the award to Tutu should be seen as a renewal of the recognition of the courage and heroism that Africans had showed in the struggle against apartheid. Aarvik went on to add that it was the Committee's opinion that the award to Tutu be recognized not only as a gesture of support of the efforts he was making to bring apartheid to an end, but also to all individuals and groups and organizations that were directing their activities toward the same objective as part of their efforts to restore human dignity to those when the system of apartheid had deprived them of it. The message to the Nationalist government was very clear: it should expect more intensified effort made by the international community to help bring about the end of apartheid.

As in the case of Luthuli, the apartheid government was angered inwardly by the action of the Nobel Peace Prize Committee in awarding a formidable adversary a recognition of his efforts to bring it to an end. At the end of the ceremonies in Oslo, Tutu returned to South Africa to be received by the government of his country with cold shoulders but with jubilation and celebration by his own people. He became an instant national and international figure in the struggle against apartheid. The fear among Africans of South Africa was whether Tutu would be subjected to the same mystery as that which surrounded the death of Luthuli.

Indeed, Tutu was entitled to more than 15 minutes of fame. This was his time in the spotlight. The Nobel prize was a recognition of his total commitment and dedication to the principles that make human beings unique in their endeavors to serve society. Although the Nationalist government never saw that service from the perspective that most people did, Tutu himself had no doubt about the role he felt he was called upon to play in the transformation of his troubled country.

At the very same time that the Nobel Peace Prize Committee was deciding to award Tutu the prestigious prize, white and black Anglican diocesan electors in Johannesburg, the South African Anglican Church's largest diocese, which at that time was predominately African, were trying to resolve a deadlock over the choice of Tutu as the diocese's new bishop. The National Anglican Committee intervened and on November 3, 1984, the committee of 11 white and 12 African bishops, meeting in the Orange Free State, elected Tutu the first African Anglican bishop of Johannesburg. Tutu responded by simply saying that the time was right for him to leave the South African Council of Churches because he considered himself fundamentally a pastor. That was what God ordained him to do.[21] What a pastor he has been! Like Huddleston, Tutu indicated that he was going to live among his people in Soweto,[22] close to them so that he could share the agony of segregation and discrimination to reinforce their determination to bring them to an end. From there he would gain strength and a new level of determination to do what he felt must be done to change the system. In 1986, while he was still getting used to his new position, Tutu was elected archbishop of Cape Town. He took his new assignment with humility, knowing that he was called upon to serve the people as their pastor in a larger context.

TUTU'S MISSION AND HIS STRATEGY FOR ACTION

Tutu's mission remained constant, a relentless opposition to apartheid. In 1924 J. B. Hertzog was instrumental in the enactment of laws that were designed to confirm his philosophy that the British should reinforce a provision in the independence constitution to protect the position of Africans.[23]

Hertzog took this action in response to the decision of the ANC in 1915 to send an official delegation to London to petition the British government to exercise its responsibility in protecting Africans whose position was being violated by Louis Botha's administration. In 1934, when Tutu was only three years old, Afrikaners were making the Transvaal the power base of racial segregation and discrimination. There, J. G. Strijdom was building a powerful system of apartheid based on Paul Kruger's philosophy of Afrikaner superiority and African inferiority.

These were among the conditions that helped define Tutu's mission.

From the moment he was aware of his world, Tutu began to see the negative effects of apartheid. He recognized that in its application apartheid destroyed self-pride among Africans, that it took away their self-esteem, that it reduced them to the level of bare existence, that it gave Afrikaners an unrealistic sense of their role in society as a group of chosen people. Because NGK had become a state church, the Afrikaners used religion to justify apartheid and tried to convince Africans that to oppose apartheid was to reject one's religious operational principles and values. Tutu was aware that African religious leaders had always rejected apartheid. He knew that John L. Dube, the first president of ANC, who served from 1912 to 1917; Zaccheus Mahabane, who served as president from 1924 to 1927 and from 1937 to 1940; and Albert J. Luthuli, who served from 1952 to 1960, were all ministers of religion who, like African Americans during the height of the civil rights struggle, came forward to offer their people leadership in the struggle to end oppression. Francis Meli concludes that Michael Scott, Joost de Blank, Zaccheus Mahabane, Allan Boesak, Manas Buthelezi, and Beyers Naude were all religious leaders who emerged at different times as outspoken champions of the oppressed people of South Africa.[24] As a religious leader Tutu could not ignore this historical precedence if he ever hoped to be effective as a national leader.

The knowledge that the problems of apartheid were compounded by the theology of NGK enabled Tutu to design a three-component strategy to confront the system that oppressed the African masses. The first component was appeal to other religious leaders to recognize the importance of their involvement in seeking an end to apartheid. The second component was to establish some form of dialogue with government to help its members understand the seriousness with which the people of South Africa opposed apartheid. The third component was to persuade Africans to resist the temptation to resort to violence to end apartheid. Tutu was aware that there had been a long-standing conflict between the English-speaking Christian organizations and the three forms of the Dutch Reformed Church, especially NGK.

For example, in December 1960, after a meeting of the World Council of Churches (WCC) held in South Africa to consider the deteriorating relationship between WCC and NGK as a response to apartheid, the Dutch Reformed Church, led by NGK, withdrew its membership from WCC in protest over a declaration that stated that the church, as the body of Christ, and as a unit within the natural diversity among people, was not annulled but sanctified. The WCC concluded that believers should not be excluded from any church on grounds of race or color[25] Tutu's strategy was not to convert the members of NGK to a new theology, but to convert their political philosophy into a pragmatic realization that the international community had unreservedly condemned apartheid. Therefore, any national institution, secular or religious, that supported it was operating outside the religious principles that had been universally accepted as a basis of human appropriate behavior.

The need to design an effective strategy is why in his first book, *Crying in the Wilderness: The Struggle for Justice in South Africa,* Tutu advances an interpretation of the Christian theology in a manner that is pertinent to the need to help those who supported apartheid see the error of their support. He suggested that Christians must avoid the temptation to use religion as a form of escape from the harsh realities of life, as most people live and experience it.

Tutu argued that just as Jesus never used religion as an opiate of the people, Christians needed to remind themselves constantly that they had an obligation to influence social change by their exemplary life, thought, and action in trying at all times to create a better world for all people to live in peace and harmony. He suggested that this objective could be accomplished by removing the chains of oppression and the yoke of injustice.[26] As Paulo Freire concluded, Tutu also knew that in the process of achieving freedom of the oppressed, achieving freedom of the oppressor becomes essential. One cannot achieve the one with the other.

Discussing the relevance of the church to conditions of human beings in the world with reference to South Africa, Tutu challenged all Christians to witnesses to the demands of society to change to ensure equality, fairness, and justice. Tutu also argued that Christians also must witness by seeing members of a community of reconciliation, a forgiving community that is needed in a world of hate and conflict. This is how Christians can influence change by service to other people. Recognizing their limitations must not inhibit their efforts to reach out to a larger world community. They must be motivated by their commitment to ideals that make all human beings unique in creation. Tutu challenged the church to be there to help those who have experienced oppression of poverty, of political injustice, of denial of basic human rights, of the soul. He concluded that Christians must proclaim that in a country of injustice and oppression where Africans received an inferior education, where they were forced to live in shantytowns, where they could not move freely and had to leave their families in the villages in order to find work in urban areas, it was important to witness to their plight.[27] He challenged the church to design methods of alleviating the suffering of those who were being evicted from their homes by the application of various laws passed under apartheid.

On September 18, 1978, Tutu resorted to what has become known among people of the Third World as theology of liberation[28] to address the importance of the church's involvement in national politics. At that time there was an increasing influence of this aspect of theology in developing areas of the world in that it was directly related to the need to address the material and spiritual welfare of the people. The emergence of this aspect of theology proved to be one important method of discussing political initiatives by the church.

On that date Tutu gave an address to the Presbyterian Church Assembly in Pretoria and used the concept of theology of liberation for the first time in his career. The basic tenet of theology of liberation is that the human being has two sides that complement each other to help him develop fully—the material side and the spiritual side. Tutu argued that the function of the church is to present these two sides as indispensable to the welfare of all people. Poverty, economic deprivation, and denial of equal political rights become the scourge that adversely affect society as a whole and must be eliminated.

In utilizing this theology, Tutu rhetorically asked the question, "Why does suffering single out black people so conspicuously, suffering, not at the hands of pagans or other unbelievers, but at the hands of white fellow Christians who claim allegiance to the same Lord and Master?"[29] The emphasis of this address was not on matters spiritual at all, but on matters material. He went on to elaborate the importance of this perspective, arguing that in South Africa the church must seek to sustain the hope of all the people who had become despondent because the powers of the world seemed to be quite rampant. The church, especially in South Africa, must preach a prophetic message to make a difference in the lives of all the people of South Africa and the world.[30] Only then could the church have a real meaning and purpose.

Tutu concluded that unless the church fulfilled this mission, it would appear that political change would have to come with considerable violence and bloodshed. If this happened the church must accept a major responsibility for failing to exercise its proper duty in teaching people the importance of respecting all human beings as equal members of society.

The second component of Tutu's strategy for confronting apartheid was his efforts to convince the Nationalist government that the policy of apartheid was wrong and should be abandoned. In discussing this strategy Tutu did not try to use elements of theology of liberation that he used to communicate with church leaders. Rather, he utilized political and diplomatic persuasion that showed his understanding of the psychology of the Nationalist government. In doing so Tutu knew that he was taking a risk of being misunderstood as being motivated by Communist-inspired influences, which the government always said came from the World Council of Churches and the South African Council of Churches. He was also aware that as an African he had limited access to the minds of Afrikaners who ran the government, because they did not have any respect for him apart from the fact that he was a church leader.

A complicating factor of Tutu's relationship with the government was the fact that he was following in the footsteps of Father Trevor Huddleston, a man who was determined to bring the Nationalist government to an end because it represented nothing positive in the expectations of the masses of the African people. The Nationalist government was unable to delineate Huddleston's opposition to apartheid and opposition to the government. Although Tutu tried to explain the reality that what both he and Huddleston opposed was the system of apartheid, not the government in itself, this fact was not fully understood until F. W. de Klerk assumed the office of president in 1989.

Until that time the Nationalist government thought that both Huddleston and Tutu were opposed to the Nationalist government because it was run by Afrikaners. In that context the government concluded that no matter what kind of policy it pursued, Tutu, like Huddleston, would still be unhappy because he wanted to influence the kind of government that reflected his own views, and the Nationalist government did not reflect those views. Of course, neither Huddleston nor Tutu was ever influenced by this line of thinking; all they wanted to see was the evolution of a system of government that was void of any elements of apartheid.

In the letter that he wrote on May 6, 1976, to John B. Vorster to warn him of the impending major uprising in Soweto in protest against the educational policy of the government, Tutu explained his position to suggest that he had authority to write it. He reminded Vorster that he was the Anglican dean of Johannesburg and therefore leader of several thousand Christians of all races in the Johannesburg diocese. He also said that he was writing to a father and grandfather who had experienced anguish and joy of parenthood, and as someone who had extended his hand to his children and grandchildren, someone who watched them when they were sick and one who had shed tears at the graveside of a relative.[31]

Finally Tutu told Vorster that he was writing the letter as someone whose race had endured the pain of discrimination and segregation. In giving this background information, Tutu hoped that he would be able to establish a personal rapport with Vorster based on things that were part of human experience without any regard to race. He had also hoped that Vorster would have an understanding of the seriousness of the issue he was about to discuss: the crisis in the schools in Soweto. To his dismay Tutu found that Vorster declined to heed the warning.

When Soweto exploded on June 16, 1976, it was too late for Vorster to understand what Tutu had been saying over a period of time. The tragedy of the uprising in Soweto is not just that it happened, but that it happened as a result of the failure of lines of communication between the people and the government sabotaged by a system that had its own way of dealing with things.

When P. W. Botha succeeded Vorster in 1978, Tutu hoped that the tragedy of Soweto had created a new climate of relationships between church leaders and the government officials. Indeed, in 1978 Botha encountered a set of conditions that Vorster, Verwoerd, Strijdom, and Malan did not experience: the determination of the Africans to refuse to compromise with apartheid. The generation of Africans of Botha's time had been hardened by the realities of oppression under various laws enacted under apartheid. Tutu recognized this reality and attempted to put it in proper perspective in dealing with Botha. Tutu found that in his response and political behavior Botha was as rigid about maintaining apartheid as his predecessors had been. How was this factor going to determine the future of the country given the climate of African increased determination not to allow any more time to the Nationalist government to do what it had always done in the past? At that time the African nationalists were more daring in launching guerrilla raids that were making it very hard for South Africa to lead a normal life.

The Organization of African Unity (OAU) was becoming more involved in supporting the ANC in its struggle to end apartheid. The international community was steadily imposing economic sanctions that were hurting the country in many ways. South Africa was being isolated from international events, such as participation in the Olympic Games. Instead of acknowledging the reality of these developments as a warning to end apartheid, Botha demanded that the international community not interfere in developments in South Africa. Although Botha later said that South Africa must adopt or die, Tutu thought that he had lost courage to face reality.[32]

In spite of his observation that Botha was too rigid and unyielding about apartheid, Tutu made a genuine effort to establish lines of communications in order to have a dialogue about the deteriorating situation the country was facing. On February 29, 1988, some 25 ministers and priests signed a letter to Botha to protest the restrictions that were placed on a number of individuals for a variety of offenses related to apartheid policy. The letter stated that the signatories were particularly horrified at the number of restrictions Botha's government had placed on people and organizations who had been in the forefront of the struggle to bring peace to the strife-torn areas of Cape Town. The individuals who had been restricted included Archie Gumede, Willie Hofmeyr, Albertina Sisulu, and these were only a few of the many examples of individuals on whom restrictions were imposed in order to silence the people.

The letter concluded by stating that it was in the interest of the government to remove these restrictions in order to establish new lines of communication between the people and the government in order to find solutions to the problems the country was facing.[33] Botha responded on March 16 to reject what he called unfortunate allegations, adding "I am sure that you will agree that the whole basis of your action is seriously in question, and that it was to a large degree, planned as a calculated public relations exercise"[34] under Communist influences. Therefore, Tutu had no better success in communicating his message to Botha than he did to Vorster. It was only after de Klerk had succeeded Botha that Tutu felt a new climate of communication existed. As a result he was able to communicate with leaders of the government in a way he had not been able to do in the past. Of course, it took de Klerk an extended period of time to come to terms with the fact that he had to yield to internal and external pressures to end apartheid.

The third component of Tutu's strategy of confronting apartheid was his effort to influence Africans to refrain from resorting to violence to bring apartheid to an end. The reason for adopting this component was not that he urged Africans to accept apartheid, but that he thought in a confrontation with the government so many Africans would be killed, as 500 students were killed on June 16, 1976, in the Soweto uprising.[35] The picture of Mbuyiselo Makhabu carrying the body of 13-year-old Hector Petersen who had been shot to death by the police in Soweto was a horrifying sight that Tutu thought must never be repeated. In responding in 1983 to what he had seen in 1976 on television, this author described the agony of Soweto as follows:

Soweto, a sprawling black ghetto outside Johannesburg, was the worst hit. Schools were closed and gangs of black youth went on a rampage of uncontrollable rage destroying anything in sight and attacking any white motorists who drove thorough the ghetto. Cars were set on fire with their occupants inside, buildings were subjected to incredible violence. For days violence converted Soweto into a towering inferno. From sunrise to sunset, throughout the night, Soweto had, indeed, become hell on earth with Lucifer commanding his forces to lay waste everything that was in their path. The innocent and the guilty, the old and the young, men and women became victims of a carnage that seemed to have no end. For days, the burning, the looting, the destruction, the smoke all descended upon Soweto with a brutal vengeance and the wrath comparable only to those of Hiroshima and Nagasaki.[36]

During a research visit to South Africa in December 1994, the author's observations confirmed this description. The problem that Tutu faced in advising Africans to refrain from violence was that they asked him to show them a better method of bringing apartheid to an end, and he did not have any except establishing lines of communications with the government and resorting to dialogue, both of which the government did not return.

However, the most persuasive method that Tutu utilized to influence Africans from resorting to violence to bring apartheid to an end was his evocation of the memory of those Africans who were either killed by the police or had died under suspicious circumstances. Tutu selected two of these Africans who represented the struggle of Africans against apartheid and whose deaths shocked the entire African community and the world. These were Robert Mangaliso Sobukwe and Steve Biko. To stress his argument that Africans must refrain from the use of violence to attain their objectives, Tutu gave an account of the life of each of these two men to show that although they were victims of violence perpetrated by the government of South Africa, they were committed to nonviolent opposition to apartheid. Tutu concluded that although each man died under suspicious circumstances, each lived a life of accomplishment by peaceful means.[37]

On March 6, 1978, Tutu paid tribute to Sobukwe during a memorial service that was held in his honor at the South African Council of Churches. Sobukwe was born in the Cape Province in 1924. He was quite active in nonviolent protest campaigns beginning in 1953 with the passage of the Bantu Education Act. He also took part in the Defiance Campaign of 1952. In that year Sobukwe was instrumental in founding the Pan-Africanist Congress (PAC), which broke away from the ANC in 1959. He was elected its president, causing the administration of Verwoerd to suspect involvement in a campaign to stage a coup. Tutu added that Sobukwe resigned his position as professor of African languages at the University of Witwatersrand in 1960 to lead the antipass protest movement. At Sharpeville these protests were met with brutal force on March 21, 1960, when the police opened fire and killed 67 Africans and wounded 186 other people.[38] Sobukwe was arrested and was sentenced to three years' imprisonment. On his release he was detained and was sent to Robben Island for six years.[39] Upon his release in 1969, Sobukwe was banned and confined to a small area in Kimberly where he died in 1958 at 54 years of age. After his death Sobukwe's reputation dramatically increased to a point where Africans now regard him as a hero and champion of nonviolent change in South Africa.

In paying tribute to Steve Biko as a champion of nonviolent opposition to apartheid, Tutu stated that the singular way in which Biko met his death at the hands of the South African police was an outrage to people all over the world.[40] Tutu gave a brief biography of Biko to suggest his commitment to nonviolent change in South Africa. Tutu said that Biko, a thinker and activist, was born in Kingwilliamstown on December 18, 1946. He was involved early in the struggle against apartheid. After the

Sharpeville massacre Biko was instrumental in forming the South African Student Organization (SASO). He wrote critical articles against apartheid and in 1973 he founded the Black Consciousness Movement, which was rapidly growing to include young people from all over the country. With a clear mind and perception of both himself and his country, Biko dedicated himself to bringing about change that would mean that all people of South Africa would be equal in every way. Biko died for that belief and commitment, rather than give them up.

On August 18, 1977, Biko was arrested and detained in Port Elizabeth under provisions of the Terrorism Act and was taken in chains to Pretoria, a trip of more than 600 miles. He died on September 12, 1977, as a result of the severe beating he had received from the police. Tutu concluded, "With his brilliant mind that always saw the heart of things, Steve realized that until blacks asserted their humanity and their personhood, there was not the remotest chance for reconciliation in South Africa."[41] Indeed, this was Tutu's own definition of the parameters of his mission, to help the Nationalist government realize that until it recognized the Africans, not as an enemy, but as allies in building a country, there was no possibility of reconciliation and peace. Instead, the road to the future of South Africa was paved with blood. Tutu also wanted the Nationalist government to know that the death of Steve Biko was galvanizing the consciousness and determination of all Africans to elevate their commitment to a higher level. The Nationalist government did not know that Biko's influence was more profoundly felt in death than in life. Tutu knew that for the Nationalist government the end was drawing near. He concluded that Sobukwe and Biko were now exerting more influence on the course of development and the struggle for change as murdered heroes of the African people by their resort to nonviolent methods of achieving change.

SUMMARY AND CONCLUSION

This chapter began with a summary discussion of events that helped shape Tutu's future from the time that he was born. From then to 1939, South Africa was under the political control of B. J. Hertzog, a hard-core Afrikaner racist who funded the Nationalist Party in 1912 out of his fear of African development and desire to preserve the assumed superiority of Afrikaners. As he was growing up, Tutu recognized that his life and the lives of the rest of the Africans were going to be a constant struggle. He soon realized that Africans had no choice but to brace themselves for the struggle that lay ahead.

Throughout the days of his education, Tutu knew that someday he would assume a major role in the Africans' struggle for self. He also recognized early in his life that apartheid was an evil system that enslaved the Africans. Just as Hertzog was determined to concede nothing to Africans, so was Tutu determined to rise above the level of oppression to which apartheid reduced them, to envisage himself as leading a struggle to restore their sense of identity and pride as a people. Such is the narrative of a national leader who had a vision of both himself and the people he led as determined to fight against evil.

In designing an effective strategy to fight against apartheid, Tutu utilized his knowledge of the philosophy of the Afrikaners and the theology of the NGK as one of the major problems that he had to confront. Having come under the influence of Father Trevor Huddleston at the age of 13 in 1944, Tutu came to understand the meaning of commitment to a noble cause. He used this understanding to exert a positive influence on the Africans' response to apartheid. As a spokesman for the South African Council of Churches, Tutu did more than was expected of a religious leader in promoting a new level of consciousness among Africans of the need to summon all their willpower to engage in a long-drawn-out war to save themselves from the jaws of an old monster, apartheid.

There is no question that Tutu measured up to expectations in playing his role in arousing a passion among his people for dignity and equality in society. This means that apartheid had to go. This also means that the government of South Africa must reflect the universal principle of majority rule. In short this means that the Nationalist government must cease to exist and the monopoly of political power the Afrikaners had been exercising since Jan van Riebeeck arrived at the Cape in April 1652 must also come to an end and be replaced by the Africans themselves. How would the Africans accomplish this seemingly impossible task?

NOTES

1. Allister Sparks, *The Mind of South Africa* (New York: Alfred A. Knopf, 1989), p. 150.

2. Ibid., p. 151.

3. Felix Gross, *Rhodes of Africa* (New York: Frederick A. Praeger, 1957), p. 53.

4. Alex La Guma (ed.), *Apartheid: A Collection of Writings on South Africa by South Africans* (New York: International Publishers, 1971), p. 35.

5. Gross, *Rhodes of Africa*, p. 57.

6. Sparks, *The Mind of South Africa*, p. 279.

7. Ibid., p. 280.

8. *The London Observer*, May 8, 1982, p. 6.

9. Francis Meli, *South Africa Belongs to Us: A History of the ANC* (Harare: Zimbabwe Publishing House, 1988), p. 128.

10. *World Almanac and Book of Facts* (Mahwah, NJ: Funk and Wagnalls, 1996), p. 792.

11. Letter from Desmond Tutu to John Vorster, quoted in Desmond Tutu, Hope and Suffering (Grand Rapids, MI: William B. Eerdmans, 1984), p. 27.

12. Ibid., p. 818.

13. Nelson Mandela, *Long Walk to Freedom* (Boston: Little, Brown, 1994), p. 421.

14. *World Almanac and Book of Facts*, p. 817.

15. Ibid., p. 818.

16. Paulo Freire, *Pedagogy of the Oppressed* (trans. M. B. Ramos) (New York: Continuum, 1983), p. 48. For a discussion of the application of this theory to relationships between the oppressor and the oppressed, see Dickson A. Mungazi, *Colonial Policy and Conflict in Zimbabwe: A Study of Cultures in Collision, 1890–1979* (New York: Crane Rusak, 1992).

17. Desmond M. Tutu, *Crying in the Wilderness: The Struggle for Justice in South Africa* (Grand Rapids, MI: William B. Eerdmans, 1982), p. 43.

18. Freire, *Pedagogy of the Oppressed*, p. 52.

19. Trevor Huddleston, "Foreword," in Desmond Tutu, *Hope and Suffering* (Grand Rapids, MI: William B. Eerdmans, 1984), p. 10.

20. Named after Alfred Nobel, a Swedish chemist who invented dynamite and other explosives, making him one of the richest men in the world by 1867. Toward the end of his life and in poor health Nobel felt guilty for inventing destructive substances. He established a fund of $9 million and the interest would be used to award annual prizes for work done to promote international peace.

21. World Almanac, *Current Biography Yearbook* (New York: Funk and Wagnalls, 1985), p. 421.

22. During a research trip to South Africa in 1994, the author made a tour of Soweto and was privileged to see Tutu's house, simple and ordinary in appearance.

23. South Africa, *Official Yearbook* (Pretoria: Government Printer, 1982), p. 47.

24. Meli, *South Africa Belongs to Us*, p. 188.

25. Ibid., p. 188.

26. Tutu, *Crying in the Wilderness*, p. 28 and 29.

27. Ibid., p. 32.

28. For example, see Dickson A. Mungazi, *The Honored Crusade: Ralph E. Dodge's Theology of Liberation and Initiative for Social Change in Zimbabwe* (Gweru: Mambo Press, 1991), for a discussion of the application of this theology.

29. Ibid., p. 35.

30. Ibid., p. 36.

31. Desmond M. Tutu, *The Rainbow People of God* (New York: Bantam Books, 1995), p. 8.

32. Ibid., p. 87.

33. Jim Wallis and Joyce Holleyday (eds.), *Crucible of Fire: The Church Confronts Apartheid* (Maryknoll, NY.: Orbis Books, 1989), p. 141.

34. Ibid., p. 145.

35. In *Crying in the Wilderness*, p. 92, Tutu gives the figure of students killed in Soweto as 500. But other estimates put the figure at more than a thousand.

36. Dickson A. Mungazi, *To Honor the Sacred Trust of Civilization: History, Politics, and Education in Southern Africa* (Cambridge, MA: Schenkman, 1983), p. 163.

The author went to South Africa in December 1994 and saw conditions as he desribed them in this passage 11 years earlier.

37. Tutu, *Crying in the Wilderness*, p. 65.

38. Ibid., p. 45.

39. In 1994 from Signal Hill the author and other tourists had a panoramic view of Robben Island, this South African Alcatraz. It was reported in the press in 1995 that the government of South Africa under Nelson Mandela was considering demolishing this notorious prison. The author holds the opinion that demolishing it would destroy an important part of the history of South Africa. It should be allowed to continue as a reminder of what could happen to a nation that lost its soul.

40. Tutu, *Crying in the Wilderness*, p. 61.

41. Ibid., p. 62.

Photo 2. Bishop Ralph E. Dodge, who served as a missionary to Angola from 1936 to 1948 and as Methodist Bishop to southern Africa from 1956 to 1964. "He who is dominated by another spiritually, economically, academically, and politically will never develop his full potential." Photo: Bishop Ralph E. Dodge.

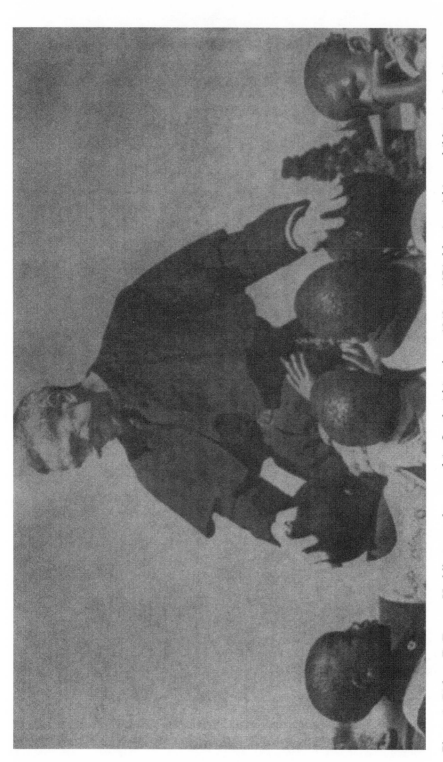

Photo 1. Bishop E. Trevor Huddleston, who served in South Africa from 1943 to 1956, blessing African children in Sophiatown, Johannesburg, 1954. "The Church is facing the challenge which it must meet now." Photo: Community of Resurrection, Mirfield, Britain.

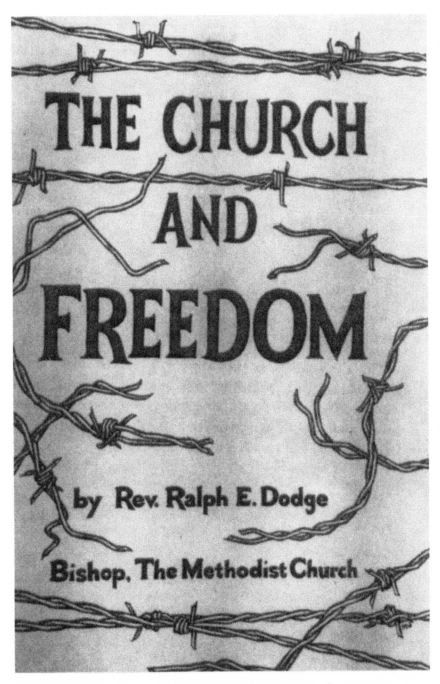

Photo 3. Cover design of a pamphlet by Bishop Ralph E. Dodge to depict oppression in Zimbabwe, *The Church and Freedom*, which Ian D. Smith and his Rhodesia Front government did not like. "He who lives by the sword will die by the sword." Design: The Methodist Church: Photo: the Author.

Photo 4. Bishop Desmond M. Tutu breaking the chains of the oppression of apartheid. "A people made desperate by despair, injustice, and oppression will use desperate means to end their oppression." Photo: Anglican Church Information Office.

Photo 5. Bishop Abel T. Muzorewa (center) with, from left to right, Chief Jeremiah Chirau, Rev. Patrick Murindagomo, who blessed the agreement, Ian D. Smith, and Rev. Ndabaningi Sithole after signing the internal agreement on March 3, 1978. "Today at the eleventh hour for Rhodesia the Africans are labeled 'Communist-inspired.' Does one have to be a Communist in order to liberate oneself?" Photo: Zimbabwe Ministry of Information.

Photo 6. Children in new South Africa, the kind that Tutu and other Africans worked hard to bring about, where there is racial equality, fairness, and cooperation. "Apartheid has been buried and will remain buried. The creation of the new South Africa has begun." Photo: South African Information Office.

Photo 7. F. W. de Klerk, president of South Africa from 1988 to 1994, and P. W. Botha, president from 1978 to 1988, following their stormy meeting in 1988. "The government has made a firm decision to release Mr. Nelson Mandela unconditionally." Photo: South African Information Office.

Photo 8. The first election held in Zimbabwe under universal voting rights, March 1980. "It will be about as easy to hold back the idea of African advancement as to stop the flow of the Victoria Falls." Photo: Zimbabwe Ministry of Information.

Photo 9. Leading ZANU nationalists in Zimbabwe during the struggle for independence, 1962. From left to right: Michael Mawema, Edgar Tekere, Edson Zwobgo, Enos Nkala, Ndabaningi Sithole, Robert Mugabe, Leopold Takawira, Morton Malianga. "Our battle cry is one man, one vote." Photo: *Moto*.

Photo 10. The author and his colleagues on the roof of the Library of the University of Zimbabwe, Harare, 1996. From Left to right: Dr. Candace Wheeler, Dr. L. Kay Walker, Professor Norman Atkinson of the University of Zimbabwe, and the author. "Every society must embrace nonracial principles to ensure its progress." Photo: Stephen Wheeler.

5

Abel T. Muzorewa: The Man and His Mission

It soon became plain to me that our theology needed to be clarified and our concerns needed a broader base. I felt at ease following in the footsteps of Bishop Ralph Dodge.
—Bishop Abel T. Muzorewa, 1978

THE METHODIST CHURCH AND THE FUTURE OF ZIMBABWE

When Abel T. Muzorewa was born on April 14, 1925, at Old Umtali Methodist Center, only ten miles north of Mutare, colonial Zimbabwe and the Methodist Church were going through a period of considerable change. In 1896 Cecil John Rhodes concluded that this frontier village was not practical in promoting his dream of building a vast colonial empire in Africa because it was inaccessible to the railway line he was building from Beira because of mountain ranges.

Rhodes decided to abandon it and establish a new town on the other side of the mountain ranges. This would have ready access to the railway line. To many settlers the move seemed a wrong policy. To abandon an already developed community in favor of starting a new one did not seem to reflect careful developmental plans. But Rhodes was not persuaded to change his mind once he made it. When he was ready to make the move, some people asked him what would happen to this developed community. Rhodes had a ready answer, "Make a mission of it."[1] What a mission it has been!

At that time the Methodist Church was sending Bishop Joseph C. Hartzell, a dedicated clergyman from Cincinnati, Ohio, to begin evangelism and education among the Africans. Hartzell seized the opportunity to convert the village Rhodes was abandoning to begin a Methodist establishment that was destined to alter permanently the life of the Africans. Hartzell named this old village Old Umtali because the new settlement Rhodes started over the mountain ranges ten miles to the south was called Umtali.

The police barracks were converted into dormitories for students, the stable that was used for horses and for the police was turned into bathroom facilities. The feeding troughs were turned into laundry facilities for the students.[2] The prison was remodeled into classrooms. Thus began a Methodist institution in colonial Zimbabwe that has since become a major center of education and service for Africans of Zimbabwe. In 1925 Old Umtali had a total of 16 missionaries conducting schools for African boys and girls. There was also a theological seminary, a printing press, a clinic, an agricultural experimental school, and a teacher training school with 40 students.[3]

Old Umtali was on its way to becoming a major institution that would transform the life of Africans into a new period of hope and aspirations. In 1984 the Methodist Church opened Africa University, offering opportunity for higher education for sons and daughters of Africa. Travelers who were appalled in 1925 at the lack of development elsewhere in southern Africa were said to be encouraged to come to Old Umtali to have their faith restored by the living proof of what the Methodist Church was doing there to promote the development of Africans.

The year 1925 also represented new challenges and opportunities to Old Umtali. Among these was to teach Africans a new set of values and purpose anchored in Christian principles. It was said that the missionaries of 1925 encountered different kinds of problems from those missionaries had encountered in the past. When Robert Moffat of the London Missionary Society opened the first school for Africans at Inyati in western Zimbabwe in 1859, he identified African resistance and traditional religious practices as being among the major problems he encountered. Hartzell experienced similar problems as he began his ministry at Old Umtali in 1898.

However, within a few years of its founding, Old Umtali provided a variety of educational activity that showed it was developing at a faster rate than Moffat had experienced at Inyati. The sight of an agricultural operation, for example, was so impressive that it offered Africans an opportunity to see a steel plow drawn by a team of 16 oxen as nothing less than a miracle in the process of training them to produce the high-quality crops they needed to feed a rapidly rising population.

Old Umtali became a fitting symbol of the most successful agent in seeking meaningful change among Africans. The practical results of this change were seen in the activities at Old Umtali. African students engaged in the process of learning to teach other Africans, or to raise better crops, or to provide medical services to a growing population. Although Hartzell and Rhodes had different objectives about how Old Umtali should prepare Africans for the future, the two men agreed that Africans must be trained for the future. It was up to Hartzell and his associates to define the nature of that preparation.

Any young African male or female who had a vision of himself or herself came to Old Umtali, this new fountain of hope, the new sanctum sanctorum of learning and the search for knowledge and the pillar of Christianity, to take a proper bearing in life. The young African man would be inspired by the educational endeavors of Kaduku Nyamurowa who became the first student there. If the young African was female she would come to Old Umtali to be inspired by the success of Tenze Mutasa, a brilliant young woman who graduated from the school in 1909 and became a celebrity by the quality of her life and work among her own people.[4]

As Old Umtali began to have a new impact on the lives of Africans, its influence began to expand into the surrounding areas, spreading out over a large distance. One of these areas was Nyakatsapa, some 25 miles to the north. From there Josiah Chimbadzwa came to Old Umtali a few years earlier than Tenze. Chimbadzwa, like Tenze, placed Nyakatsapa on the map of accomplishments of the Methodist Church in Zimbabwe by distinguishing himself as a student.

Forty years later, in 1940, Ezikiel Makunike, a successful journalist, came from Nyakatsapa to Old Umtali where he, too, distinguished himself as a student. From different parts of eastern Zimbabwe Edward Mazaiwana, Susan Ngonyama, Harriet Zwinoira, and later Oliver Musuka, Eliot Musumhi, William Kodzai—all prominent educators—came to Old Umtali to prepare themselves for the future.

Sixty miles to the south of Old Umtali was Mutambara Methodist Center, which developed into a thriving center from which Benjamin Mutambara came to Old Umtali to train as a teacher. Here a strong industrial and educational center was rapidly developing. In 1925 the colonial government inspector of schools commented about the learning activities at Mutambara School, stating that at no mission in Rhodesia had he seen such rapid and sound progress as had taken place at Mutambara during the last two years. He added that not long before there were 40 to 50 pupils receiving instruction in reading and writing with practically no industrial training. Now, he added, here were 283 pupils attending fairly regularly and the organization throughout was sound.[5]

In its endeavor to provide Africans a new sense of hope, Mutambara obtained its inspiration and example from the success of Old Umtali. In 1924 Nyadiri Methodist Center and Mrewa Methodist Center, both in northeast Zimbabwe, carried out their work in accordance with the expectations and standards that Old Umtali had set. To Murewa came Alec Chibanguza who accepted the challenge of new opportunities for further schooling, steadily moving from primary school to secondary school at Goromonzi. After attending Morningside College in Sioux City, Iowa, from 1961 to 1964, Chibanguza returned to Zimbabwe to serve as teacher and principal of Murewa Secondary School. Among Africans who graduated from Old Umtali and Morningside College with Alec Chibanguza were Eliot Musumhi and Oliver Musuka.[6]

A short distance north of Old Umtali, between it and Nyakatsapa, Mundenda Methodist School developed rapidly and provided a new hope for Africans. From there, Amon Dangarembga came to Old Umtali, where he distinguished himself as a student earning his way to the training school there. He went to South Africa to attend college following his success at Goromonzi Secondary School, and then to Britain to pursue graduate studies, giving Old Umtali credit for providing him the educational background he needed for success in the future.

On his return, Dangarembga served with distinction as principal of Old Umtali Center for over a decade beginning in 1965. Oliver Musuka, also educated at Old Umtali and Morningside College, later returned to serve with distinction as principal of Nyamuzuwe Methodist Center, a short distance from Mtoko in northeastern Zimbabwe.

The success of Old Umtali was not limited to these few examples; it was felt throughout the region of southern Africa including Angola, South Africa, Mozambique, and the Belgian Congo. In 1925 the Methodist Church made a projection of its work in Zimbabwe, expressing the hope that the movement toward Christianity would set in strongly in this region and that it was not far too much to expect a Christian following of from 15,000 to 20,000 within a year.[7] This development suggests that Africa was on the march toward a new life. The old ways and traditions that had controlled the lives of Africans were giving way to new ways of thinking on life.

The practice of worshipping the spirits of the ancestors was slowly giving way to the practice of Christianity. Although Africans still revered their ancestral spirits, as people all over the world should do, they recognized that balance between their respect of them and the need to carve new lifestyles that Christianity represented was an important part of the new life they were trying to build. Abel Muzorewa would fit into this new climate well to accept the challenge that Old Umtali offered.

THE RISE OF GODFREY HUGGINS

One cannot complete a discussion of the role that the Methodist Church played in influencing the future of Zimbabwe and Muzorewa's life without discussing Godfrey Huggins, prime minister from September 12, 1933, to September 6, 1953. In 1933 Huggins helped create an environment of conflict between his government and the church—a conflict that eventually led to the collapse of the colonial government itself.

The circumstances that brought Huggins to power were typical of the conditions that influenced colonial political behavior in the past. A physician who arrived in Zimbabwe in 1911, Huggins was known among his patients as a conservative and unorthodox general practitioner who had no time for innovative ideas. Indeed, Huggins practiced medicine not because he wanted to make it his career but because he wanted to establish a political base. The national debate in 1923 about the referendum to determine the future of the British South Africa Company administration brought him into the political arena. Instead of talking to his patients about their medical problems, he talked about the political future of the country.

Recognizing an opportunity for assuming the reins of power in a political vacuum, Huggins withdrew his support of Moffat and formed the Rhodesia Reform Party, drawing his support mainly from the dissident elements of Moffat's Rhodesia Party.[8] During the election campaign of 1928, Huggins attracted national attention with his strong anti-African rhetoric. Such rhetoric had been an important part of colonial politics since Cecil John Rhodes used it successfully to come to power in the Cape Parliament in 1895. Any person who sought political power used anti-African rhetoric to climb the colonial political ladder to the top. It was the only viable route to national prominence, and Huggins was only being true to a colonial tradition that had paid heavy political dividends in the past.

But because Huggins was a relative newcomer to the political leadership of the country, the voters preferred to return Moffat to power. However, in 1930, when Moffat opposed the Land Apportionment Act of 1929 in favor of moderation in the government's approach to African advancement, his popularity among whites began to decline. Moffat had lost the leadership that he once exercised effectively. The action that his government took in 1930 to protect the economy shattered by the Great Depression, and the purchase of mineral rights from the defunct British

South Africa Company for $4 million when many thought they should have been acquired free of charge, brought sharp criticism from Huggins. Hence Huggins's image among the whites was suddenly elevated as someone to whom they could entrust their future by exercising this kind of new leadership.

Deciding that he needed a new mandate from the voters, George Mitchell dissolved Parliament in August 1933, less than two months after he had succeeded Moffat as prime minister, and called for new elections. Huggins had the chance of a lifetime. Extreme members of the Rhodesia Party abandoned Mitchell and joined the ranks of the Rhodesia Reform Party. The election campaign was marked by a lack of clearly articulated issues, except for the continuation of anti-African rhetoric and the problem of finding ways to minimize the effects of the Depression. When the election results were known in September, Huggins had won with a slim majority. Mitchell, like his mentor Moffat, went into the cave of political oblivion. Huggins became prime minister on September 12. He remained in office until he retired in 1953.

While he was working on his political strategy to win the new elections, Huggins was having secret discussions with George Stark, Harold Jowitt's successor, about formulating an educational policy for Africans that the white business community would support. The reason for secrecy was that neither man wanted to subject the major features of that policy to public scrutiny while it was being developed. That Huggins used it as a major political strategy to win the elections of 1934 with a comfortable majority shows how cruel colonial politics were. What appealed to the voters was what Huggins called parallel development for the two racial groups.[9]

Huggins's underlying philosophy was that each race should be allowed to develop under its own conditions, the whites according to their Western cultural traditions and the Africans according to their tribal traditions. As Huggins and Stark saw it, the two races had nothing in common except only in a master-servant relationship. Without any political leverage through the electoral process, the Africans were at the mercy of Huggins and Stark.

It was not by coincidence that the introduction of compulsory education for white students in 1935, which the whites hoped would protect them from the threat of the Africans, occurred in the same year that Stark was confirmed as Director of Native Education. In 1938, when Stark felt secure in his position, Huggins decided that it was time to state clearly the policy of his government on the place of the Africans in society.

After consulting with Stark, Huggins spoke in Parliament in a way that surprised only a few, when he argued that the Europeans in this country could be likened to an island in a sea of black, with the artisan and tradesman forming the shore and the professional class the highland in the center. He rhetorically asked if Africans were to be allowed to invade the shores and gradually attack the highland. He concluded that to permit this to happen would mean that the haven of civilization that he said whites represented would be removed from the country and Africans would revert to a barbarism worse than before.[10]

There is no question that this line of thinking was intended to strengthen and defend the laager. Huggins's position was exactly the same position Stark had taken as inspector of schools in 1930. Huggins went on to indicate that while there was still time, the country must be developed between white areas and native areas to protect both racial shores of the island[11] To accomplish this objective, Huggins and Stark decided that the educational policy for Africans must be developed from the perspective of its intended objectives, which had always been the primary concern among whites.

Huggins could not have been happier. These were the circumstances that he took into consideration in outlining the essential elements of the new educational policy of his government in order to convince the voters that academic education for Africans would not be considered then or for the future. He argued that providing academic education for Africans would pose a threat to the political power and influence the whites had enjoyed in the past.

Both Huggins and Stark knew that this position was the kind of leadership needed to formulate policy that the white voters would support. In adding that good academic education was critically important for the white students, Huggins stated, "This is essential if all our children are to be given equal opportunity for progress and to keep their position of influence and power. It will prevent the creation of a poor white class. Constant adjustment will take place and the result should be a system of education Rhodesian in character, and especially suited to our own requirements."[12]

MUZOREWA DEFINES THE PARAMETERS OF HIS MISSION

When Muzorewa and his family returned to Zimbabwe from the United States in June 1963, Africa as a whole was going through tremendous political turmoil. The rise of African nationalism was at its height. In Angola and Mozambique a brutal war of independence was raging out of control. In South Africa the application of the policy of apartheid was having a devastating effect on the lives of the Africans. The Sharpeville massacre, the South African withdrawal from the British Commonwealth of Nations, and the banning of the African National Congress were among the events that represented the lowest point in the administration of Hendrik F. Verwoerd. South Africa was slowly but steadily degenerating into a state of political and social decay.[13]

The Federation of Rhodesia and Nyasaland under the leadership of the erratic and emotional Roy Welensky was going through the last phases of its life, giving the Africans in Northern Rhodesia and Nyasaland the opportunity they were looking for to advance themselves without interference from the whites in Southern Rhodesia who were promoting a political agenda of their own. As soon as the federation came to an end in December 1963, Zimbabwe was in the grip of the Rhodesia Front party led by Winston J. Field, a wealthy tobacco farmer from Marondera. Under the RF Zimbabwe was going thorough a period of testing. The general political situation in southern Africa was extremely unstable. On arriving at the airport in Harare, Muzorewa was subjected to humiliating treatment and discrimination.

The RF appointed individuals of unquestionable loyalty to key positions all over the country, including immigration officials, who were trained to behave toward Africans in such a way as to show that the RF was there to stay for at least a thousand years, as its leaders claimed. The RF immigration officials searched him and interrogated him for hours, asking him why he went to study in the United States.[14]

As was often the case in colonial Africa, discriminatory treatment of Africans by colonial officials led to anger, and anger led to a decision to fight the injustice. The RF government did not know that by treating Muzorewa in a discriminatory manner at the airport, it was creating a new hard-core nationalist and a formidable adversary within a few years. For the time being Muzorewa was appointed pastor of Old Umtali Methodist Center, where he remained for three years.

Muzorewa's salary was to be the same as other pastors in the Methodist Church in Zimbabwe, about 25 pounds per month. In 1965 Muzorewa was appointed secretary to the Rhodesia Student Christian Movement. In that capacity he had the opportunity to travel widely and learn about the conditions that affected young Zimbabweans.

Muzorewa came to know that throughout the country young Africans showed tremendous interest in politics.[15] He felt this was a very healthy development as these young people would one day provide the political leadership that was needed to free the country from the RF. In his realization of the conditions that affected the country, Muzorewa was defining the parameters of his mission.

Muzorewa was also compelled to define the parameters of his mission by a series of events he could not control. The humiliating treatment he had received at the airport convinced him that Africans not only had a right to demand an end to colonial oppression, but had also a duty to liberate themselves. He was aware that in the policy of the RF Africans were subjected to conditions of life that they had not experienced in the past. He was aware that in its behavior the RF had become totalitarian in every way and was slowly converting Zimbabwe into a police state. He immediately decided as he was traveling from the airport that "Our people needed to hear a total gospel that God created man and woman as a total person, having a body, a mind and spirit" whose needs must be addressed fully.[16]

Muzorewa concluded that for this total person to realize his full potential as a human being, restrictions that were placed on him in the form of inadequate opportunity for creative thought on the political process must be removed. These included the right to vote, freedom of expression, and the right to run for public office. He regarded the RF as the greatest threat to African advancement since the days of Godfrey Huggins, and he decided that he was going to play his role fully in bringing about the change that would enable Africans to realize their political ambitions and aspirations.

The first occasion for Muzorewa to put these ideas into action, as the first step in defining the parameters of his mission, came on March 13, 1964, when he was part of the organization of the day of prayer and unity which brought together 18,000 people from the townships of Salisbury. When Ian Smith assumed the office of prime minister in April 1964 as a result of his leading a political coup that removed Winston J. Field from that office, relations between the Africans and the RF took a dramatic turn for the worse. Smith felt that in Field's failure to take decisive action against the demonstrations staged by Africans he was committing errors of leadership and that he must be replaced as a new national leader. But it was Smith's action that the Africans needed to bolster their own opportunity and that Muzorewa used to sharpen his own definition of the parameters of his mission.

Among the events Muzorewa could not control but that would help define his mission was the deportation of Bishop Ralph E. Dodge in July 1964. Muzorewa admired Dodge for his philosophy of the "total gospel for the total man."[17] This was a new concept among preachers of the this period. Many embraced the thinking of liberation theology that suggested that the human being must be free to develop his mind in political, social, economic, and religious settings to be complete.[18] Because Smith felt that liberation theology carried a more political message demanding the collapse of his government, he could not tolerate Dodge's message.

But in deporting him Smith created a larger problem for his government than Dodge created by his message. Muzorewa explained how the deportation accentuated the crisis between the Smith government and the church in general, saying that his first contact with white officials of the government came over this issue with other church leaders. He said he joined in a fruitless attempt to persuade the government officials to cancel the order to deport Bishop Dodge and Rev. Robert Hughes. He added that a lawyer advised him and other church officials to write a formal letter of protest to the government, but he let them know that he held no hope that anyone would listen to their plea.[19]

The problems that Smith created by formulating and implementing the policy of his government were a high level of insensitivity to the feelings of Africans. Throughout his political career, Smith did not make any efforts to bridge the gap that existed between him and the church leaders in an effort to find solutions to the problems he was creating by both his attitudes and policies. His desire for political power seriously inhibited his ability to see the issues that divided him and church leaders from their proper perspective. His action in banning the *African Daily News* in 1964 came as result of his desire to eliminate all opposition to his policy. In the same way the banning of the African political organizations in 1964 created more serious problems than Smith would encounter if he had allowed them to operate.

In 1990 F. W. de Klerk fully recognized this reality by unbanning all the political parties that had been outlawed in South Africa in 1964. Once de Klerk took that action he opened avenues of dialogue with Africans, and finally solutions to the problems that apartheid had created for many years were now found. If Smith had recognized this reality he would have spared his country the agony of a painful transformation that resulted in his loss of the power that he was trying to preserve for whites. The continuation of the African political parties would have facilitated the dialogue that would have led to solutions of the political problems the country was facing.

The deportation of Bishop Dodge was merely a prelude of more serious events to come. For the next four years following his deportation, he tried to discharge his episcopal duties from Zambia with the work that his assistant, Rev. Jonah B. Kawadza, did in Zimbabwe and the work of the Methodist Church went on fairly well. Members of the Methodist Church refused to elect a successor to Dodge because they feared that Smith would exploit the situation to his own political advantage.

However, the deportation of Dodge plus the banning of African political organizations and African newspapers gave Smith the opportunity that he needed to seize power and declare the country independent unilaterally. This action came on November 11, 1965. Smith claimed that he took this action because "the mantle of the pioneers has fallen on our shoulders to sustain civilization in a primitive country."[20] From that time to the end of his government in 1979 the behavior of the Smith government manifested nothing to show that it was civilized. He simply equated his own behavior with civilization. Therefore his definition of civilization was much narrower than the universal definition.

Two weeks following Smith's unilateral declaration of independence

(UDI), on November 26, the Christian Council of Rhodesia, of which Dodge was president, issued a statement condemning the illegal seizure of power saying:

We affirm our present loyalty to Her Majesty the Queen within the constitution which is at present the constitution accepted by the lawful parliament of Rhodesia in 1961. We judge the proclamation of a new constitution by a group of ministers without assent of the parliament of the Crown to be an unlawful act and only further enchantments of parliament to be unlawful confirmed by the lawful governor. We look forwards earnestly to pledge ourselves to work for the rapid restoration of constitutional government in our land.[21]

Due to press censorship that Smith imposed immediately before the UDI, the statement was not published, giving Smith an erroneous impression that things were just fine. This is why he thought that the declaration of independence was Rhodesia's finest hour, paraphrasing Winston Churchill's remarks made during the battle of Britain in the Second World War.

Among the events that Muzorewa utilized to define the parameters of his mission was his election as bishop of the Methodist Church on August 28, 1968, to succeed Dodge who had decided to retire. At the age of 43 Muzorewa was both the youngest and the first African to hold the office of bishop in Zimbabwe. Since Dodge's deportation the administrative work of the Methodist Church in Zimbabwe was carried out by Rev. Kawadza, who was Muzorewa's classmate in theological school at Old Umtali. Kawadza was an articulate and perceptive leader with a charming personality, a captivating smile, and an imposing physical stature. A ruggedly handsome man, Kawadza did not have any adversaries in the church—except that in carrying out his duties as assistant to Dodge, he was so concerned about not doing anything different from Dodge that he was considered to lack the ability to make decisions that many Methodists felt must be made in the interest of the Methodist Church. Some people felt that he operated too much in Dodge's shadow in a way that did not allow him to define his own philosophical and administrative identity.

However, Kawadza was admired by many and supported by most missionaries because he was less controversial in his views on any subject than Muzorewa, who was known to be outspoken about some ways the Methodist Church did things, especially lingering discriminatory practices that Dodge had stopped but resurfaced after his deportation. As most of the missionaries came from the United States, it was believed that they carried some discriminatory practices in the United States with them to Africa. Muzorewa resented this and argued that if discriminatory tendencies remained characteristics of the Methodist missionaries, how could the Methodist Church possibly fight against the discriminatory policy of the RF government?

The election of bishops in the Methodist Church in southern Africa was conducted by the Central Conference, which met in Botswana in 1968. Delegates from several countries of southern Africa met there to discharge their responsibility. The delegates from Zimbabwe traveled to Botswana by bus. Muzorewa described the social climate that surrounded the Zimbabwe delegation during this trip, saying that he found himself sitting alone in the bus carrying church delegates to the Central Conference. No one wished to side with him openly lest it was found later that they supported a losing candidate. He understood then the level of loneliness that political candidates must feel at times amid crowds of anonymous well-wishers.[22]

Every delegate was assuming that Kawadza would be elected bishop. In fact many people in Zimbabwe during the previous four years addressed him as Bishop Kawadza, simply because of the stature that he brought to the office of the Methodist Church in Dodge's absence. But somehow between the time the Zimbabwe delegation left for Botswana and the time the balloting began, the delegates reached the conclusion that although he was a likable man with considerable experience, Kawadza was too soft to deal with the emerging critical issues that the Methodist Church and the country were going to face soon. They also concluded that controversial as Muzorewa was, he stood a much better chance of leading the Methodist Church in its forthcoming struggle against the RF government. Muzorewa was elected on the first ballot with 56 votes out of a total of 70.

Kawadza took his defeat in humility. He and his family left immediately for study at Drew University in Madison, New Jersey. In June 1971 the author visited him there and had an opportunity to listen to him express his feelings about the election, saying, among other things, that the election was not conducted in a fair manner. Although the charge was incorrect, Muzorewa remained worried by it all.

THE ELEMENTS OF MUZOREWA'S MISSION: THE DILEMMA OF AN EFFECTIVE CHURCH LEADER

As the conference came to an end, Muzorewa began to feel the heavy responsibility he was soon to shoulder as leader of the Methodist Church and as the first African leader of a major denomination in Zimbabwe. It was therefore appropriate that Dodge, the leader he was now about to succeed and the man who was his mentor, gave him his charge. In that charge Dodge stated five principles that he believed defined the essence of Muzorewa's mission:

1. Maintain your integrity, be honest in dealing with issues.

2. Maintain your concern for the welfare of all people. Do not forget those of different classes, those who walk far from where you normally walk. Do not forget the dispossessed.

3. Maintain an open mind so that you learn from others as well as teaching them. Listen as well as speak. Admit your mistakes, but learn to avoid them.

4. Maintain vision and foresight. Remember: Where there is no vision the people perish. He who leads people must be ahead of them. You must look into the future. You must begin now to build the foundation in Africa upon which our church of the year 2000 will stand.

5. Maintain contact with the true vine. Your ministry will fail if you are out of harmony with God's plan and purpose.[23]

Muzorewa did not have to wait long to put in place the elements of his mission. He immediately decided to base his entire administration on the model that Dodge had created. He explained, "It soon became plain to me that our theology needed to be clarified and our concerns needed a broader base. I felt at ease in following in the footsteps of Bishop Ralph Dodge. He had stressed that the Christian faith must be proclaimed as a total gospel for the total person."[24]

In 1969 the Smith government introduced two elements into national politics that entrenched racism at a higher level than it did in the past. The first element was the introduction of a republican constitution that the RF believed erased the last vestiges of the British control and influence. From now on the RF was the master of its own destiny and that of Zimbabwe. The second element was the enactment of the Land Tenure Act, which replaced the Land Apportionment Act of 1929. On June 5, 1969, church leaders across the country, both Catholic and Protestant, issued a joint statement in response to the Land Tenure Act, saying what the implications would mean to the country:

1. The majority of people will be given no opportunity to express their opinion by democratic means.

2. The new constitution will decide Africans and whites by replacing a common voters' roll with separate rolls and by its distribution of land.

3. It will use the payment of income tax as the assessment of a people's right to representation.

4. It will take away from the individuals and from the judicious basic rights and safeguards, and place absolute power in the hands of the government.[25]

An examination of the provisions of the Land Tenure Act furnishes evidence to show that Africans and church leaders had reason to worry about what the RF government was doing. The main provision was that the law divided the country into two equal halves, one half for a 250,000 whites and the other half for 6.1 million Africans. Each racial group was prohibited from owning land in the area reserved for the other.

There was no public input before the bill became law. At that time all 50 seats reserved for whites in Parliament were held by RF members. The remaining 15 seats were reserved for Africans. For all practical purposes the RF government was virtually a one-party state. In their individual ways church leaders initiated an official response to register protests against the new law. This is why on June 12–13, 1970, Muzorewa convened an emergency session of the Methodist Church Conference for the purpose of debating the new law and to pass a resolution, which read: "We view with great alarm the passing though parliament of the Land Tenure Act. The philosophy behind this act and the possible grave results ensuing from the enforcement of it, will, in our opinion, not avoid racial friction but, on the contrary, will seriously intensify it."[26]

The special session of the conference was also addressed by two Catholic priests, Bishop Donal Lamont of Umtali, and Father Richard Randolph of Salisbury. Randolph gave a portrait of the implications of the Land Tenure Act that many people had not fully understood. He painted a grim picture of the new law, saying that the church was no longer at liberty to move freely among people of all races to carry out its mission. He added that people of different races may no longer freely associate for the worship of God in churches outside their own prescribed racial areas. He concluded that in such case the church no longer had the right to admit in its schools whomever it wanted because the church was now forbidden to admit to its hospitals people of a race different from that of the prescribed area.[27] Until that time the church operated both schools and hospitals for both races. Now they had to obtain permission to do so.

In March 1970 Muzorewa was invited to his alma mater, Central Methodist College in a country in which he cautioned whites to exercise restraint in their euphoria about the apparent success the RF government was claiming it was scoring against both the Africans and the British government in the battle of wills. He began by saying that since he was going out of the country for a lengthy period of time, he felt he should address himself to the electorate. He said since only 2 percent of the total Zimbabwe population could vote, they carried a heavy responsibility to the voteless masses. He argued that the country needed free men and women free from fear. He argued that even the RF was not free from fear of Africans and loss of privilege. In that context the RF could not really be free until the Africans were free.

Muzorewa concluded, "I am sorry to think that at the very time when scientists and theologians are coming to a common understanding of the basic common nature of man, the rulers of Rhodesia are still believers in the false doctrine of racial superiority and inferiority."[28] In entering the political arena of Zimbabwe, Muzorewa was facing the dilemma of a church leader. On the one hand he was aware that he had a responsibility to preach the total gospel for the total human being. On the other hand he faced the prospects of criticism that he was exploiting his position as church leader to make maximum political gain. This dilemma did not remain unknown to Smith, who did every thing to exploit it. But without constitutional provision to ensure the separation between church and state, there was little that Smith could do to stop Muzorewa other than to treat him as an ordinary person. But he was not an ordinary person. Therefore Smith himself faced a dilemma of his own.

THE INAUGURATION OF THE AFRICAN NATIONAL COUNCIL: THE BEGINNING OF MUZOREWA'S MISSION

This appeal made Muzorewa an instant national figure. His star was rising rapidly as he began to articulate positions consistent with the political aspirations of the Africans. Throughout 1971 the British Conservative government made secret contact with Smith, beginning with the visit of Lord Goodman in April for purposes of seeking a solution to the question of independence. After another visit in June the British government concluded that there was a different climate between Smith and itself and that Smith was now willing to negotiate seriously because he was facing increasing problems he was unable to resolve.

This conclusion led to further secret discussions between the two sides. In November the British government sent Sir Alec Douglas-Home, the British Foreign and Commonwealth secretary, to have discussions with Smith. Beginning in 1964, when Smith began to demand independence from Britain, the British government formulated the famous five principles that it said the RF must respect to guide the negotiations and could not be violated:

1. There must be unimpeded progress toward majority rule.

2. There would have to be guarantees against retrogressive amendment of the constitution.

3. There would have to immediate improvement in the political status of the African population.

4. There would have to be progress toward ending racial discrimination.

5. The British government would need to be satisfied that any basis proposed for independence was acceptable to the people of Rhodesia as a whole.[29]

From the time that Smith assumed the office of prime minister in April 1964 to November 1971 he made it very clear that there would never be an African government in his lifetime, not in a thousand years, as he often repeated. If it was true that in 1971 he accepted the five British principles for independence, was he aware that their implementation would lead to an African government to which he dedicated his entire life from becoming a reality?

The answer is that apart from the last principle, Smith believed that he could accept the principles without giving up power to the Africans. He also concluded that the test of acceptability required by the fifth principle would prove what he had always argued, that he had the support of all segments of Zimbabwean society including the Africans. Therefore, Smith never envisaged the actual turning of political power to the African majority as a result of his accepting the five principles. This was why in November 1971 he signed an agreement with Douglas-Home.

In order to implement that fifth principle the British government appointed a commission under the chairmanship of Lord Pearce, an expert on constitutional law, to travel to Zimbabwe and conduct a test of acceptability in all the major areas of the country. The commission arrived in Zimbabwe on January 11, 1972, under Smith's impression that it would return a positive verdict on the proposals. With African political leaders in prison, a vicious state of emergency, which made it virtually impossible for the Africans to have any political activity and with conditions of a police state, Smith's excitement over the prospects for a legal independence and recognition of his government reached a new level of euphoria. Things seemed to go on well for Smith because there was no political opposition of any kind.

As the Africans studied the settlement proposals closely, they came to the conclusion that Britain was about to abandon its responsibility to the future of Africans by its failure to protect the interests of Africans and granting independence to Smith. Faced with this possibility, the Africans decided to do something under very difficult conditions to express their views to the Pearce Commission. As the Pearce Commission was arriving, a number of individuals held a meeting and decided to form an organization known as the African National Council and asked Bishop Muzorewa to be its president. Rev. Canaan Banana was elected vice president. The executive committee thus formed called a news conference to explain four major objectives that would guide its views before the Pearce Commission.

The first objective was to represent the voice and will of the silenced African majority in the country. The second objective was to call all Africans to realize the essential power of unity at this critical moment and to move as one people to achieve their ultimate goal of freedom. The third objective was to explain and expose the dangerous implications

that would result if Africans accepted the Anglo-Rhodesian constitutional settlement proposals. The fourth objective was to raise funds for
the promotion of the organization.[30] The African National Council executive committee concluded that after the test of acceptability was completed, the Pearce Commission would conclude that the people of
Rhodesia as a whole rejected the proposals.

The Council immediately launched a national campaign to inform and
advise Africans of the dangers of accepting the Smith–Douglas-Home
proposals. For the first time in the history of Zimbabwe the Africans had
an opportunity to express their opinion on a major national issue on
equal terms with whites. Unknown to Smith, this occasion represented
the principle of one person, one vote, a principle the Africans first enunciated at the formation of the African National Council in 1957, but a
principle that Smith rejected until now.[31]   At a news conference on December 16, 1971, Muzorewa read a statement saying,

The Anglo-Rhodesian proposals for a settlement have been critically studied,
analyzed and found to be a vicious and subtle device for recognition of UDI by
the British government. The proposals as contained in the White Paper do not
reflect a single suggestion made by African leaders. Their views were completely
ignored. We are convinced beyond a shadow of doubt that acceptance of these
proposals by Africans would be their betrayal. We cannot be vendors of our
heritage and rights. Therefore the African's responsible answer should be an
emphatic No![32]

With these words Muzorewa had completed the definition of his mission; now he was going to design a strategy of accomplishing it. That
mission was now just beginning.

After several months of gathering the evidence it needed to reach its
conclusion and make its recommendation, the Pearce Commission released its report and stated that the terms of independence were acceptable to the whites but they were unacceptable to the Africans. Therefore
these terms were unacceptable to the people of Zimbabwe as a whole.
Muzorewa became an instant national figure. The first phase of his mission had been successful. Instead of criticizing his policy, Smith decided
to place the blame for the rejection of the proposals at the doorsteps of
the Pearce Commission and the Africans.[33]

SUMMARY AND CONCLUSION

This chapter traced the major developments from the time Muzorewa
was born in April 1925 to the dramatic political events that were unfolding in 1971. Related important events were taking place beginning
in 1927. By the time Muzorewa went to school at the age of 9 these events

were already having an impact on all the people of Zimbabwe, both white and African.

As Muzorewa was growing up he was introduced to painful experiences of racism that alerted him of the need to do something to fight it. Early in his life he made a decision that he was not going to stand by and watch the colonial government abuse him and his people by denying them their legitimate rights as people. This is why he pursued his studies with a purpose only he could understand. During the height of the Smith government from 1964 to 1979, Muzorewa became increasingly aware that he would have to play a role effectively in the struggle for freedom for Africans in Zimbabwe. That, too, was a mission only he could understand and undertake.

NOTES

1. Ralph E. Diffendorfer (ed.), *The World Service of the Methodist Episcopal Church* (Chicago: Council of Board of Benevolencies, 1925), p. 123.

2. When Muzorewa arrived at Old Umtali in 1940 to go to school, these facilities were still there and continued to exist until they were replaced in 1966.

3. Diffendorfer, *The World Service*, p. 123.

4. For details of this remarkable woman, see Dickson A. Mungazi, *Colonial Policy and Conflict in Zimbabwe: A Study of Cultures in Collision, 1890–1979* (New York: Crane Russak, 1992).

5. Quoted in Diffendorfer, *The World Service*, p. 123.

6. This author was a member of this group, which attended Morningside College from 1961 to 1965. The group included students from the Belgian Congo, Zimbabwe, and Angola. All were supported by the Methodist Church during the episcopal leadership of Bishop Ralph E. Dodge.

7. Diffendorfer, *The World Service*, p. 124.

8. The influence of this event on future developments cannot be ignored. In 1962, when Huggins's United Federal Party was weakened by circumstances he could not control, Ian Smith and Winston Field broke away to form the Rhodesia Front and drew their support from dissident members of the UFP.

9. At that time the Africans did not have the vote. The Bantu Voters Association concerned itself with township elections. Africans were not allowed to claim the right to vote until the introduction of the constitution of 1961. Even then voting was by race until the elections of 1980. This is why the colonial politicians ignored the Africans.

10. Godfrey Huggins, during a debate in parliament, in Southern Rhodesia: *Legislative Debates*, 1938, p. 21.

11. Ibid., p. 22.

12. Godfrey Huggins, "Education in Southern Rhodesia: Notes on Certain Features," (Zimbabwe National Archives, 1939).

13. Francis Meli, *South Africa Belongs to Us: A History of the ANC* (Harare: Zimbabwe Publishing House, 1988), p. 277.

14. Abel T. Muzorewa, *Rise Up and Walk: The Autobiography of Abel Tendekai Muzorewa* (Nashville: Abingdon Press, 1978), p. 53.

15. Ibid.

16. Ibid., p. 56.

17. Ibid., p. 59.

18. For a detailed discussion of this theology, see Dickson A. Mungazi, *The Honored Crusade: Ralph E. Dodge's Theology of Liberation and Initiative for Social Change in Zimbabwe* (Gweru: Mambo Press, 1991).

19. Muzorewa, *Rise Up and Walk*, p. 59.

20. Ian D. Smith, "Rhodesia's Finest Hour: Unilateral Declaration of Independence" (Salisbury: November 11, 1965). Zimbabwe National Archives.

21. Christian Council of Rhodesia, Response to Unilateral Declaration of Independence," November 26, 1965. Zimbabwe National Archives.

22. Muzorewa, *Rise Up and Walk*, p. 64.

23. Ibid., p. 67.

24. Ibid., p. 68.

25. Ibid., p. 73.

26. Ibid., p. 79.

27. Ibid., p. 81.

28. Ibid., p. 71.

29. Judith Todd, *The Right to Say No: Rhodesia 1972* (Harare: Longman, 1987), p. 13.

30. Muzorewa, *Rise Up and Walk*, p. 95.

31. The reader should not confuse the African National Congress that was formed in South Africa in 1912 with the African National Council formed in Zimbabwe in 1957.

32. Ibid.

33. Todd, *The Right to Say No*, p. 153.

6

Tutu's Role in the Political Transformation of South Africa

A people made desperate by despair, injustice, and oppression will use desperate means to end their oppression.
—Desmond M. Tutu, 1983

Tutu argued that without freedom of the human person, the mind is totally oppressed and cannot function to bring out the best in human creative activity. Creativity is an indispensable quality of the human being. Without it constructive innovation, that part of human endeavor that makes it possible to improve society, is rendered meaningless. Tutu adds that freedom is the soul of society, the hub on which the social wheel rotates to move forward the vehicle that moves society to its destination: human fulfillment as a prerequisite of the development of society itself.

Tutu was of the opinion that in South Africa, where these components of freedom were denied to individuals, the South African society itself lost the purpose for which it existed. It began to die a slow and painful death, unable to recover from the social cancer that was destroying its vital tissue. In this situation those who denied freedom and those who are denied it suffer the same fate. Those who denied freedom fared no better in society than those who were denied it.

Does Tutu see any other functions of freedom? The answer is definitely yes. First, he says there must be freedom of thought, that central tenet of being human. It is this kind of freedom that produces an inventor, a philosopher, an entrepreneur, a theologian, a statesman, a music composer, a poet, a novelist, a historian, a medical scientist, a mathematician, a physicist, an economist. Freedom of thought generates new ideas about various aspects of society. It brings to the fore a new John Maynard Keynes, a Helen Keller, a John Keats, a Steve Biko, an Edison Sithole. It is this kind of freedom that allows movement of concept in the human mind to allow expression of human horizons. Tutu concluded that any society that impinges or inhibits this kind of freedom, such as apartheid did, is destroying the very essence of its own existence and development.[1] Apartheid, unconscious as to what it was, would not enable its authors to see the importance of human freedom on the quality of society from this perspective. It was too narrow and repressive to allow individuals to acquire this freedom in order to benefit society itself.

Tutu then addressed the importance of freedom of human association without regard to race. He fully recognized the effect of the attitude that the Dutch settlers at the Cape adopted toward Africans in 1652 as having a negative impact on human relationships. He believed that because human intellect is found in all people of all cultures and races,[2] there is no reason to restrict human association on any basis. He also sees freedom of association as being essential to human development, the sharing of the most valuable resources that any nation needs to ensure its own development. He concluded that freedom of association enables both the individual and society to place their confidence in the ability of all its people to create and re-create for their mutual benefit. Creativity and creation are unique attributes of the human mind made possible by freedom of association. Tutu acknowledged the adverse effect of apartheid in this regard, stating that South Africa was starved of the great things many of its children could create because of the artificial barriers and the refusal of the Nationalist government to let people develop to their fullest potential.[3]

Tutu concluded that freedom of association, like freedom of thought and freedom of the human person, is an inherent part of being human and cannot be restricted without inflicting severe damage to society itself. This is exactly what apartheid did to South Africa: it offered no benefits to the Afrikaners by denying them freedom of association with Africans. For this reason the Afrikaners never came to know the Africans. How could this level of ignorance help build a country?

In projecting his vision for South Africa, Tutu utilized an African concept of humanity, *Bantu*, which is a rare gift of sharing. In African philosophy something is not valuable or meaningful unless it is shared. Love, food, ideas, thoughts, understanding, and a sense of belonging are fundamental tenets of human association that elevate both human beings and society to a level where its priceless values determine its character.

Under these tenets, discrimination of any kind robs both individuals and society of an opportunity to achieve greatness. But Tutu was aware that important as it is, the concept of *Bantu* is what the Afrikaners belittled as an operational principle of human association. However, Tutu underscored the significance of this concept when he argued that the concept of sharing, as a basic thrust of human association, is often exemplified at African gatherings where food is served.

This concept is relevant today when people eat together from the same dishes, rather than from separate or individual dishes.[4] Tutu recognized that a major problem of applying this concept under apartheid was that the Afrikaners did not believe it had any significance or role in the kind of society they were trying to preserve. He mourned the loss that the value of sharing represented in taking a meal from common dishes, because Africans had been subjected to excessive individuality associated with Western material objectives. His vision of South Africa was that all its people have an opportunity to learn the importance of human association based upon the value of sharing. Only then would human association have meaning for the benefit of society.

Tutu projected a vision of equality and consideration of the needs of all people, adding that his vision included a society that was more compassionate and caring in which superfluous appendages were unthinkable, and where the young and the old were made to feel wanted because they had different contributions to society.[5] Tutu also decried the practice that existed under apartheid, creating what he regarded as a distorted community that forced certain members of society into heartless and soulless institutions. He also mourned the loss of collective and accumulated wisdom and experience needed to restructure South African society so that it could recapture the values that once made the traditional African society what it was before apartheid.

A critical component of Tutu's vision for South Africa was his hope for justice, both in society and in the legal system. For years the concept of justice under apartheid was totally foreign to Africans. The Nationalist government appointed to the legal system hard-core Afrikaners who subverted the legal system to subject Africans to a position that forced them to feel less than human. What Tutu regarded as particularly painful was that once an African was arrested for any possible offenses related to various laws under apartheid, he was presumed guilty until he proved himself innocent. The universal principle that one was presumed innocent until proven guilty in a court of law was completely ignored when Africans were involved. The right to vote as citizens was denied to Africans solely on the basis of color. Tutu expressed his vision in this aspect of national life, saying that South Africa would need the integrity of territory with a common citizenship and equal rights for all people.[6]

Tutu also called for the end of the equally notorious Bantu Education Act and a move toward a unitary system of education that would bring students of all races together for purposes of learning to live together for the benefit of the country. He also advised the Nationalist government to suspend the application of apartheid laws and regulations and call a convention or initiate dialogue between itself and other groups for purposes of putting in place a new climate that would help heal the wounds inflicted by apartheid over many years. Tutu expressed an urgency over this goal as time was running out.

TUTU'S VIEWS ON CRITICAL ISSUES NEEDING IMMEDIATE ACTION

In February 1979 Tutu was profoundly troubled by his observation that apartheid was having a paralyzing effect on South Africa. Black and white were totally unable to communicate on any issues of national importance. At that time the international community was increasingly taking the position that apartheid was a crime against humanity and that international cooperation was needed to apply pressure on the Nationalist government to end it. As a result South Africa was being isolated from having any relationships with other nations including sport. At the beginning of 1979 it was announced that John Tate, an African American boxer, would go to South Africa to fight Gerrie Coetzee, an Afrikaner fighter and local boxing champion.

Although the announcement of Tate's impending visit to South Africa was highly controversial among members of the international community, Tate himself decided to make the trip. Before the match the Afrikaners were hailing Coetzee as their local folk hero who had an opportunity to beat Tate decisively to prove their superiority over Africans. In turn the Africans universally supported Tate as a champion of their political struggle. As Tutu had noticed, the excitement that was building on both sides before the match was having a paralyzing effect on race relations.

As he was working away from home until midnight on the night of the big match, Tutu noticed that the quiet of Soweto was suddenly shattered by blaring sounds of cars often associated with new year's celebrations. At first he could not understand what was going on. Then it occurred to him that this was the night of the Tate-Coetzee match. From the manner in which the Africans in Soweto were celebrating, he came to the conclusion that Tate must have won the match. As he turned on the radio he learned that indeed the Africans were celebrating Tate's victory over Coetzee. Tutu concluded that Africans were thrilled that Tate, a black man, had won. His victory gave even those who were opposed to Tate's visit to South Africa and the match itself in the first place to celebrate because he had made an Afrikaner bite the dust. But most Afrikaners were quite despondent over Coetzee's loss.[7] Racial tension suddenly increased and there was nothing anyone could do to ease it.

Tutu concluded that like Nazi Germany, sport in South Africa was acquiring heavy racial dimensions that did not serve the interests of the country in any way because it was having a paralyzing effect. He cited another example to prove his point. Most Afrikaners were delighted when the British Lions, a major rugby team, came to play in South Africa. But most Africans were displeased. Tutu expressed his vision that in the best interest of the country the Nationalist government must initiate an end to this racial polarization and help create a new national identity to which all South Africans could contribute. He also concluded that a national initiative in this area of life could yield successful results if the Nationalist government decided to end apartheid. Of course, Tutu was aware that the end of apartheid would have to take a lot more than persuasion to have the Nationalist government end it.

The second area that Tutu said needed immediate action had to do with the standards of behavior of the Nationalist government itself. For years the government observed no standards and respected no conventions in its actions to silence the critics of apartheid. It resorted to the practice of detention without trial under the Terrorism Act of 1967. The police were given absolute power to arrest and detain opponents of apartheid for unspecified periods of time. Those who were arrested had no recourse of any kind except to appeal to the government itself. They were not allowed to have an access to the legal process. They could not obtain legal representation. They could not demand a speedy trial. Anyone arrested under provisions of the Terrorism Act was subject to detention for five years without trial. The Terrorism Act was itself a definite form of terrorism. It terrorized mostly innocent Africans and those who were expressing their legitimate opposition to an extremely oppressive system, apartheid.

Tutu's greatest concern was that so few whites seemed to care about this violation of the rule of law.[8] There was no doubt that the government itself was acting in a lawless manner in engaging in behaviors that were contrary to universal practices. He also concluded that by passing laws such as the Terrorism Act, the government itself was engaging in acts of terrorism far worse than for what it was arresting and detaining Africans. Tutu urged the government to move aggressively to remove this gross injustice because it was hurting the country.

The third area that Tutu felt needed immediate action was to initiate the transformation of South Africa in order to end the system of banning opponents of its policy. Banning orders were routinely issued against Africans who opposed apartheid. Those who were banned were often placed under house arrest and could not have any association or communication with more than one person. They could not be quoted in any publication or distribution for public consumption. A banned person was prohibited from traveling outside his house for any reason. In 1979 Tutu explained how petty and cruel the system of banning was. During a sermon he preached in Kingston, Jamaica, he told of what often happened when someone was banned. For example, he visited Winnie Mandela, who was a banned person. At that time her husband, Nelson Mandela, was serving a life sentence on Robben Island, a maximum security prison.[9] Tutu had arranged for Winnie to take Holy Communion as part of his ministry to the dispossessed and oppressed. But the police told him he could not enter her house because she was a banned person. The Holy Communion was celebrated in his car. On a second occasion Tutu went to see Winnie her restriction order was even more tightened. She could not leave her yard. Therefore the Holy Commission was celebrated with her on one side of the fence to her house and Tutu on the other side. Tutu expressed his vision that the Nationalist government must take action to end once and for all this inhuman treatment of its own people.[10]

The fourth area that Tutu felt the Nationalist government must address was to stop inciting Africans to engage in activity to provide an excuse for arresting them. Because the Nationalist government feared its own people, it imposed conditions of a police state that made it very hard for Africans to conduct their normal business. Beginning in 1935 the government designed a strategy for creating conflict among African mineworkers so as to create division among them. From that time to 1979 the government improved this method until it designed a system of creating instability among urban Africans. When Africans felt harassed they responded in ways that suggested a situation of riot to the police. This is what happened in June 1980 when a policeman was killed. The government would move in against them, disrupting their normal daily life by mass arrests.

On June 17 Tutu issued a press statement in which he decried the action of the police, saying that the death of the policeman was regretted, but he wished to emphasize the fact that when the police repeatedly interfered with funerals of the people they had killed under the guise of maintaining law and order, there was bound to be trouble. He also recognized that the racial situation was extremely volatile and that the government must exercise restraint in reacting to a situation that had a potential for a major conflict. Tutu projected his vision in this aspect of national life, saying that the only way to bring about real peace and trust between Africans and the government was to end apartheid. He suggested that the government call a conference to resolve the issues that were causing conflict between it and the Africans.[11]

The fifth area of national life that Tutu felt the government must initiate was to stop its practice of using armed forces and the police to occupy African townships. On March 31, 1978, the police, with cooperation of the army, carried out raids that the media described as a form of blitz. While a senior police officer described the raids as routine, Africans regarded them as nothing less than an act of terrorism by the police and the army. Tutu concluded that nowhere in the world was such a practice considered routine—where there was no civil disturbance or a breakdown of law and order the army and the police moved against the people in an unprovoked way—as was done on that day. In that operation the police and the army units carried out searches on women at roadblocks. The police and the army required the public to cooperate in subjecting African women to this indignity and concluded that it was routine.[12]

Africans from all walks of life as well as religious and civic leaders came to recognize a hard reality of the apartheid system: if they did nothing to bring it to an end, apartheid itself would engulf the entire population, causing massive destruction that would take years to heal. Tutu concluded that all South Africans had a duty and responsibility to end apartheid before apartheid enslaved them all. This was not an easy task, but it had to be undertaken in order to save South Africa from a major national disaster. Tutu's vision of South Africa provided an incentive that made it possible to undertake this task. If the people of South Africa failed to undertake this task, they would have only themselves to blame, because the international community was supportive of any effort that was intended to bring it to an end.

TUTU'S ROLE IN THE TRANSFORMATION OF SOUTH AFRICA

In expressing his vision for South Africa, Tutu was defining the parameters of his action in the future. That action was intended to initiate the transformation of South Africa from apartheid to an internationally accepted form of government. He recognized that when Hendrik F. Verwoerd was assassinated in August 1966 and was succeeded by John B. Vorster, another hard-core Afrikaner segregationist, South Africa was going through a period of major crisis. The fact that the Nationalist Party elected Vorster to succeeded Verwoerd as prime minister meant that Afrikaners failed to read something far more serious from Verwoerd's assassination. The year 1966 is also important in that the Tutu family lived in London, where he was part-time curate of St. Albion's. He also received his B.A. honors and Master of Theology from King's College. This educational accomplishment was an accumulation of a period of study that had begun in 1962.[13]

In 1964 Alan Paton, the author of *Cry, the Beloved Country*, described the action that the Nationalist government took against Fort Hare, saying

Prior to 1959 the staff of Fort Hare included white liberals, and its students Africans, Indians and Colored people. But in 1959 the government summarily dismissed most of the white liberals from the staff because it claimed that they were sabotaging apartheid. Several African members known to oppose apartheid were also fired, or else resigned in sympathy with their white colleagues. The policy now is to admit no more Colored or Indian students, and a government appointee now heads the staff, which is gradually being Afrikanized. Students who protest against the order are dismissed, and the number of security police in Alice had been increased.[14]

The conditions that the Nationalist government created to control every aspect of national life, including higher education, inevitably led to a police state. African members of the faculty who demonstrated an intellectual level higher than the ordinary were served with notice to go elsewhere. For example, Professor Z. K. Matthews, a distinguished African scholar and chairman of the Department of Anthropology, was subjected to the indignity of apartheid in such painful ways that he was forced to resign. Matthews entered the services of the government of Botswana, serving as its ambassador to the United Nations until 1968. These conditions had deteriorated rapidly by the time Tutu began his campaign to initiate the transformation of South Africa. These conditions also made that campaign very difficult.

When Steve Biko formed the South African Student Organization in 1968 to spearhead the Black Consciousness Movement, the Nationalist government became alarmed, forcing it to ban the group in 1973. Even this action was not enough. It continued to watch Biko closely for the next two years as a dangerous opponent of apartheid. With the ANC and other African political organizations outlawed, the Nationalist government thought it had designed an instrument of combating the threat Africans were posing to the supremacy of apartheid, totally unaware that it had placed the country on the tip of a volcano. Once it became a reality, black consciousness of the kind Biko was promoting could not be eliminated. In an introduction to Biko's I Write What I Like, published posthumously in 1978 and revised in 1996, Tutu described the Black Consciousness Movement saying that it sought to awaken in Africans a sense of their infinite value and worth because they are all created in God's image so that their worth was intrinsic to who they were and not dependent on biological irrelevance such as ethnicity, skin color, or race.[15]

These were among the conditions that inspired Tutu to play his role in seeking the transformation of South Africa. He had taken to heart Edmund Burke's idea that for evil to continue all it required was for good people to do nothing. Tutu felt that he was a good man, a man of God, a man who had responsibility to play that role well, unmindful of any consequences of his action to himself. Tutu began to play that role by confronting the head of the Nationalist government itself. In the letter he wrote to John B. Vorster on May 6, 1976, Tutu moved from expressing his vision for South Africa to suggesting specific action to ensure the transformation of South Africa to democracy as it is universally known by freeing it from the grip of apartheid. He recognized the fact that Africans were no longer willing to live under apartheid. He wanted an immediate change from a government that imposed a police state to a representative democracy. Nothing less than this change was acceptable any longer.

Tutu did not decide lightly to write the letter to Vorster. But once he decided to write it, he did so with absolute conviction of the rightness of his action. Further, this was the first time that an Afrikaner leader had received a letter directly addressing the evils of apartheid. Tutu did not even stop to consider how Vorster might respond. He considered what he had to say more important than Vorster's response. He warned Vorster that the application of apartheid to the educational process would sooner than later cause a major conflict and must be abandoned immediately in favor of a unitary system that provided equal opportunity to all students without regard to race.[16]

Tutu then made an impassioned appeal to Vorster to remove apartheid entirely from South Africa. He attempted to compare the aspirations of Africans with Afrikaners themselves in their struggle against the British, beginning with the British occupation of the Cape Province in 1806.[17] He observed that Africans faced tremendous odds, they braved the unknown, and faced daunting challenges and countless dangers, rather than be held as subjugated people.[18] Tutu concluded that Africans under apartheid were now at that point and that Vorster ought to understand the anguish they were going through in being subjected to inhuman treatment. While Vorster understood the Afrikaner struggle against the British, he simply did not have any understanding of the pain Africans were enduring in being subjected to the indignities of apartheid. Therefore, for Tutu to expect Vorster to understand the agony Africans were enduring under apartheid was to expect a patient who has been treated by Dr. Jekyll to seek second medical opinion from Mr. Hyde. It cannot be done. Nevertheless Tutu made his point.

Tutu advised Vorster to move immediately to terminate the practice of using the police and the army from terrorizing Africans. He said he was speaking with all the eloquence he could command that the so-called security forces were inflicting terror on the Africans by instilling fear among them. He argued that the security of South Africa rested on goodwill and government respect of Africans as a people with dignity. He warned that the police were using draconian methods to exercise power over Africans and to do virtually as they pleased without being accountable to the legal system of the country. Tutu argued that the police terrorized all Africans, both innocent and under arrest or detention. This was why he said Africans must continue to call for the release of all political prisoners or they must be brought before the courts charged with specific criminal offenses.

Tutu then compared the plight of Africans in South Africa with that of other oppressed people elsewhere in Africa and in other parts of the world to suggest that when people are oppressed they resort to desperate action to free themselves. He suggested that the people of Vietnam, those of Angola and Mozambique, and in Kenya during the Mau Mau uprising[19] all resorted to desperate action to free themselves. Tutu concluded that a people made desperate by despair, injustice, and oppression would use desperate means to end their oppression.[20]

Tutu warned Vorster that unless he did something to resolve the situation, events would generate a momentum of their own and nothing would stop their approaching a point where a major national disaster could not be avoided. He indicated that he was frightened by this prospect because he had seen the escalation of violence in the Middle East, Ethiopia, Nigeria, Northern Ireland where Catholics and Protestants were fighting, and in Uganda. He concluded that what made the South African situation unique was the application of apartheid laws. Tutu concluded his letter to Vorster by quoting the famous prayer of St. Francis of Assisi about understanding, consolation, love, and forgiveness.[21]

Tutu took time to study the effects of apartheid based upon the kinds of questions people all over the world asked him during his speeches. When he answered these questions he denied that he was an expert on South Africa. He came through to his audiences as someone who was motivated by humane feelings toward the oppressor of his people. At no time did he show anger or rancor toward the government of South Africa or the Afrikaners who supported it without condition. He also refrained from personal attack of the leadership of the Nationalist government. Like his mentor, Father Trevor Huddleston, Tutu learned to direct his attack toward a system, rather than its authors. He operated by the biblical teaching to love one's enemy. In this manner he became an undisputed and accepted crusader for social change in South Africa.

No one else spoke with so much eloquence and knowledge of what apartheid was doing to the people of South Africa, both African and Afrikaner. As he practiced the art of delivering a good speech, the messenger became the message sought after by the business executive, the civil rights leader, the religious leader, and the ordinary investor who had interest in investing in South Africa.

Recognition came quickly for Tutu. In 1979 he received an honorary degree from Harvard University. This gave him the exposure that he needed for the international community to condemn apartheid. With the

Nobel prize in December 1984 Tutu became an instant international figure whose campaign against apartheid was recognized across the world. Following a police massacre of 19 African demonstrators in Uitenhage and 700 in the townships in September of the same year,[22] Tutu decided to intensify his campaign against apartheid both at home and abroad. Recognizing that the Nationalist government sustained itself by having trade with other countries, Tutu began to persuade members of the international community to impose economic sanctions and boycott South African products. Since Tutu had become the message, members of the international community responded by doing what he was asking them to do.

In 1986 the Congress of the United States enacted the Comprehensive Anti-Apartheid Act, imposing comprehensive sanctions as Tutu had suggested. European nations followed the U.S. example and imposed sanctions against South Africa. African nations also imposed economic sanctions. In 1987 South Africa was virtually isolated and with no friends in the world. In October 1988 President George Bush submitted a report to the Congress in which he stated that the administration had concluded that the additional U.S. economic sanctions mandated by the act had not been successful in moving the South African government toward a set of goals outlined in Title 1 of the act.[23]

Bush added that because these sanctions had not been completely successful in influencing the South African government to end apartheid, he suggested more sanctions be added. This was bad news for the Nationalist government and good news for Tutu. Bush added that the purpose of sanctions was to convince the Nationalist government that the United States shared the view expressed by other members of the international community that the policy of apartheid had to go or South Africa would face even harder times in the future.

As Tutu had suggested, the U.S. legislation on economic sanctions against South Africa identified five specific areas that South Africa must resolve quickly to have sanctions removed:

1. Release of Nelson Mandela, Govan Mbeki, Walter Sisulu, African trade union leaders, and all other political prisoners.

2. Permit the full exercise of all races the right to form political parties, express political opinions, and participate in the political process.

3. Establish a timetable for the elimination of all apartheid laws and run the South African society on a nonracial basis.

4. Negotiate with representatives of all racial groups in South Africa the future political system in the country.

5. End military and police action against the Africans of South Africa, and paramilitary activities against neighboring states.[24]

If the Nationalist government had ever thought that sanctions would be eliminated, it had to think again. This means that the government of South Africa faced a dilemma of choice. If it refused to accept these conditions, the economy of the country would continue to deteriorate rapidly to a point where it would have a devastating effect on its ability to govern. If it accepted these conditions the Nationalist government would come to an end soon. Whatever its choice was, the Nationalist government knew that its days of absolute political power were seriously numbered.

Bush then gave an account of the political situation in South Africa to recommend that economic sanctions should be intensified. He hoped that freedom of expression, association, movement, and the press had been severely restricted during the 1987–1988 period. During that time activities on campuses across South Africa, including academic activity, had also been restricted. All antiapartheid organizations, including the United Democratic Front and the National Education Crisis Committee, had been outlawed. Political activities of the Congress of South African Trade Unions were also severely restricted. The End Conscription Campaign was effectively banned.

Throughout this period events in South Africa proved that the Nationalist government did not seem to care about the concern expressed by the international community about the need to end apartheid as a condition of South Africa's acceptance back into the circle of the international family. Bush also observed that in June 1987 the state of emergency was renewed for another year. Although Govan Mbeki was released from political prison in November, new restrictions were imposed on his activity, movement, and association soon after the release. At the same time new political detentions continued to occur every week. Since the imposition of new economic sanctions in 1986, the South African government had been far less responsive to U.S. and other government representatives on behalf of antiapartheid initiatives.[25]

In spite of Bush's view that U.S. sanctions against South Africa were less than effective in seeking an end to apartheid, and in spite of the claim made by the leader of the Nationalist government, P. W. Botha, that the international sanctions had no effect on its policy of apartheid, the year 1988 proved that sanctions were having a devastating effect on the economy of both black and white South Africa and were eroding away the political power of the Nationalist government. Since that year the Nationalist Party was rocked by internal strife as its members began to react to sanctions in ways that showed serious disagreement about policy. At that point a wing of the party led by F. W. de Klerk challenged Botha's leadership of the party and the government. A rebellion was developing rapidly that would cause Botha's fall from power. In November 1988 more than 300 African squatters from the shantytown of Crossroads near Cape Town showed up at Tutu's official residency in the city to demand a stop in his campaign against sanctions because, they argued, it was ruining them financially. They were losing their jobs much faster than sanctions were taking effect.

Because Tutu was attending an All-Africa conference in Kenya, the protesters were met by Colin Jones, the vicar-general of Cape Town and an aide to Tutu, to discuss their concern. Writing for the *Washington Times* of November 3, 1988, Peter Youngblood quoted a spokesman of the group as saying, "People are without work and are hungry because of these sanctions. We feel that we have been betrayed. People are saying now that Tutu is a false prophet. We do not like the government and we want to see it go. But we do not wish to see our children starve for the sake of sanctions. There must be another way of changing the government that does not take away our jobs and make us starve."[26] Two observations arise from this sad development. The first is that the Nationalist government would never admit that sanctions were having the intended effect. What it would do was simply to turn on the impoverished Africans to wage a campaign against Tutu for promoting sanctions. Instead of accepting responsibility for the adverse effect of apartheid, the Nationalist government elected to manipulate the poor Africans into blaming Tutu for his action.

The second observation is that the reaction of the Nationalist government to sanctions was quite typical of the reaction of a system of government that was less than representative. From 1966 to 1979 Ian D. Smith, the leader of a rebel administration in Zimbabwe, reacted in exactly the same way. In manipulating Africans to stage a demonstration against Tutu, the Nationalist government tried to give the false impression that it had the support of Africans. The ploy did not work. On his return from Kenya, Tutu continued to convince the Africans that the effect of economic sanctions was short-lived while the effect of applying them to end apartheid was long-term, because they were intended to ensure their economic and political freedom. He also convinced them that it was in their best interest to support sanctions in order to bring both apartheid and the Nationalist government to an end. He argued that while this was happening Africans needed to make sacrifices to ensure that their future was better than the past, and that the future would be ensured by cooperation among Africans in seeking an end of conditions that oppressed them.

In August 1989, three weeks before P. W. Botha fell from power, Tutu participated in the Defiance of Unjust Laws Campaign, a movement that Nelson Mandela and Oliver Tambo began in 1952. In 1989 the campaign movement acquired characteristics of the civil disobedience campaign of Mohandas K. Gandhi and Martin Luther King, Jr. The disobedience campaign of 1989 had its origin in the plans that Tambo had evolved from exile in Lusaka, Zambia, where he had been living for nearly 30 years. In the campaign Africans boarded buses meant for whites.

William Claiborne concluded that protesters also went into segregated parks and spread panic among whites, making them think that a revolution was about to begin.[27] Botha, embattled by political dissension within his own party and facing a formidable challenge from a rebel group led by de Klerk, was totally unable to respond to events he did not fully understand. As the campaign continued, African parents announced that they would soon begin to send their children to white schools. The African workers refused to work for income less than the white workers were earning. Normal daily business, transport, and educational processes came to a halt.

TUTU VERSUS DE KLERK: THE TRIUMPH OF A CRUSADER

Two weeks later, on September 15, Botha, at the age of 73 and in poor health, was at the end of his political career. Botha resigned the office of president in favor of F. W. de Klerk. While Tutu was sorry to see Botha endure this humiliating defeat, he had no regrets for his action in causing his demise. Suddenly Tutu's reputation as an uncompromising foe of apartheid grew to a new level. He warned de Klerk that unless he moved quickly to dismantle apartheid, South Africa was on the brink of a major national catastrophe. De Klerk, unsure of how to respond, simply stated his view that Africans could not allow those who propagated violence and intimidation in the name of peaceful protest to succeed in their plans.[28] By speaking the language of his predecessor and by adopting his attitude, de Klerk was raising the stakes for conflict to a much higher level than was done in the past. In the face of a combination between crippling sanctions and determination of the Africans to bring about change, did he really know what was waiting for him? It was clear that Tutu and de Klerk were on a collision course.

De Klerk was an Afrikaner bureaucrat who went into politics in 1972 to preserve the Afrikaner domination of Africans. His father had been a senior member of the Nationalist Party under the leadership of J. G. Strijdom, who was related to the de Klerk family by marriage. De Klerk's father held the position of minister of education, the position he used to implement apartheid policy. For a number of years F. W. de Klerk did the same in the administration led by Botha before the two men had serious differences on how to plan for the future. De Klerk tried to operate by the old principles that had kept the Nationalist Party in power since 1948. But as soon as he settled into the position of power and responsibility, he came face to face with the reality that things had changed quite a lot and he had to accept new realities. Meanwhile Tutu was bracing himself for a new round of struggle and confrontation.

The old issues were still alive, but the game plan had changed on both sides. With the intensification of economic sanctions and an increase in political violence as a reaction to apartheid laws aided by both the action of the World Council of Churches and the Organization of African Unity, de Klerk soon found that he was rapidly losing control of the situation. While this was happening, Tutu was relentless in warning de Klerk of an impending national catastrophe, just as he had done in May 1976 when he warned Vorster of the disaster that was to unfold in Soweto. Tutu also increased pressure on de Klerk to release all political prisoners and unban all political parties opposed to apartheid.

Recognizing that he was fighting with his back to wall, de Klerk felt compelled to do something that he believed would give him some room. On October 10, 1989, he announced that he was ordering the unconditional release of eight prominent African political prisoners that included Walter Sisulu, the former general secretary of the ANC, and four other African nationalists who were sentenced to life imprisonment in 1964. De Klerk indicated that "the release of Nelson Mandela was not on the agenda."[29] However, de Klerk indicated that Mandela would be released only when conditions for negotiations were fully outlined. This statement gave the impression that it was now a matter of time before Mandela would be released. It also meant that de Klerk was the first Nationalist leader to include negotiations with African representatives as a condition of deciding the future. Clearly he knew that the pressure from the international community was combining with the pressure from within South Africa for him to recognize that conditions that had been outlined for the removal of sanctions had to be met. Preparation for Mandela's possible release began immediately as Tutu played a critical role in the developments of the next few months.

On that same day, October 11, 1989, de Klerk agreed to hold a meeting with Tutu and two other clergymen, Allan Boesak and Frank Chikane, to discuss how apartheid was hurting the country and to seek ways of ending it. Tutu told de Klerk that he was willing to advise the international community to suspend economic sanctions if de Klerk was willing to meet the five conditions that Bush announced in his report to Congress on October 3, 1988. De Klerk was accompanied by the minister of constitutional development, Gerrit Viljoen. The three clergymen gave de Klerk a list of five steps he should take immediately to start negotiations with representatives of the African people. But to take this action de Klerk first had to be convinced of the rightness of that course. Facing prospects of the intensification of sanctions and an increase in political violence, de Klerk was left with no choice but to acquiesce to the demands.

These conditions had been drawn up by the outlawed ANC and included lifting the state of emergency, removing restrictions on political activity, release of all political prisoners, unbanning the ANC and other outlawed political parties, repealing all apartheid laws, and agreeing to free elections under the principle of universal voting rights for all people. The United States had fully endorsed these conditions, and President George Bush had taken them into account in specifying what South Africa needed to do to comply so that sanctions could be removed. De Klerk responded to the three clergymen by saying that lifting the state of emergency was a priority of his administration, but that other conditions would have to be fulfilled as a result of negotiations. John D. Battersby observed that less than 24 hours before the talks began, the government announced it had decided to release eight more prominent black leaders from jail. He concluded that the move followed criticism of the government that de Klerk had spoken about making fundamental changes in South Africa but had done little to match statements with action.[30]

During the next three months the lines of communication remained open between de Klerk and Tutu. During that time de Klerk also received more bad news than did Botha about the general conditions of the country. He learned that the security situation was deteriorating rapidly. The ANC guerrillas were becoming more daring in launching raids in all parts of the country, both rural and urban. These guerrillas were using more sophisticated weapons that made any part of South Africa vulnerable to instant attack. Public buildings, railway stations, bus depots, post offices, and cinemas were subjected to attack without warning.

There was also information before de Klerk that at any moment the country could explode into massive violence such as it had never seen in the past. This is exactly what Tutu had been saying, that the policy of apartheid was steadily placing South Africa on the brink of a major catastrophe. There was also a general deterioration in morale and confidence among Afrikaners. They had never seen this situation in the past, not even when they were fighting the British from 1899 to 1902. Their sense of superiority over the Africans was rapidly disappearing. In addition to all this South Africans were barred from participating in international events such as the Olympic Games. They were denied visas to travel to other countries. Economic sanctions were intensifying to a point where the economy was deteriorating rapidly. Like Botha before him, de Klerk was at the end of the road; the end was near for him sooner than he and the Nationalist Party would have wished. He and his administration spent these months examining all options. For weeks the country was held in suspense of what de Klerk was likely to do.

Suddenly on February 2, 1990, de Klerk released a bombshell during a major speech in Parliament in Cape Town. During a presidential address de Klerk claimed that practically all the leaders agreed that negotiations were the key to reconciliation, peace, and new and just solutions to the problems of South Africa.[31] Assuming that he was referring to the position of the church leaders, the ANC, and the international community when he said "all leaders," many people understood de Klerk to say that he was now willing to hold discussions with the ANC. He went on to outline seven steps that his administration was going to take to bring about that peace and transformation of South Africa, which he called a new and just dispensation:

1. The prohibition of the ANC, the Pan Africanist Congress, the South African Communist Party, and a number of subsidiary organizations was being rescinded.

2. People serving prison sentences merely because they were members of one of those organizations, or because they had committed political offenses that were merely offenses because a prohibition on one of the organizations was in force, would be identified and released. Prisoners who had been sentenced following conviction on charges of other offenses such as murder, terrorism, or arson, were not affected by this action.

3. The media emergency regulations as well as the education emergency regulations were being abolished in their entirety.

4. The security emergency regulations would be amended to make provision for effective control over visual materials pertaining to scenes of unrest.

5. The restrictions in terms of the emergency regulations on 33 organizations were being rescinded. These organizations included National Education Crisis Committee, South African National Students Congress, United Democratic Front, and Congress of South Africa Trade Unions.

6. Conditions imposed in terms of the security emergency regulations on 374 people on their release were being rescinded and the regulations which provided fore such conditions were being abolished.

7. The period of detention in terms of the security emergency regulations would be limited to six months. Detainees would also acquire the right to legal representation and a medical practitioner of their choice.[32]

De Klerk then concluded, "I wish to put it plainly that the government has taken a firm decision to release Mr. Nelson Mandela unconditionally. I am serious about bringing this matter to finality without delay. The government will take a decision soon on the date of his release."[33]

De Klerk did not indicate if his government was ending the apartheid laws as was required by both the ANC and the international community as a condition of ceasing guerrilla warfare and termination of economic sanctions, except that he indicated that anything else, including ending apartheid laws and negotiating a new constitution, would have to be resolved through negotiations. Tutu was among those who watched de Klerk's address to Parliament and was at a loss for words to express his reaction.

However, his joy at this turn of events was overwhelming. He knew that at last the end of apartheid was in sight. The humiliation and suffering that he and all Africans had endured under apartheid and the Nationalist Party would soon be a thing of the past. For Tutu, the man who gave everything that he had to bring apartheid to an end, this moment in time was the victory and triumph of a relentless crusader. The confrontations that he had with Vorster, Botha, and de Klerk had finally yielded expected results. Now all the people of South Africa could look to the future with great expectations. Tutu felt that from this moment on his crusade had been completed and that the ANC should now take over to allow him to return to the pulpit.

SUMMARY AND CONCLUSION

There is no question that Tutu played a decisive role in the transformation of South Africa from May 1976 to February 1990. That role began with his vision for South Africa. In expressing it Tutu recognized some basic things that he felt the Nationalist government must do to avoid a major national conflict. He also initiated contact with the leaders of the government beginning with Vorster in 1976, for purposes of establishing lines of communication to resolve the issues that were paralyzing the country. Tutu then moved from expressing his vision to initiating specific action to ensure the transformation of South Africa. He did this in two ways.

The first way was to initiate dialogue with leaders of the government on how change could be accomplished. Although Tutu did not receive any response from Vorster and Botha, he did not give up the effort. It finally paid off in 1989 when de Klerk agreed to meet with him and two other clergymen. For the first time in the history of the Nationalist Party an Afrikaner was compelled by conditions beyond his control to have an exchange of views with Africans to plan the future of the country.

The second way was to persuade the international community to impose economic sanctions to pressure the Nationalist government to end apartheid. Both methods proved so successful that negotiations between the government and the ANC followed. The release of Nelson Mandela on February 11, 1990, led to negotiations on a new constitution, which led to elections in April 1994, resulting in Mandela being elected president of South Africa. Tutu had played his role well. Now he could go back to the pulpit full time to pastor his flock.

NOTES

1. Trevor Huddleston, "Foreword," in Desmond M. Tutu, *Crying in the Wilderness: The Struggle for Justice in South Africa* (Grand Rapids, MI: William B. Eerdmans, 1982) p. 7.

2. Bishop Ralph E. Dodge made this line of thinking a principal tenet of his advocacy of equal opportunity for Africans, saying "God has divided His gifts fairly evenly among His various children of all races so that in the end there is no overall superiority or inferiority. Achievement and failure are both known to all." *The Unpopular Missionary* (Westwood, NJ: Fleming H. Revell, 1964), p. 86.

3. Tutu, *Crying in the Wilderness*, p. 99.

4. Ibid., p. 100.

5. Ibid., p. 101.

6. Ibid., p. 102.

7. Ibid., p. 67.

8. Ibid., p. 69.

9. In December 1994 the author had an opportunity to see this South African Alcatraz Island prison. Situated off the coast near Cape Town, Robben Island Prison, like Alcratraz, was a prison for hard-core criminals. Mandela was not a hard-core criminal, he was a political prisoner. While Alcatraz lasted from 1933 to 1963, Robben Island Prison continued.

10. Tutu, *Crying in the Wilderness*, p. 69.

11. Ibid., p. 70.

12. Ibid., p. 71.

13. Naomi Tutu, *The Words of Desmond Tutu* (New York: Newmarket Press, 1989), p. 101.

14. Alan Paton, *The Land and People of South Africa* (New York: J. B. Lippincott, 1964), p. 134.

15. Desmond M. Tutu, "Preface," in Steve Biko, *I Write What I like* (London: Bowerdean Publishers, 1996), p. v.

16. Desmond M. Tutu, "Open Letter to Mr. John B. Vorster," in *Hope and Suffering* (Grand Rapids, MI: William B. Eerdmans, 1984), p. 29.

17. Britain took this action to protect its interests against the action that Napoleon had taken in launching his continental policy, which was designed to eliminate the British from Africa.

18. Tutu, "Open Letter to Mr. John B. Vorster," p. 30.

19. For detailed discussion of the effect of the Mau Mau uprising in Kenya, see Dickson A. Mungazi, *The Last British Liberals in Africa: Michael Blundell and Garfield Todd* (Westport, CT: Praeger Publishers, 1999).

20. Tutu, "Open Letter to Mr. John B. Vorster," p. 33.

21. Ibid. p. 35.

22. N. Tutu, *The Words of Desmond Tutu*, p. 103.

23. George Bush, Report to Congress on the effect of the Comprehensive Anti-Apartheid Act of 1986 for the year ending October 2, 1988.

24. Ibid.

25. Ibid.

26. Peter Youngblood, "Destitute Blacks Urge Tutu to Halt Bid for Sanctions," in *Washington Times* (November 3, 1988), p. 2.

27. William Claiborne, "Familiar Turmoil Unfolds in South Africa," in *Washington Times* (August 27, 1989), p. 4.

28. Ibid.

29. William Claiborne, "South Africa to Release ANC Chiefs," in *Washington Times* (October 11, 1989), p. 1.

30. John D. Battersby, "Tutu and de Klerk Talk about Talks," in *New York Times* (October 13, 1989), p. 2.

31. F. W. de Klerk, *Address to Parliament of the Republic of South Africa*, February 2, 1990 (Pretoria: Government Printer, 1990).

32. Ibid.

33. Ibid.

7

Muzorewa's Role in the Political Transformation of Zimbabwe

> Until there is peace, Rhodesia will continue to endure the agonies of protracted conflict and social disorientation.
> —David Lagon, 1978

THE GENEVA CONFERENCE

There are three major events in which Muzorewa participated in the transformation of Zimbabwe: the Geneva conference of 1976, the internal agreement of March 1978, and the negotiations for independence in September 1979. This last event set the stage for the independence of Zimbabwe to begin on April 18, 1980. In 1976 the political crisis in Zimbabwe was entering a critical stage. In seizing power on November 11, 1965, in a unilateral declaration of independence, Ian Smith had grossly underestimated the determination of the African nationalists in Zimbabwe, the international community, and the British government to bring his illegal government to an end.

The economic sanctions that the United Nations imposed in 1965 began to have immediate effect. Gasoline was severely rationed, essential supplies were reduced to dangerous levels. Those traveling on Rhodesian passports were denied entry into the countries to which they wished to travel. Trade with other countries came to a halt except with South Africa, itself a target of international sanctions in protest of apartheid. The decline in the economic and political fortunes of Smith and his Rhodesia Front government soon after the economic sanctions were imposed is what led him to seek a negotiated settlement with Britain.

These are the conditions that compelled Smith to meet on December 2, 1966, with Harold Wilson, then British prime minister, on the H.M.S *Tiger* to try to resolve the crisis that his own action had created.[1] But given the demands and terms of independence Britain had outlined, Smith found himself unable to reach agreement with Wilson. Thus, the decline in political and economic conditions in Zimbabwe and of the RF government continued at a faster pace than at the beginning of sanctions in 1965. Realizing that no nation had extended recognition of his government and that the economic situations were causing rapid economic deterioration, Smith sought another opportunity to reach agreement with the British government. He had his wish on October 9, 1968, when he met one more time with Wilson aboard H.M.S. *Fearless*.

The atmosphere this time was friendlier than when the two men met on the *Tiger*. However, when Wilson indicated his unwillingness to compromise the terms that Britain had outlined and used in the past to grant independence to its colonies in Africa under an African government, Smith once again found himself unable to accept them. Therefore, the deadlock between the two sides continued.

In September 1976, fearing that the Soviet Union would exploit the continuing crisis in Zimbabwe to promote its own national interests, President Gerald Ford dispatched U.S. Secretary of State Henry Kissinger to southern Africa to explore the possibility of a new initiative between Smith and Britain. Ford had hoped that the Kissinger shuttle diplomacy, which he had initiated during the war in Vietnam, would divert attention from the negative response in the United States to his pardon of former President Richard M. Nixon in 1975 for his role in the Watergate scandal. That was not to be. However, as the first part of his initiative, Kissinger was reported to have warned the Soviet Union against meddling in the explosive racial situation in southern Africa. He urged Soviet leader Andrei Gromyko to call off Moscow's campaign of criticism of his African peace-making bid.[2]

On September 29, 1976, British Secretary for Foreign and Commonwealth Affairs Anthony Crosland, announced in the House of Commons that he was going to convene a conference to begin on October 21 in an effort to resolve the constitutional crisis in Zimbabwe. However, the conference did not begin until October 28. Crosland also announced that the conference would convene in Geneva under the chairmanship of Ivor Richard, British ambassador to the United Nations. The announcement followed a number of ministerial visits to southern Africa, including that of British Minister of State for African Affairs Edward Rawlands. On his return to London, Rawlands reported that Britain and other parties were on course as far as arrangements for the conference were concerned. He indicated that he would recommend the location of the conference, but could not say where it was. He added that the conference had been agreed to by all parties concerned.[3] Crosland did not make any reference to the Kissinger initiative, making everyone wonder whether there was any coordination or consultation between the United States and Britain.

However, Crosland indicated that the next step in preparation for the conference was to organize a meeting between African nationalist leaders and Smith in order to work out the structure of the interim government. He told the House of Commons that he was going to invite Robert Mugabe, the leader of the Zimbabwe African National Union; Joshua Nkomo, leader of the Zimbabwe African Peoples Union; and Bishop Abel T. Muzorewa, leader of the African National Council, to represent Africans and their parties at the conference. He asked these leaders and Smith to nominate additional delegates to their negotiating teams. Crosland then added that he was most anxious to do everything within his power to ensure a successful outcome of the conference. He said that he had most useful exchange of views in New York and London with a number of African foreign ministers about various aspects of the conference.[4]

During the parliamentary debate in the House of Commons on the prospects of the conference, David Steel, the leader of the Liberal Party, suggested that since there was some criticism of Richard's appointment as chairman of the conference, Richard himself must move aggressively to assert himself and establish his authority because he enjoyed the confidence and support of the British government. Crosland accepted Steel's suggestion, adding that Richard's appointment as the chairman of the Geneva conference on the future of Zimbabwe had been cleared by all the parties concerned.[5] However, there was another problem that participants in the Geneva conference did not anticipate: on October 8 Mugabe and Nkomo announced in Dar es Salaam that their delegations would recognize Smith's delegation to the conference only as part of the British delegation. The two leaders warned that guerrilla warfare against the Smith government would continue. Nkomo stressed the African position that Africans sought the restoration of Zimbabwe, and that should Smith or any of his colleagues attend the conference, he and his delegation could only regard them as an extension of the British delegation.[6]

For Smith, a man who had argued at the time of the unilateral declaration of independence on November 11, 1965, Nkomo's remarks added insult to injury. On the same day the RF reported the death in action against guerrillas of Army Sergeant Anthony Stainthorpe. Muzorewa refrained from making remarks that, in his opinion, would jeopardize the chances of success of the conference. He would prefer to stake out the position of his delegation in the conference room. While Mugabe and Nkomo stated their position that they did not accept the so-called

Smith-Kissinger agreement because it did not take their views into account, Muzorewa remained silent on the issue in order to enhance the prospects of success of the conference.

Mugabe and Nkomo argued that while Kissinger had consulted presidents of the front-line states,[7] he had not consulted them before he held discussions with Smith, and therefore he could not possibly represent their views. However, Nkomo stressed his view that the two-year period of transition to majority government, which Smith and Kissinger had agreed upon, was negotiable. Nkomo concluded, "There is no such a thing as the Pretoria agreement,"[8] referring to the agreement reached between Kissinger and Smith in Pretoria in September.

THE CLIMATE OF THE CONFERENCE

While this was happening Smith had time to reassess his position with respect to the transitional period to majority government. Did he really think that this dreadful thing, as he repeatedly called the advent of an African government, was inevitable given the rapid pace of change in Africa and the hostile attitude of the international community toward his government? Was it realistic to expect Smith, a white man born to despise the Africans, to regard them as his social equals? For years he had seen them at his grandfather's farm in Shurugwe performing functions no higher than cheap labor. Suddenly in 1976 he was expected to shake off his stereotypical view of them in connection with making plans for the future of the country. How could he possibly do that?

Was it realistic to expect Smith and other whites to live under a government run by Africans, the people they considered inferior in every way? Smith concluded that the trend in governments in Africa, most of them dictatorships worse than his, did not necessarily set a precedent that his government could not defy. He also concluded that if an African government was installed in accordance with British principles, it would introduce a socialist program that would force him to give up most of his 22,000 acres of prime farm land. He concluded that with agreement reached at Geneva, the rights and privileges whites had enjoyed for so long would come to an end. He began to believe that he and other white people in Zimbabwe would lose more by accepting majority government than they would gain.

Smith began to count on the help that he was receiving from South Africa in violation of the UN sanctions and from the Byrd Amendment of 1971.[9] He counted on the mercenaries that he was successfully recruiting in Europe and North America to keep his government in office. His government had launched a reasonably successful campaign to make the Western world believe that his government was in the front line in the war against Communist aggression, which the African political leaders and leaders of the African delegations to Geneva represented. Before the conference he had already made up his mind to sabotage it. On October 21, soon after arriving in Geneva, Smith was quick to respond to the statement of October 4 that there was no such a thing as the Pretoria agreement. He said that his delegation would walk out of the conference if the African leaders made demands that he thought would undermine the whole concept that brought them to Geneva.[10]

Caught between two conflicting positions, Smith appears to have reacted to the conference with both sides of his mind, giving the impression that he would exercise restraint to make it possible for the conference to succeed, and adherence to principle making it impossible to succeed. In this conflicting situation, Smith said that he had come to Geneva in a positive frame of mind. He indicated a flexibility and would lean over backward to make the conference succeed. He said that his delegation had come to Geneva to confirm what was now known as the Kissinger agreement that was endorsed by the American and British governments and the black presidents. He said he believed it was possible that his delegation might arrive at a situation where, in all honesty, it would have to say that the whole concept that brought the conference there had been undermined and defeated, and therefore there was no point in continuing the conference.[11]

Smith's unwillingness to accept modifications to the Kissinger plan made his claim to accept the principle of majority rule questionable. The African delegations failed to see how a man who made public statements accepting the principle of majority before he left Zimbabwe would now resist even the slightest suggestion to enable him to understand why the so-called Kissinger plan was unacceptable to them.

Therefore, the climate of the conference was marred by Smith's refusal to accept suggestions to improve that basis of discussion. Kissinger himself had reiterated that apart from the transitional period of two years to the African majority government, the rest of the terms of the agreement between him and Smith were subject to negotiation at the conference. Smith said that this was not the case. He believed that the conference had the function of formalizing the agreement between him and Kissinger, and in no way must the terms of that agreement be open to negotiation between his delegation and the African delegations. Thus, Smith's refusal to accept suggestions was seriously hurting the chances of success of the conference.

The difference of opinion between Smith's delegation and the African delegations over the terms of the Smith-Kissinger agreement, even before the conference actually started, was so great that it would require a Herculean effort made by Richard to bridge it so that the conference could have a reasonable chance of success. Michael Snitowsky described this difference as follows: "The diversity of the delegations alone promises to detract considerably from the dignified air of such an occasion. As a result, idealistic images of black men and white men working together to build a viable dynamic society quickly gave way to visions of a modern day Tower of Babel."[12] Even a religious leader like Bishop Muzorewa found it hard to compromise principle in order to accommodate the position of white segregationists.

The one issue that threatened to wreck the conference even before it began was: Who should control the army and the police during the transitional period? To many, the question may be irrelevant because the army and the police were associated with normal government operations and functions. But both sides knew that throughout history the colonial government used the army and police as instruments of political action to subdue the Africans. Smith argued that whites should control the army and police to give them confidence in the future. The Africans argued that if meaningful change in the conditions that controlled them should come about, they should control the army and police.

Richard knew from the arguments advanced by either side that whoever controlled the army and police controlled the political process and the country. Both Smith and Kissinger disregarded the fact that if majority government was to come in two years, it was natural that Africans should control them as the first step in establishing a new government system. There was nothing in the Kissinger plan that would stop Smith from using the army and police in exactly the same way he had done in the past in suppressing the Africans. Since he took office in April 1964, Smith admitted that he had turned Zimbabwe into a police state, placing the Africans at the mercy of army and police.[13]

As Richard pondered the responsibility he faced as chairman of the conference, some questions loomed in his mind. Could he succeed in persuading Ian Smith, Peter van der Byl, Mark Partridge, and David Smith on one side of the conference table, and Robert Mugabe, Joshua Nkomo, Ndabaningi Sithole, and Abel Muzorewa on the other side to believe that they all had one purpose in coming to Geneva: to work together for the death of Rhodesia and the birth of Zimbabwe? Would he be able to convince Smith that the interests of Zimbabwe were far above those of his own political ideology and philosophy, which were the basis of his low regard of Africans? Could Richard convince the African delegations that by agreeing to share power with the white extremists for a transitional period of two years, they gave the whites an opportunity to place their confidence in the new African government that would control their lives in the future? Could he convince them that after years of oppressive rule, Smith was finally and genuinely seeking to relinquish the reins of power as a price of the termination of the devastating guerrilla warfare?

THE COLLAPSE OF THE CONFERENCE

As the delegates began to arrive at Palais des Nations on October 28, the suspicions that each side had about the intentions of the other had not abated. One by one the participants paced into the conference hall with serious doubts about the wisdom of attending a conference that had so much potential for failure. Sithole was the first to arrive, and Richard, puffing his pipe, was next. Nkomo and Mugabe, partners in the Patriotic Front (PF), arrived next. Twenty minutes later Muzorewa arrived without his two close associates, Edison Sithole, who had disappeared without trace, and Enos Nkala, who was still in detention in Zimbabwe. Finally, Smith arrived and took his seat without talking to or greeting anybody. He was accompanied by Peter van der Byl and David Smith, close associates and members of his cabinet.

Thus, the Geneva conference on the death of Rhodesia and the birth of Zimbabwe opened with ominous signs of failure. David Spanier, the diplomatic corespondent of the *Times of London*, was present at the opening session and wrote, "It was an unemotional opening, although everyone was on edge until it took place. The single gesture of cordiality among the delegations was when Mr. Nkomo shook hands with Mr. Sithole."[14] Richard made a declaration that the conference was a major effort to resolve the political and constitutional problems to pave way to an African majority government.

The conference then adjourned for the rest of the day to allow delegations to reflect upon the important preliminaries. When it resumed the next day, Muzorewa, speaking on behalf of the African delegations, indicated that there was total agreement among them that they rejected the Smith-Kissinger agreement and that the major responsibility of the conference was to evolve a constitution that would result in an immediate African government. Muzorewa added that the Africans were quite prepared to take the country by force, if necessary.[15] He also added that the position of the African delegations was that the interim government must be elected on the basis of one person, one vote.

The interim government should then be charged with the responsibility of drawing up a new constitution within one year. He then concluded that either the people take power completely, or the people's armed struggle would continue because Africans stood solidly united in their demand for majority.[16]

Nkomo added that the conference must only work out a process of complete transfer of power to an African majority. But when Smith reiterated his position that his delegation was unwilling to move away from the agreement he reached with Kissinger, Richard had a distinctive feeling that the delegations were not going to agree on the purpose of the conference. He adjourned the session for the weekend to allow him time to meet separately with each delegation in order to break the obvious deadlock.

Richard was made painfully aware of the fear among African delegations of the police and army. When one member of the African delegations refused to compromise on who should control the army and police, Richard's spokesman responded by saying that the British government understood his feelings. Richard had found out that the delegate had just been released a day or so earlier in order to attend this conference after nine years in political prison.[17] Richard himself added that Smith would have to yield on his rigid refusal to depart from the Kissinger package if the conference had a reasonable chance of success.[18]

Smith regarded Richard's views as totally biased against his delegation. He did not think that Richard was impartial anymore. This is why he threatened to pull his delegation out of the conference. After consulting the British government Richard proposed a compromise solution, which meant that the police and army would be controlled by neither the Africans nor the RF government, but by a Commonwealth peacekeeping force consisting of units from member nations of the British Commonwealth of Nations. The African delegations accepted this compromise but Smith's delegation refused.

Richard and members of the African delegations cast a long shadow of doubt on Smith's claimed acceptance of the two-year transitional period to an African government. Smith responded by arguing that he believed this was part of the tactic of African nationalist extremists. He added that they were deliberately going out of their way to say that he could not be trusted. They did not believe that he meant what he said. He asked how was it that a few months ago he was saying something completely different. He concluded that they were correct that a few months previously he was saying a different thing, and admitted that he had been forced to come to the conclusion that if the free world was not going to give his government any support, there was not much hope for Rhodesia if the friends of his government in the world were not going to give them any support. That was the reason for the change of his position.[19]

As the conference failed to resolve the question of who must control the army and police during the period of transition, there was strong indication that it would fail because Smith was deliberately sabotaging it by diverting attention from the real issues to his attack of the British government and on Richard himself. Once more Smith said the British were trying to humiliate his delegation. He suggested that they must be small people who were still seeking revenge for UDI.[20] This is why he told them that if they tried to push around his delegation, they would come off second best.[21]

With these words Smith decided to pull his delegation out of the conference. Smith repeated his claim that he was given the understanding by Kissinger that if the conference failed, he would receive military help from the United States to keep the Communists from taking control of his country. In Washington, D.C., the U.S. State Department denied that Kissinger had ever given Smith that understanding. For all practical purposes, the conference was over. Muzorewa warned Smith that severe consequences would follow his fateful decision and that he must accept full responsibility for those consequences.

Michael Blundell, a former political leader who was involved in the struggle launched by the Mau Mau in Kenya from 1952 to 1956, advised the whites in Zimbabwe to accept the principle of an African majority rule while it was still possible, because time would soon come when they would be forced to accept terms completely unfavorable to them.[22] Blundell also felt that the Geneva conference was a genuine effort made by the African delegations to reach a compromise, and he urged the Smith delegation to accept the new proposals for a settlement. He warned that to remain rigid about the Kissinger plan was unwise.[23]

Although the Smith delegation rejected Blundell's advice, the whites took it seriously and began to emigrate in increasing numbers, not because they feared the African government, but because they feared that Smith's refusal to accommodate African political aspirations would intensify the struggle with severe consequences for all. When a solution was finally found in December 1979, Smith and the RF had lost everything they had fought for, just as Blundell and Muzorewa had advised.

MUZOREWA AND THE INTERNAL AGREEMENT, 1978

The failure of the Geneva conference placed parties in the Zimbabwean crisis at the crossroads. Nobody seemed to know exactly what to do next. The British government had come to the end of the road except to insist that independence would not be granted unless it reflected the principle of African majority rule, the principle that Smith continued to reject. The failure of the Douglas-Home–Smith initiative of 1971, which brought Muzorewa to national politics for the first time, had left the situation more confused than in the past. For the next three years differences of opinion among African leaders as to what to do next caused a split between them. The declaration of unity that Muzorewa, Nkomo, Mugabe, Ndabaningi Sithole, and James Chikerema signed in Lusaka on December 7, 1974,[24] did not keep them together.

At the United Nations, Andrew Young (U.S. ambassador to the UN) regarded the move as similar to suggestions of elections that excluded the Viet Cong during the war in Vietnam. Josiah Chinamano, a respected veteran black politician who spent many years in prison under the Smith government, characterized Smith's offer of holding negotiations as an exercise in futility and as political gimmickry at its worst. Chinamano added that an internal settlement could not succeed because Zimbabwe was not the personal property of the Rhodesia Front to be given away to its African political puppets.[25]

In London, British Foreign Secretary David Owen reiterated the British official position that independence for Zimbabwe must involve a genuine transfer of power to an African government based on free elections. He expressed his conviction that Smith was unlikely to give his black negotiating partners what Africans had been fighting for all these years—unconditional free elections leading to an unconditionally free Zimbabwe.

At a press conference following the announcement, Smith told reporters in Harare (then called Salisbury) that his government was offering what he termed safe return to any guerrillas who were willing to lay down their arms. At that point, about 5,000 people had been killed. In his announcement of a search for an internal settlement, Smith remarked that the whole world was sick and tired of the Rhodesian issue.[26] However, he neglected to say that the entire international community was, in fact, tired of Smith himself.

Both the PF and Britain warned Smith and the African leaders negotiating with him that an internal settlement would be unacceptable to the international community because it would mean, in essence, the continuation of the RF itself On January 30, 1978, Owen and Young met with Nkomo and Mugabe in Malta to discuss ways of implementing the plan that the United States and Britain had worked out for the independence of Zimbabwe. Smith told both the United States and Britain to get off his back and let him continue his search for an internal settlement. Mugabe warned that an internal settlement would mean a civil war in Zimbabwe. Nkomo added that there would be no agreement reached by Smith and what he called his puppet African leaders that could ever be recognized by African nationalist parties. He concluded that the primary objective was the creation of a sovereign and independent state of Zimbabwe whose government would operate in complete freedom of any controls.[27]

On March 3, 1978, Muzorewa, Sithole, Chirau, and Smith emerged from a two-hour plenary session to announce to the waiting journalists, and thus to the world, that they had reached an agreement. The major terms included the following: There would be a legislative assembly consisting of 100 members, 72 would be African and 28 would be white. The 28 white members would have a veto power. These would be elected by white voters, and the 72 African members would be elected by African voters.

This constitution would be reviewed in ten years to see what changes needed to be made. It was quite obvious to observers that the internal agreement represented racial division of the country at its worst. Reaction to the agreement began to come in immediately from all over the world. Britain stated that any settlement that excluded the PF would have little chance of succeeding. At the United Nations, Andrew Young warned Smith and his three African negotiating partners that what they had done was not to settle the situation but to create a situation for a civil war in which Africans would fight Africans. The PF simply dismissed the agreement as a meaningless piece of paper and resolved that the fighting would continue.

Radio Mozambique broadcast messages to warn Zimbabweans that the agreement was dictated to by an illegal government to its African puppets. Zambian Foreign Minister Siteke Mwale said that Smith was playing his usual game of trying to hoodwink the world. UN Secretary-General Kurt Waldheim expressed concern that the agreement would not result in a genuinely independent Zimbabwe. President Kenneth Kaunda of Zambia warned that the war of liberation would intensify.

In Dar es Salaam, the *Daily News* called on Britain and the United States to reject the agreement because it was reached between Smith and some black participants calling themselves ministers of this and that, but with Ian Smith retaining the power to decide their fate.[28] In Harare, whites seemed to have a mixed reaction to the agreement. Bryan Waddacor, chairman of the stock exchange, observed that there were all sorts of questions still to be answered, such as whether those in power would be pro- or anticapitalism. Waddacor expressed his hope that things in general looked promising and that there was a degree of optimism.[29] A few days earlier, Smith had told William McWhirtier during an interview that, whether people liked it or not, there was a (1969) constitution under which Parliament had been elected and that he was the leader of the party in power. He concluded that there was nothing anybody in the world could do to change that position.[30]

This is exactly why the international community refused to recognize the internal agreement. For Muzorewa, the man who had come forward in 1971 to lead a campaign against a government that had placed him under house arrest for five years, the agreement with Smith presented a painful problem of trying to persuade those who opposed it to accept it.

WHITE REFERENDUM AND GENERAL ELECTIONS, 1979

On January 30, 1979, the frightened and dwindling white community voted in a referendum to ratify the internal agreement. The African people did not vote. The RF campaigned vigorously for a "yes" vote, arguing that this was the last hope of survival of whites in a country that the partners to the internal settlement agreement would call "Zimbabwe Rhodesia." The RF warned that if whites voted "no," Nkomo and Mugabe would dance with joy in the streets of Moscow.

But the extreme right-wing all-white Rhodesian Action Party (RAP) campaigned for a "no" vote, arguing that if a "yes" vote was returned, Nkomo and Mugabe would dance with joy in the streets of Salisbury. Between these two extreme positions was the multiracial National Unifying Force (NUF), which argued that the referendum was totally irrelevant to the racial problems of the country. The NUF warned that the country needed peace and recognition, neither of which the internal settlement was able to achieve.

The referendum therefore posed a dilemma to the whites. A "yes" vote would amount to playing their last political card. The resulting regime would be unable to end either the international economic sanctions or the guerrilla war. A "no" vote would appear to be a rejection of the majority rule. It was a dilemma that the whites pondered seriously. When the votes were counted, nearly 85 percent decided to ratify the agreement, which they knew would enable them to control the army, the police, and the civil service for at least five years. Thus, Smith scored a victory over the issue that had wrecked the Geneva conference in 1976.

Farmers in the war-torn eastern districts drove to the polling stations in armored cars with rifles and machine guns ready for action against a guerrilla ambush. At the polls, most of those voting appeared somber. Robert Cross, a Salisbury automobile mechanic who braved a rainstorm to vote, remarked that the situation was hopeless if whites rejected the agreement and only slightly less hopeless if they accepted it. He concluded that they may as well go along with Smith and pray that he could pull it off.[31] Smith himself expressed a somber mood when he said during the campaign earlier on that this was the most difficult exercise he had ever undertaken and he was trying to sell whites something he had tried to avoid[32]—African participation in government on the basis of equal opportunity in all aspects of national life.

Observers concluded that the intransigence of Smith government, reinforced by the support given him by three black political leaders, resulted in a devastating racial war with serious consequences to the people. David Lagon described some of these consequences as follows:

Prominent among the signs of social upheaval is the divorce rate, the highest in the world at almost 40%. Marital infidelity became rife. The suicide rate has skyrocketed in the past two years. Prostitution is on the upswing. Children are growing up with a war mentality. Hundreds of people have lost limbs in land mine explosions and automatic weapon crossfire. There is the problem of mental and physical rehabilitation, a surge in petty crimes among children, theft, purse snatching, rape and auto theft. Until there is peace, Rhodesia will continue to endure the agonies of protracted conflict and social disorientation.[33]

Following ratification of the internal agreement by white voters, Joshua Nkomo threatened an orgy of violence and of total destruction of Colonial Zimbabwe if the elections scheduled for the week of April 20, 1979, were held. Smith regarded the ratification as the only alternative to what he said to be a takeover by the PF. In order to eliminate Nkomo's threat of an orgy of violence, the Smith forces began a series of raids into Mozambique, Zambia, Angola, and Botswana, destroying anything in sight, causing extensive damage to human life and property.

By thus putting the guerrilla movement on the defensive, the Smith government now campaigned vigorously for support. The election campaign became more heated. The 66-member legislature was dissolved to make way for a 100-member Parliament. All predictions showed that Muzorewa would be the next prime minister because he appeared to enjoy more popular support than Sithole and Chirau. During the campaign, Muzorewa assured voters that security forces would protect them as they had done before, during, and after they had voted, and he urged them to turn out in large numbers to prove to the United States and Britain that the internal agreement had the support of the black masses.

On April 12 the whites voted for their 28 white members to the legislature. On that same day, commandos staged a surprise raid on Nkomo's house in Lusaka, destroying it and killing about ten people. The home was located in the Woodlands suburb of Lusaka, 60 miles from the border with Zimbabwe. The commandos wanted to kidnap Nkomo and take him back to Salisbury as hostage. But Nkomo escaped unharmed. On April 16, guerrillas blew up the second largest oil depot in Rhodesia, located at Fort Victoria. However, Sithole predicted that peace would be restored soon after the elections.

Both Britain and the United States regretted the escalation of violence. On April 17, the first day of voting, black students at the University of Rhodesia staged a demonstration against the elections, singing and shouting freedom songs in support of the Patriotic Front. It was obvious that many Africans did not know what they were voting for. One black man in white uniform and a chef's hat told reporters that he was going to vote with his (white) boss because he said that all people wanted peace.[34]

On April 24, early election returns showed that Muzorewa might win with a landslide. But after the votes were all counted, Muzorewa won 51 seats, Sithole 12, K. Ndiweni 9, and Chirau none. Therefore, with an overall majority of one, Muzorewa would certainly have to depend on the support of other parties to carry out any meaningful programs. This is exactly what Smith wanted: the fragmentation of the parties so that whoever emerged the winner would have to play to his tune. As the election results became known, Sithole charged gross irregularities at the polls and accused Muzorewa and Smith of stage-managing the elections to have Muzorewa appear the winner. He said that the elections were, in fact, a fraud. Indeed, in a number of districts, voter turnout was reported to be well in excess of 100 percent of the registered voters. In one Mashonaland district, a stronghold of Muzorewa, voter turnout was reported to be 108.1 percent.

With Sithole's charges of irregularities, the prospects of an immediate recognition appeared to decline sharply, and the charge of irregularities seemed to have gained some ground. Reports of police harassment against those who hesitated to endorse the agreement were widespread. Farmers in the rural areas were asked to provide their tractors to carry black laborers to the polls. Army trucks were also used for a similar purpose. At every polling station, troops appeared to outnumber the voters, making Muzorewa's promise of protection good. The presence of soldiers suggested that only the ruling alliance between Smith and the black leaders would bring stability to Rhodesia.

As Muzorewa prepared to take office as interim prime minister, there were reports that the guerrilla movement was losing morale to fight. Some guerrilla fighters were reported to be returning to Rhodesia to undergo rehabilitation and join the regime's army; others were reported to seek refuge in some African countries or Europe. But Nkomo and Mugabe told Dan Rather of CBS on April 22 that the war would go on until Zimbabwe was unconditionally free. On April 28 the UN Security Council voted to reiterate its resolution of March 8 that the elections were null and void. Britain and the United States abstained, suggesting that they wanted to leave their options open. As the war showed signs of escalation, both Muzorewa and Smith seemed to want to put the elections behind them and pay more attention to finding ways of ending the war.

In this stance Muzorewa was, in fact, fanning the fires of controversy at a time when he needed moderation in an effort to bridge the gap between himself and other black political leaders. By speaking the language Smith had been speaking for years, Muzorewa was making it harder for a peaceful solution to the problems of the country to be found. Although both Muzorewa and Sithole suffered a crushing defeat in the elections of 1980, these two men of God gave everything they had for the freedom of Zimbabwe. This author pays tribute to both men for relentlessly working toward attainment of the goals and objectives that had for many years been the dream of Zimbabweans. Both men made incredible personal sacrifices. It was unfortunate that both men signed the internal agreement that was not recognized by the international community. But with the advent of Zimbabwe, Muzorewa and Sithole could, therefore, not be regarded as losers. The real loser, however, was Ian Smith, the misguided politician who misled them. This writer also extends his congratulations to Muzorewa and Sithole for accepting defeat with grace and dignity, recognizing, as very few have done, that the wishes of the voters must be respected. It is a lesson that all people must learn.

THE NYERERE-THATCHER PLAN: THE END OF MUZOREWA'S ADMINISTRATION

Following the announcement of the April election results, Sithole accused Muzorewa and Smith of cheating and stated that his ZANU would not allow the installation of an administration that came to power as a result of stage-managed election tactics. Sithole even warned that ZANU would consider resorting to violence similar to that of the 1960s to sabotage the Smith-Muzorewa administration.

Sithole then persuaded his ZANU successful candidates to refuse to take their 12 seats in the legislature until there was a thorough and complete investigation of his charges of election fraud. Both Smith and Muzorewa ignored Sithole's claims and charges. In August, ZANU members took their seats in the legislature as a result of Sithole's failure to arouse any interest in his opposition to the Smith-Muzorewa alliance. Sithole had forgotten that he had been part of the agreement that had led to the election.

Muzorewa sent a delegation to Britain and the United States in an attempt to persuade leading Western nations to recognize the administration that he was leading. While this was happening, Nkomo and Mugabe were holding consultations with front-line states. As a result they decided to intensify the military struggle as a result of the policy adopted by the Smith–Muzorewa administration. It was estimated that at that point Nkomo's ZAPU forces had increased to 15,000 and Mugabe's ZALA (Zimbabwe African Liberation Army) had increased to 24,000. ZAPU and ZALA were also reviewing their joint military strategies. There was, therefore, no hope that Smith and Muzorewa could come to terms with the PF. Everything pointed to the intensification of the armed struggle.

In the United States, a wide difference of opinion was increasingly becoming evident between President Carter and the Congress with respect to U.S. policy toward the Smith-Muzorewa administration. On May 15, the U.S. Senate voted 75–19 to urge the Carter administration to lift economic sanctions against Rhodesia and to recognize the Muzorewa administration. On May 23, however, U.S. Secretary of State Cyrus Vance said that the new Rhodesian regime was a new reality for the Carter administration. Vance made the remark after holding a meeting with British Foreign Secretary Lord Carrington. Obviously, Vance's announcement was music to Muzorewa, who felt he wanted to end Sithole's political career. On June 2, Muzorewa announced that 11 members of Sithole's party had plotted to assassinate him and that a good number of people were arrested for the plot.

On June 12, the Senate voted 52–41 to end Carter's attempts to maintain sanctions against the Smith-Muzorewa regime. But Carter argued that ending sanctions would deal a devastating blow to U.S. policy in Africa, where U.S. influence was needed. This is the position that Andrew Young had always taken, and Carter believed that policy was good for U.S. interests in Africa. The controversy was left in abeyance with the resolution passed in the House of Representatives urging President Carter to lift economic sanctions against Rhodesia if that action was in the best interests of the United States. The motion leading to the resolution was made by Stephen Solarz (D-N.Y.). However, the events of the next few weeks proved the resolution to be unnecessary.

On June 20, Muzorewa suffered a severe setback in Parliament. Eight members of his ANC resigned from the party and set up their own party to oppose him. James Chikerema, Muzorewa's vice president and a former militant, led this defection, which caused Muzorewa to lose his parliamentary majority. The defecting members accused Muzorewa of "nepotism and Mafia-like practices."[35] The defections left Muzorewa's party with only 43 of the 100-seat Parliament. Immediately, Muzorewa received assurances from Smith that the 28 white members would support him and that he would be in no danger of losing a no-confidence vote. These assurances raised new doubts, both in Zimbabwe and overseas, of Muzorewa's claim of leading a black majority government free from control by Smith.

During the British election campaign of 1979, the Labour Party, led by James Callaghan, and the Conservative Party, led by Margaret Thatcher, espoused opposing views regarding the situation in Zimbabwe. Callaghan stated that if the Labour Party was returned to power, he would try to arrange an all-party conference, a move both Smith and Muzorewa opposed. Thatcher stated that if the Conservative Party was returned to power, her government was more likely to recognize the Muzorewa administration. An unidentified senior Conservative member remarked, "In her heart Margaret has decided to recognize the Muzorewa government, but it will have to be played coolly."[36]

Soon after Thatcher took office following the Conservative Party victory on May 2, she dispatched Lord Carrington, her foreign secretary, on a fact-finding mission to southern Africa, with particular reference to British policy toward the Muzorewa administration. This was presumably to pave way for British recognition of the Muzorewa administration.

Carrington reported to Thatcher what she did not expect to hear: an intense opposition throughout black Africa to the Muzorewa administration.

British recognition of Muzorewa's administration, reported Carrington, would seriously damage British relations with black Africa, including African members of the Commonwealth. Thatcher then decided to do nothing about the Zimbabwean situation until after she had assessed the views of the Commonwealth conference to be held in Lusaka, Zambia, in August. But while visiting Australia, Thatcher reiterated her view that her government would move quickly to recognize the new administration in Zimbabwe.

As Commonwealth members began to arrive in Lusaka at the end of July, Thatcher knew that she was under heavy pressure not to recognize the new colonial administration in Zimbabwe. As she arrived in Lusaka, African demonstrators jeered and booed her. Immediately, Thatcher knew that she had two choices to make: to recognize the new Rhodesian administration and risk seriously strained relations with black Africa or to make a new bold start in a search for an equitable solution to the problem of Zimbabwe. Thatcher then indicated that she had come to Lusaka to listen to the views of black Africa and to take those views into consideration in formulating British Conservative government policy toward the question of true independence for Rhodesia. This sudden change of position by Thatcher took many people, including Smith and Muzorewa, by surprise.

Why did Thatcher suddenly change her position to recognize the new Rhodesian regime? The African states had warned that if she recognized the new regime in Rhodesia, they would increase their military aid to the PF. The consequences of such a military escalation of war in Rhodesia would have serious political implications for Thatcher. Behind the scenes, President Julius Nyerere of Tanzania had held open and frank discussions with Thatcher on a number of proposals aimed at resolving the Rhodesian crisis. Nyerere helped Thatcher see the urgency of making a new start in an effort to find a solution to the problem.

For the first time, Thatcher fully acknowledged African discontent with her views. She knew that the only course of action open to her was simply to abandon her intention of recognizing the new Rhodesian regime. She then stated clearly that the internal agreement constitution of March 3, 1978, was unacceptable to Britain and that it was a sure recipe for national disaster for Zimbabwe. She added that it was invalid and of no consequences as far as the British government and the international community were concerned.

Therefore, a new start must be made. At a press conference in Lusaka on August 1, 1979, Thatcher added, "The British Government is wholly committed to genuine black majority rule. The aim is to return Rhodesia to legal independence on a basis which the Commonwealth and international community as a whole will find acceptable."[37] This position was devastating to Muzorewa. He knew that his role in the transformation of Zimbabwe from colonial status to African government was now seriously limited.

It later turned out that Thatcher and Nyerere had worked closely together as soon as they arrived in Lusaka on a new peace plan for Zimbabwe. The following were the major points of the Thatcher-Nyerere plan: Britain would call a constitutional conference to be attended by all parties to the Rhodesian conflict. The Smith-Muzorewa constitution would be abandoned. A British governor would be sent to Rhodesia to arrange new elections and take control of the army and police. The veto power given to whites by the Smith-Muzorewa constitution would be removed. The number of white seats would be reduced to 20. Zimbabwe would be the name of the new independent state. If agreement was reached on these important points, then Britain would urge the United Nations to lift economic sanctions, provided new elections were held. Smith would be urged to resign from politics.

Reaction to the announcement came quickly from President Carter, the PF, Smith, and Muzorewa. Carter supported the plan as a basis for a just and lasting peace settlement for Zimbabwe. The PF expressed doubt that Britain would be impartial in supervising the elections because it was looking after its economic interests in Rhodesia. Muzorewa said that the plan was an insult to him. However, by August 21 he had accepted the invitation to attend the conference. He announced that he would lead a 12-member delegation to London. Smith was to be a member of that delegation as well as two other whites. From Dar es Salaam, the PF announced its intention to attend.

Suddenly, in an attempt to allay persistent criticism against the ineffectiveness of his administration, Muzorewa announced on August 25 that "Rhodesia" would be dropped from the name of the country, which he said would be known henceforth simply as Zimbabwe. He said that his 19-member cabinet, including five whites, had reached this decision because, he claimed, that was what the people wanted. He added that the change would be passed by Parliament before the London constitutional conference. But for reasons that were not clearly known, this action was not taken. It was speculated that Smith had objected to the change in the name of the country and that Muzorewa did not wish to irritate an ally on whose help and support he depended.

These were among the factors that forced Smith and Muzorewa to accept Thatcher's invitation to attend the conference, although the prior conditions she had stipulated were totally unacceptable to them, especially to Smith, because his acceptance of them meant in essence that he was giving up 14 years of illegal seizure of independence. The participants began to arrive in London on September 8 for the official opening on September 10. There was little hope for the success of the conference; however, the racial bitterness that characterized the Geneva conference of 1976 was now substituted for the rancor and hostility between the two sides. On one side were Smith and Muzorewa, who regarded the other side as a potential new dictatorship for Rhodesia. On the other were Nkomo and Mugabe, who regarded Muzorewa as a traitor to the black struggle for freedom.

The PF announced that it would only talk to Britain, not to Muzorewa and Smith, because, it maintained, the Salisbury regime was an alliance of conspirators against the legitimate interests of Zimbabwe.

As the conference got under way, the participants argued over details of seating arrangements, and observers feared that it would be wrecked before it even started. Garfield Todd, an adviser to Nkomo at the Geneva conference and an observer at the London conference, expressed the hope that the London conference would succeed where the Geneva conference failed because, he said, the British government was a full participant. He said he hoped that Carrington would negotiate with the warring parties, that he would not just mediate, as Richard did at the Geneva Conference.[38]

Heavily armed police guarded the conference hall because the British government believed that after years of a bitter racial war, the warring parties were far less inclined to talk than they were at the Geneva conference. As Smith arrived in London, he was greeted at the airport by demonstrators chanting, "Murderer, murderer." This was his first visit to London since 1965 when he seized power, an action that was the major cause of the war. To attend the conference, Smith had to receive special immunity from arrest by the British government for his action in the seizure of power.[39] There was speculation that Smith and Muzorewa wanted the conference to fail because they believed the British government would let sanctions expire in November.[40]

Although a spokesman for Muzorewa remarked that if only sanctions would end, the Rhodesian regime would fight till hell froze, Muzorewa himself was not party to this position. Smith and Muzorewa hoped that the end of sanctions would enable them to gain international acceptance. However, this turned out to be a misplaced hope. Like Ivor Richard during the Geneva conference, Lord Carrington appealed to the participants to do everything possible to make the conference succeed. He warned that the price of failure would be prolonged bloodshed and further destruction of Zimbabwe, adding that all parties carried a heavy responsibility for the situation. He said he did not believe that the people of Zimbabwe would readily forgive any party that deprived them of the opportunity to settle their future by peaceful means. He concluded that the responsibility for preventing an opportunity to reach an agreement would further prolong bloodshed and the destruction of the country.[41]

Having reached agreement on the substance of the constitution with the PF, the British government decided to request the queen to appoint a governor to the colony of Colonial Zimbabwe. On December 7, Queen Elizabeth II appointed Lord Christopher Soames, son-in-law of Winston Churchill, as the governor. While the parties were negotiating a cease-fire, Lord Soames was making plans to assume his colonial duties in Southern Rhodesia and to make preparations for new elections, scheduled for the end of February 1980, as the first step toward independence for Zimbabwe. This action marked the end of 14 years of Smith's rebellion and of the sanctions against the Rhodesian regime.

In Rhodesia itself, the appointment of Soames was welcomed by many Africans and some whites. Muzorewa was particularly pleased. His spokesman remarked that the appointment of Soames was as good a guarantee as could be expected that British supervision of the transitional period to majority rule would be impartial. Although the RF voted to accept the governor, Smith lashed out his anger by saying that the British governor could go to Zimbabwe and raise his Union Jack and sing "God Save the Queen" until he was blue in the face. He suggested that it was of no consequences to him because he had children and grandchildren in the country and he needed to ensure their future. He concluded that the governor's assignment was to extricate the British government from the Rhodesian problem at whatever cost to the whites who had made their home there.[42] Smith did not care to mention that the Rhodesian problem was the product of his own policy and action. Instead of blaming Britain, he should have blamed himself for that problem.

However, Britain ignored Smith's protest, and as Soames prepared to go to Southern Rhodesia, the colonial governor's residency was being refurbished. A Commonwealth peacekeeping force of 1,200 would monitor both the Rhodesian regime forces and the guerrillas to ensure that they did not break the cease-fire. On December 11, after five hours of debate, the Rhodesian Parliament voted to dissolve itself in favor of Soames.

This action was a painful experience for Smith. The appointment of Soames, the hoisting of the Union Jack, the dissolution of Parliament, the presence of a Commonwealth force, and a new constitution providing for African majority government—all of which Smith had flatly rejected during the past 14 years as prior conditions for return to legality, peace, and independence—signaled to him and his white supporters that, indeed, the era of white supremacy was coming to an end and that a genuine African government was about to begin. On December 12, 1979, Soames arrived in Salisbury on a British Royal Air Force VC 10.

He was welcomed by a number of people, including Muzorewa, David Smith, and Chris Anderson, both members of Smith's RF. Ian Smith was invited, but he decided to boycott the welcoming ceremonies.

A band made up of African policemen played "God Save the Queen," an event Smith had vowed would never take place again in Rhodesia. At the airport, Soames was greeted by chanting African demonstrators carrying placards reading, "Down with Rhodesia Front, down with Smith, down with racism." Among the whites who came to welcome Soames was Sir Humphrey Gibbs, aged 71, the governor whom Smith pushed from office when he seized power in 1965, and whom he told to go back to his farm and produce more milk from his cows. For Gibbs, this was a moment of joy; Smith had finally been brought to his knees, the rebellion he led was at last over.

On December 21, 1979, the seventh anniversary of the start of the war, the constitutional conference on the future of Zimbabwe came to an end with signing ceremonies. On the same day, Soames signed a number of decrees, including one lifting the ban on political activities by ZANU and ZAPU, led respectively by Mugabe and Nkomo. Soames released most of the political prisoners held by the Smith government. He also granted amnesty to Smith for leading a rebellion in 1965 and to those who were accused of murdering civilians during the height of the war. He also lifted the ban on three newspapers, *Umbowo*, *Moto*, and the *Zimbabwe Times*, all of which had, before they were banned, criticized the policies of the Smith government and had supported the PF. Public meetings were once again allowed for the first time since Smith banned them in 1964.

As the cease-fire began to take effect, guerrillas moved back into Zimbabwe in large numbers to occupy the 16 assembly areas designated to them under the terms of the Lancaster House agreement. Suddenly, the peace agreement was seriously threatened when two men in a car fired a submachine gun and threw a bomb into the house occupied by Mugabe's sister and mother in Salisbury, injuring Mugabe's two nephews. It was reported that Muzorewa's supporters were responsible for the attack, but Muzorewa denied the charges. Thousands of people marched in Salisbury in support of Mugabe, while another large crowd marched in Bulawayo in support of Nkomo. A third group marched in Gweru to demonstrate against Muzorewa. Soames promised to put an end to violence, but it appeared he was unable to do much about it.

ELECTIONS OF FEBRUARY 1980

As the precarious peace seemed to hold, there was increasing expectation and hope that the PF would come home to campaign for elections, scheduled for the end of February. As soon as the peace agreement was signed on December 21, Muzorewa and his aides rushed to Rhodesia to campaign against the PF. Both Mugabe and Nkomo were making plans to return to Rhodesia, but they had to do that in stages. On December 26, 87 guerrilla officers flew into Salisbury from their bases in Mozambique and Zambia. Thousands of chanting blacks gave them a hero's welcome. The crowds broke down an airport fence and smashed the windows of a bus carrying Mugabe and Nkomo in order to reach and touch them. Robyn Wright, reporting for ABC-TV, observed that the tumultuous welcome extended to Nkomo and Mugabe suggested that there was a momentum building behind the Patriotic Front.[43]

As the elections campaign got under way, predictions seemed to give Mugabe a substantial lead over Muzorewa and Nkomo. Several attempts were made on Mugabe's life, and Muzorewa's supporters were held responsible. On February 9, Garfield Todd was arrested and charged with aiding guerrillas. Todd was later released from prison on condition that he remain in his home area of Shabani. On February 11, Mugabe threatened to return to guerrilla war because he accused Soames of failing to stop Muzorewa's supporters from violence and intimidation. The auxiliary forces loyal to Muzorewa, operating under the name of "Pfumo Rewanhu"[44] (People's Army), was allowed to solicit support for the ANC, while similar activity by supporters of the PF was regarded as intimidation. Soames had, in fact, banned some PF politicians from campaigning, and Mugabe indicated that if Soames took one more action against ZANU, then the whole peace agreement would go down the drain. The Selous Scouts (the special security branch of the army) were secretly planting bombs all over the country.

On February 15, 240,000 white voters elected 20 white members to the legislature in accordance with the Lancaster House agreement. Ian Smith's RF won all the seats. All but six candidates were returned unopposed. Smith had token opposition from Johannes Hulley and Donald Speedie, two white "liberals." By the time the election results were known, Smith was on a lecture tour of the United States. In the midst of all this, Soames once again moved against the PF. On February 20, Justin Nyoka, a journalist and aide to Mugabe, was arrested on charges of making inflammatory remarks during an election campaign speech.

In London, Amnesty International sharply criticized Soames for failing to end torture methods and illegal arrests of blacks. The International Red Cross also criticized Soames for adopting exactly the policies of the Smith regime.[45] Nyoka's arrest seemed to confirm reports that Soames had, in fact, ordered the arrest of many PF supporters in an effort to promote the African National Council of Muzorewa.

Nearly 3 million African voters cast their ballots February 27–29. As counting of the ballots began on March 3, Mugabe took an early lead.

When the results were made official the next day, whites and Muzorewa were stunned to discover that Mugabe's ZANU had won 57 seats, Nkomo's ZAPU 20, and Muzorewa's Council 3. Mugabe's party had, in fact, captured 90 percent of the total vote cast. Independent international observers and British and American officials declared the elections free and fair. ZANU's 57 seats and ZAPU's 20 seats gave the PF more than the two-thirds majority needed to pass a constitutional amendment without the support of any other party. The landslide victory scored by the PF suddenly became a nightmare among the whites. The state of the parties in the first Zimbabwean Parliament, 1980, is as follows:

Name of Party	Leader	Number of Seats
Patriotic Front (ZANU)	Robert Mugabe	57
Patriotic Front (ZAPU)	Joshua Nkomo	20
United African National Council	Abel Muzorewa	3
Rhodesia Front (RF)	Ian Smith	20*
Total		100

*These are reserved seats for whites.

The following were other parties that contested the elections but failed to gain any seats:

Name of Party	Leader
National Democratic Union	H. Chihota
National Front of Zimbabwe	P. Mandaza
United National Federal Party	K. Ndiweni
United People's Association of Matabeleland	F. Bertrand
Zimbabwe Democratic Party	J. Chikerema
Zimbabwe African National Union	N. Sithole

SUMMARY AND CONCLUSION

As Mugabe began the task of forming the first Zimbabwean government, he appealed for unity and reconciliation. He also indicated that Nkomo would have a role in that government. Soames and Peter Walls, an RF army general, also appealed for calm. During polling, Walls made a trip to South Africa to warn the Botha regime not to interfere in the affairs of Zimbabwe because, he said, if it did, the consequences of such action would be severe for South Africa itself. With the election results made official, one era closed and another began. Both Southern Rhodesia and Ian Smith, as far as the Zimbabweans were concerned, belonged to the unwanted past. All they were looking to was the future. Thus, the transformation of Zimbabwe was finally completed.

Two days after the results were known, some whites were reported to be planning to burn down their farms and homes and go away. The first action Mugabe took was to end the 15-year state of emergency Smith had been utilizing to impose a white minority dictatorship. It was also announced that Nkomo was unwilling to serve as first president of Zimbabwe; he finally accepted the position of prime minister of Home Affairs. With this new alliance, the PF appeared to consolidate its power. Zimbabwe was free at last.

The discussion in this chapter shows that three major events began to take place in the struggle for independence and in which Muzorewa was involved. The first event was the Geneva conference in 1976, the second was the internal agreement of 1978, and the third was the Lancaster House conference of 1979. Although he lost the elections of 1980, Muzorewa had played his role well except for the internal agreement which eliminated the PF from participation. This proved to be a fatal error because the British government refused to accept the agreement as a basis for independence for Zimbabwe. One sad outcome of this political saga was the continuing conflict between Muzorewa and Mugabe. It would be in the best interest of Zimbabwe to find ways of ending this conflict once and for all.

NOTES

1. For detailed discussion of the *Tiger* meeting, see Dickson A. Mungazi, *The Cross Between Rhodesia and Zimbabwe: Racial Conflict in Zimbabwe, 1962–1979* (New York: Vantage Press, 1981), p. 75.

2. *Lincoln Evening Journal* (Lincoln, Neb.), (September 25, 1976), p. 1.

3. *Time* (October 12, 1976), p. 6.

4. Ibid., p. 7.

5. *Times of London* (October 12, 1976), p. 8.

6. Ibid., p. 9.

7. Front-line states was a term that was used to refer to black-ruled countries of southern Africa that shared common borders with white-ruled countries. In 1976 the front-line states were Zambia, Mozambique, and Angola. However, the ones that had a profound influence on the struggle for independence in southern Africa were Zambia and Tanzania.

8. *Lincoln Evening Journal* (October 4, 1976), p. 1.

9. Named after its author, U.S. conservative Republican Senator from Virginia Harry Byrd, the Byrd Amendment was part of a defense budget that allowed the United States to violate sanctions against Smith to import chromium that the United Sates needed for defense purposes.

10. *Lincoln Evening Journal* (October 21, 1976), p. 1.

11. Ibid., p. 2.

12. Michael Snitowsky, "Rhodesia Talks: Fiery Black Nationalists Versus Hard-core White Segregationists," in *Lincoln Evening Journal* (October 29, 1976), p. 20.

13. G. Sparrow, *The Rhodesian Rebellion* (London: Brighton, 1966), p. 20.

14. Ibid., p. 1.

15. *Lincoln Evening Journal* (October 29, 1976), p. 1.

16. Ibid., p. 2.

17. Ibid.

18. Ibid., p. 1.

19. *Time* (November 16, 1986), p. 61. Subsequent events proved that Smith was not sincere in claiming this change of mind.

20. Unilateral declaration of independence, which Smith made on November 11, 1965. The international community regarded the action as illegal and urged nations of the world not to extend any recognition of his government. In addition, economic sanctions were imposed, making it difficult for Smith to have a government that had the confidence of Zimbabweans for the good of the country.

21. *Times of London* (November 6, 1976), p. 6.

22. For a detailed discussion of the role that this remarkable man played in the events in Kenya during the Mau Mau rebellion, see Mungazi, *The Last British Liberals in Africa: Michael Blundell and Garfield Todd* (Westport, CT: Praeger Publishers, 1999).

23. *Lincoln Evening Journal* (December 19, 1976), p. 2.

24. For the full text of the declaration, see Mungazi, *The Cross Between Rhodesia and Zimbabwe, p. 284.*

25. *Lincoln Evening Journal* (November 25, 1977), p. 1.

26. Ibid.

27. *Lincoln Evening Journal* (January 27, 1978), p. 1.

28. *Lincoln Evening Journal* (March 3, 1978), p. 1.

29. *Lincoln Evening Journal* (February 16, 1978), p. 3.

30. *Time*, (March 6, 1978), p. 46.

31. *Lincoln Evening Journal* (January 31, 1979), p. 1.

32. Ibid.

33. *Globe and Mail* (Toronto) (December 16, 1978), p. 1.

34. *Omaha World Herald* (April 18, 1979), p. 46.

35. *Lincoln Evening Journal* (June 21, 1979), p. 12.

36. *Time* (July 7, 1979), p. 31.

37. *Time* (August 13, 1979), p. 25.

38. Basil Davidson, *Modern Africa: A Social and Political History* (London: Longman, 1994), p. 124.

39. The reader will recall that Smith refused to grant immunity to members of the black delegation at the 1975 Victoria Falls conference. His refusal aborted the conference. What would have happened if Britain had refused to grant immunity to Smith is simply a matter of speculation. But at this point it might very well be that the conference would have gone underway without him.

40. Snitowsky, "Rhodesia Talks," p. 20.

41. *Lincoln Evening Journal* (September 10, 1979), p. 5.

42. *Lincoln Evening Journal* (February 21, 1980), p. 4.

43. Robin Wright, Reporting for the ABC-TV, January 13, 1980.

44. This Shona translation comes from the Zulu expression *Umkhonto we Sizwe*, meaning people's army. For a detailed discussion of this concept, see Francis Meli, *South Africa Belongs to Us: The History of the ANC* (Harare: Zimbabwe Publishing House, 1988), p. 145.

45. In December 1979, Russia invaded neighboring Afghanistan and installed a puppet regime. The invasion triggered a worldwide condemnation of Russia, threatening the Olympic Games scheduled for summer 1980 in Moscow. There was also stiff resistance to Russian occupation inside Afghanistan itself. President Jimmy Carter indicated that the United States would boycott the Moscow games and urged other nations to do the same. A number of Third World countries, including Africa, indicated they would boycott the games in protest against the invasion.

8

Tutu and Muzorewa in the Footsteps of the Masters: Summary, Conclusion, and Implications

We believe that the government, in its action over recent years, has chosen the path which will lead to violence, bloodshed, and instability.
                    —Desmond Tutu, letter to President P. W. Botha, 1988

Whether I am in the best hotel of Oxford or London or New York, or anywhere in the world, . . . I feel a slave in the country of my birth.
                    —Abel Muzorewa, 1973

HUDDLESTON'S LEGACY AND TUTU'S ROLE IN SOUTH AFRICA

This book has addressed the roles that Bishop Desmond M. Tutu and Bishop Abel T. Muzorewa played in the political transformations of South Africa and Zimbabwe, respectively. It has based that discussion on the work that was done by their predecessors, Bishop E. Trevor Huddleston who served in South Africa from 1943 to 1956, and Bishop Ralph Dodge who served in Zimbabwe from 1956 to 1964. Both Huddleston and Dodge believed profoundly in the prophetic role of the church in seeking an improvement of society in religious, political, social, and economic areas. Both men subscribed to the creed that the church must preach the gospel of the total human being, meaning that it must address human needs in all aspects of life, both spiritual and physical. Huddleston argued that while he would defend the right of the church to take part in the political life of the country, he would deny categorically its right to align itself with any one political party.[1] Bishop Tutu took this identical position as well.

This approach enabled church leaders, not just Huddleston and Dodge, to rise above the limitations of party politics placed on politicians to address larger national issues: the need for society to practice social justice, equality, fairness, and recognizing fundamental freedoms of people—issues that political parties can address only to promote themselves. In both South Africa and Zimbabwe these issues were directly related to race, and race was the basis of apartheid and various forms of discriminatory legislation that were arbitrarily imposed on Africans in both countries. Since the settlement of the Boers in South Africa in 1652, race was the only criterion used to determine a person's place in society, nothing else mattered. Until the advent of an African government in April 1994, the Afrikaners never pretended that they based their policies on principles of equality. While Huddleston recognized the fact that apartheid was a vicious system that enslaved Africans, he was equally certain that Africans would sooner than later fight to bring it to an end. Just before he was expelled from South Africa in 1956, Huddleston commented that of the future of South Africa he was in no doubt at all. He said that it was inconceivable to him that 2.5 million whites would rule the country forever with no justifiable claim to moral leadership. He warned that whites should not hope to mold the continent of Africa to their pattern because over 200 million Africans, increasingly conscious of their common past and of their exciting present, were certainly not going to accept leadership of their continent from heirs of Paul Kruger and Cecil John Rhodes. Therefore, white South Africa would be fortunate if, 50 years from then, it was still a tolerated minority group, allowed to remain where it has been since the founding of colonies in the 19th century.[2]

The change of government from Afrikaners to Africans beat Huddleston's prediction by 12 years. Huddleston also recognized the fact that national leaders such as J. G. Strijdom, who were so anxious to maintain power under the Afrikaners as their definition of civilization, did so by using military force to maintain themselves in office. Huddleston argued that it was the function of the church to warn the government of the consequences of adopting such a policy. He expressed his view the Afrikaner nationalism was destroying the spirit of racial harmony that was crucial to national development, and its obsession with race would prove to be the demise of the Nationalist government.[3]

Throughout his service in South Africa and in his book, Huddleston warned the Nationalist government that Africans would continue to resist oppression and injustice until a crisis point was reached, at which time an explosion might occur.[4] Instead of heeding that message, the

Nationalist government deported him. In doing so the government forgot that killing the messenger intensifies the message. Huddleston also argued that because of the oppressive methods the government was using, it created the impression that it was invincible, forcing it to increase the oppression of apartheid. However, there would come a time when with all the power at its disposal, the government would be subject to judgment by others. That would be the time of reckoning.

Huddleston warned the Africans that their day would come, and when it came they must not adopt the same oppressive methods that the Nationalist government was using. They must arise above the periphery of human nature to exercise magnanimity. They must learn not to revile their former persecutors for that would make them just as bad. They must embrace a reconciliatory approach in their efforts to rebuild a non-racial society in which the worth of the human being is protected by policies of fairness and justice.

Huddleston said Africans must act in ways that would bring their former oppressors to shame. They must respect democracy. They must seek to discover past abuses and expose them in the interest of healing the nation, but they must not be vindictive. They must reject the thinking of the old Afrikaner school of thought that once black and white were divided, they would happily be together for ever after,[5] because true happiness came from practicing human brotherhood based on communication and free association in social matters and business practices. The evil of apartheid was that it denied people an opportunity to know each other by living together and cooperating in building a vibrant community that served the needs of all people.

In writing *Naught for Your Comfort*, Huddleston took some precaution to ensure that his views were not misunderstood by the framers of the apartheid system. Because the Community of Resurrection did not permit the use of "I" and "me," Huddleston wanted to make sure that these views were not taken as the views of the Anglican Church. He explained that he must ask the Community's forgiveness for doing so in his book. But he had done so for two reasons: first was for the obvious one of literary style; the second reason was because the opinions expressed in the book were entirely his own responsibility. They did not in any way reflect the common mind of the Community, although he believed that many of his brethren were in substantial agreement with them.[6]

Using these first-person pronouncements in Huddleston's book enabled Tutu to separate his own views from those of the Anglican Church. He did not want the Nationalist government to accuse the Anglican Church of expressing views that were critical of the government. In his book Huddleston discussed all the evils of apartheid that characterized the South African society: racial prejudice, discrimination, psychological harm to both perpetrator and victim, alienation, failure to appreciate the

richness of diversity, physical oppression, a lack of justice, daily humiliation suffered by the Africans, poverty that was the lot of the African
population, and claimed superiority by the Afrikaners. There was no
escape from the timeless shackles that oppressed both Afrikaners and
Africans alike. Life was a daily circle of pain and suffering that extended
beyond the realm of imagination.

Huddleston's legacy is what Tutu utilized to carry the campaign Huddleston started to end apartheid to a new level. David Welsh describes
Tutu's qualities as a human being and leader, observing that the first
quality that impressed him about Tutu was his infectious laughter and
expressively mobile face. He said that Tutu was capable of great merri-
ment and had an immense zest for life. It was precisely these qualities
that had so often served as tension breakers. His clerical career had been
eventful, even stormy. Contrary to what his detractors claimed, Tutu
never had political ambitions. In spite of the fame he achieved as a Nobel
Peace prize winner (1984) and the huge publicity his activities received,
Tutu remained at heart the humble parish priest that he had always
been.[7] Welsh goes on to say that Tutu's forthright advocacy of sanctions
to force an end to apartheid alienated many affluent whites and poor
Africans. His political activity has been regarded as a form of naiveté by
his critics.

Against this view of Tutu it must always be remembered that he assumed the role of spokesman for the cause of African freedom at a time
when major nationalist organizations and leaders had been outlawed
and were in political prison. Since the lifting of the ban on political organizations on February 2, 1990, Tutu consciously returned to his clerical
role, insisting that the church must not be seen as an advocate of partisan
political positions.[8]

Huddleston also traveled extensively internationally to promote his
antiapartheid campaign, and held meetings with world leaders. For example, in 1982 he addressed the UN General Assembly on the evils of
apartheid. In 1984 he toured the front-line states of southern Africa that
included Botswana, Mozambique, Tanzania, Zimbabwe, and Zambia to
discuss with leaders of those countries various ways of honoring sanctions against South Africa. In 1984 he returned to the United Nations to
deliver a petition calling for the release of Nelson Mandela. He also addressed the UN Special Committee Against Apartheid. In the same year
he traveled to India, New Zealand, and Australia to meet with respective
national leaders. In April 1989 he was the honored guest of the head of
state in Nigeria for a week-long nationwide tour.[9]

Like Huddleston, Tutu tended to minimize his own role in the confrontation that emerged between the church and the Nationalist government. He explained this by saying that although individual persons are
important, the fight has got nothing to do with individuals because it is
the duty of all to fight for justice. He also believed that as individuals,

members of a society may help to force things. But, if one were to pass off center stage, it would not be the end of the movement because the movement is much, much bigger than the individual.[10] It was in this spirit of collective effort that Tutu participated in the campaign to end apartheid.

This is why on February 20, 1988, Tutu wrote a letter to P. W. Botha, just as he had done on May 6, 1976, to John Vorster, to warn him about the consequences of trying to maintain apartheid. In the letter to Botha Tutu said Africans were deeply distressed at, and therefore protested in the strongest of terms possible, the restrictions that were placed on the activities of 17 members of the South African Christian Council, on the Congress of South African Trade Unions, and on 18 of their leaders. He stated his belief that the government, in its action over recent years, had chosen a path for the future that would lead to violence, bloodshed, and instability.[11]

On February 29, 1988, Tutu and 25 other clergymen wrote a petition to Botha and members of the South African Parliament to reiterate their call for lifting the ban on the 17 organizations, to unbar political organizations, and to begin negotiations with leaders of political organizations to initiate a new constitution and end apartheid before it was too late.[12]

Learning from the mistake that John Vorster made in refusing to respond to Tutu's letter in 1976, Botha responded on March 16, 1988, but took the same attitude that the Nationalist Party always used as an excuse for maintaining apartheid, saying that Tutu's letter raised a question of whether it is possible to come to any other conclusion than that actions such as the march to Parliament may have been seen as part of the campaign by the ANC propaganda. He reminded Tutu that he was no doubt aware that the expressed intention of the planned revolution was to transform South Africa into an atheistic Marxist state, where freedom of faith and worship would surely be among the first casualties.[13]

It was quite sad for Tutu and other clergymen to learn from Botha's response that this line of thinking was still a central tenet of the philosophy of the Nationalist Party and its desire to maintain apartheid. It was a philosophy that had been the basis of all of apartheid laws. It was the basis that the international community had repeatedly condemned, and was one the Africans were fighting against. Botha had not learned anything new. This is why the following year, on September 15, 1989, he was forced out of office and replaced by F. W. de Klerk. On February 2, 1990, de Klerk took the action that Tutu and other clergymen had suggested as a condition of beginning negotiations with the ANC.

TUTU'S ROLE IN CHANGING OF THE GUARD

By the time de Klerk made his proposals in an address to Parliament on February 2, 1990, he took all the conditions that Tutu had suggested into consideration. Indeed, he began to observe these conditions in the address, saying that his government had taken a firm decision to release Nelson Mandela unconditionally. Nine days later, on February 11, Mandela was actually released. Hundreds of other political prisoners had been released shortly before. These included Walter Sisulu, Raymond Mhlaba, Ahmed Kathrada, Andrew Mbugeni, Wilton Mkwayi, and Osacar Mpethu. Hundreds of exiles were to return soon, including Oliver Tambo and Tabo Mbeki, both of whom were running ANC operations from bases in Zambia.

Immediately on his release Mandela issued a statement in Cape Town, saying in the traditional ANC salute and slogan: "Amandla! Amandla!" (power! power!). The huge crowd that came to welcome him roared back, "Ngawethu!" (is ours!). He went on to add that he greeted them all in the name of peace, democracy, and freedom for all. Then he told his audience, "I stand before you not as a prophet, but as your humble servant and of the people. Your tireless and heroic sacrifices have made it possible for me to be here today. I therefore pledge the remaining years of my life[14] in your hands."[15] Mandela went on to thank the ANC and Oliver Tambo for refusing to give up the struggle against apartheid. He paid tribute to the work that Tutu had been doing since 1976 to bring apartheid to an end.

Mandela also recognized the fact that de Klerk had gone further than any previous Nationalist leader in taking steps to restore South Africa to its proper place among nations of Africa and the world. He added, "Mr. de Klerk is acutely aware of the dangers of a public figure not honoring his undertakings. As an organization we have our policy and strategy. On the harsh reality we are still suffering under the policy of the Nationalist government. Our struggle has reached a decisive moment."[16] The final phase of the negotiations proved to be the final act of bringing the apartheid system to an unconditional end.

On August 14, 1990, after three months of preparation, the first session of negotiations between the Nationalist government and the ANC was held in Cape Town. After this preliminary session the participants issued a communiqué stressing agreement on five essential considerations:

1. The establishment of a working group to make accommodation on a definition of political offenses and to advise on norms and mechanisms for dealing with the release of political prisoners still being held.

2. The working group would define and recommend conditions of immunity from arrest for political offenses. At this point Tutu began to fall in the background of things to allow politicians an opportunity to map out the future of the country.

3. The Nationalist government would undertake to review existing security leg-

islation to bring it into line with the new situation in order to ensure normal and free political activity.

4. Ask the government to reiterate its commitment to work toward lifting the state of emergency.

5. Efficient channels of communication between the government and the ANC be developed in order to curb the possibility of misunderstanding, which could lead into conflict. The Nationalist government agreed to introduce legislation to repeal all apartheid laws.[17]

The success of this first session was measured in terms of de Klerk's willingness to meet all the conditions that the ANC had outlined in 1989. From this point on the negotiations focused on other critical issues remaining to be resolved. These included the constitution and voting rights. Ending all discriminatory laws was addressed by the introduction of legislation repealing all apartheid laws. All indications were that the ANC would easily have its way prevail as de Klerk seemed more than willing to bring apartheid to an end as a condition of ensuring the future of Afrikaners in the country. The absolute power that they had exercised over many years was about to come to an end before their very eyes.

In January 1992, as negotiations between the ANC and the Nationalists appeared to experience some problems, de Klerk and his Nationalist government suffered a series of defeats in special elections, forcing them to seek the approval of white voters to continue the negotiations. In February de Klerk announced that a national referendum would be held on March 17, 1992, to provide an answer to a single question: "Do you support the continuation of the reform process which the State President began on February 2, 1990, and which is aimed at a new constitution through negotiation?" De Klerk considered the referendum so important that his government decided to make arrangements for voters living outside South Africa to cast their ballots on March 11 and 12. The slow progress in the negotiations with ANC created a political climate that forced some members of both African and white communities to take extreme positions.

Two examples must be presented to substantiate this conclusion. The first example is that Thami Mcerwa, president of the Azanian Youth Organization, opposed the negotiations because, he said, Africans wanted total liberation, not cosmetic changes. They may go into civil war struggle, but quick-fix solutions would not work. He quoted Steve Biko,[18] who said that it was better to die for an idea that will live than to live for an idea that will die.[19] Mcerwa was in no mood to compromise his political beliefs.

The second example is that Pieter Rudolph, a member of the Neo-Nazi Afrikaner Resistance Movement, considered de Klerk a traitor to Afrikaner interests. Rudolph argued that Afrikaners inherited South Africa as a glorious national legacy. Rudolph added that he received South Africa as he received his mother's milk and that he was a son of Africa more than Africans.[20]

The extreme positions taken by Mcerwa and Rudolph represented the positions taken by the antagonists, who placed South Africa at the crossroads until Nelson Mandela assumed office as president following elections that were held in April 1994. Rudolph and the other extreme Afrikaners were overwhelmed by the rapid pace of events they could not understand and control. Mcerwa was pleased to see that things finally came out the way he had hoped and wanted.

The sad part of it all is that de Klerk agreed to be part of a national referendum that allowed only whites to vote on an issue of great national importance. Since he claimed to be committed to bringing about social reform, what better opportunity for him to start bringing the Africans into his confidence than initiating a process for their involvement in the referendum?

This is why on March 12, 1992, 17 people and on March 13 another 24 people were killed in violence related to the forthcoming referendum. Reporting from Johannesburg on March 13, Alan Pizzey put the conflict between the Afrikaner psychology and the determination of Africans to bring about fundamental political change in its proper context, saying, "There is still a belief among the Afrikaners that God has ordained them as the master race of South Africa. But the Africans believe that the future belongs to them."[21] This conflict evinces the tragedy of apartheid.

On March 18, 1992, when the referendum results showed that the "yes" vote had carried the day by a margin of 2:1 out of the total white electorate of 2.8 million voters, de Klerk went into a state of euphoria; his government had closed the chapter on apartheid.[22] While generally pleased with the outcome of the referendum, Nelson Mandela had a more somber reaction, saying that because Africans could not vote in their country, he could not say that apartheid was gone.[23] De Klerk also saw the result, coming on his 56th birthday, as the real birthday of the real South Africa.[24]

In a similar manner Allister Sparks, the South African author of *The Mind of South Africa*, recognized the perils of a national crisis cast in the context of the determination of the Africans, saying "The danger now is that the right-wing may turn to violence. White South Africa has rejected apartheid and must now embrace a non-racial approach to its problems. The talk of power-sharing is a code word for white veto."[25]

It is a known fact that Africans are quite capable of grasping this reality and demanding that South Africa move into the realm of a completely nonracial society. Gary Player, a South African professional golf player, added that change was the price of survival.[26] But Pieter W. Botha, aged 76, reacted by saying that he would not support a reform process that would lead to the suicide of his people.[27] It was not possible for the old and tired horse to see things from their proper perspective. After failing to recognize the need for change during his own administration, how could he possibly accept change initiated by others?

When the referendum was over, the task of negotiations resumed, giving de Klerk freedom to make more concessions to the ANC. But on April 5 violence in black townships broke out on a larger scale than before the referendum. As hundreds were killed, Mandela called for a UN peacekeeping force, arguing that the South African security forces were behind the violence and that was the only way to contain it. But de Klerk rejected both the call and the charge, arguing that the violence was caused by Africans themselves struggling for power.

On April 11, in a strange turn of events, de Klerk tried to campaign in a black neighborhood outside Cape Town in an effort to recruit Africans into the ranks of the Nationalist Party. As he tried to make a speech, he was jeered and shouted down, but he managed to tell his audience that apartheid had been buried and would remain buried. He also told them that the creation of the new South Africa had begun.[28] One angry African reacted angrily saying that Africans were still discriminated against, and that they still could not vote. He asked de Klerk what he was campaigning for?[29]

Unconvinced of his sincerity, ANC called de Klerk's action "a case of political opportunism."[30] De Klerk was forced to cancel the rest of the speech and hurriedly moved out of the neighborhood. The spiral of conflict took an ominous and tragic turn on June 18, 1992, when 39 Africans were massacred in cold blood at Boipatong, reportedly by members of Inkatha Freedom Party headed by Manas Buthelezi with what ANC identified as the assistance from the government.[31]

Although de Klerk denied the charge, an African mine-security guard told a government-appointed commission that the police from a former paramilitary unit had joined in the Boipatong killings.[32] Negotiations between ANC and the government were suspended as the result of the killings to allow the parties to assess the situation and to determine the next move. Instead of dealing forthrightly with the situation that his government had created, de Klerk threatened to reimpose the notorious state of emergency, an easy strategy the apartheid government had utilized for so many years to control the Africans.

On August 3, 1992, over a million African workers went on strike for two days in protest against the refusal of the government to end apartheid. This action paralyzed major industries and services. On September 18, 28 Africans were massacred in the Bantustan Homeland of Ciskei while protesting peacefully against the puppet regime of Brigadier Oupa Gqozo, who was promoted to his position in the government of South Africa for his service against the demand of the Africans to dismantle apartheid. According to *Time*, when the 60,000 chanting ANC supporters moved closer to the capital, trigger-happy troops of the Ciskei army began shooting directly into the crowd. After two prolonged bursts of gunfire, 28 people lay dead in pools of blood, another 400 were wounded,[33] dragging the country closer to the edge of a major civil conflict.

There is no doubt that the racial confrontation that apartheid has created over many years was destined to intensify with the passage of time. This situation actually led to one thing: a major racial war that produced a national tragedy such as the one that occurred in Zimbabwe from 1966 to 1979. Apartheid has been a cancer that has destroyed the delicate tissue of the South African vitality—human resources without which no nation can prosper. Even Brian Nel, a Herstige Nationale Party organizer, seemed to agree when he said ironically in 1980 that the cancer of apartheid was spreading and was going to follow Africans wherever they went.[34]

In the determination of Afrikaners to sustain apartheid at all costs and in the determination of oppressed Africans to rise and envisage the restoration of their selves as the seeds of the tragedy of apartheid in the South African system. Although the world community has exercised its moral duty to help Afrikaners see the tragic course they have charted for the country, apartheid has extended beyond the boundaries of South Africa, and it must therefore be viewed from a global perspective.

Indeed, by 1992, the international community came to realize that in apartheid's oppression of the black masses of South Africa humanity as a whole was inescapably enslaved. This is the reality that de Klerk took into account in deciding to hold serious discussions with the ANC on a new constitution that would bring true democracy to South Africa.

After months of negotiations, the parties finally agreed to hold free elections on April 26–18, 1994. Immediately the ANC designed a strategy to "capture at least 67 percent of the 22.4 million eligible voters."[35] This would mean that the ANC would take 328 of the 490 seats in Parliament. As the election campaign got under way, it was clear that de Klerk was hoping for no more than a respectable showing. He was pleased that he had made it possible to turn over power to the Africans in a way that would ensure the future of the whites in a new country. An African government would not match the brutality of apartheid by utilizing methods that would make them uncomfortable to live in.

As was expected, when the election results were known on May 2, the ANC won with more than the two-thirds majority it had needed to form the first black majority government in the history of South Africa. Nelson Mandela, the man who spent 27 years in prison for opposing apartheid, emerged as the new man in the incredible saga of the transformation of South Africa. With a sense of duty and humbled by it all, Mandela responded,

It is not the individual that matters, but the group that is important. I come to you as a servant, not a leader above others. We must together begin to mobilize our minds and build a better life for all South Africans. We are here to honor our promise. If we fail we betray the trust placed on us by our people. As we form the government of national unity, we must set the tone for the future."[36]

After conceding defeat, de Klerk pledged the support of his party to the new government that Mandela was about to lead, saying that after 300 years all the people of South Africa were now free.[37] When Mandela was inaugurated on May 9 the entire African continent had eliminated the last vestiges of colonial domination, raising Africans to a new level of hope for the future. Mandela made an impressive inaugural address as he reflected upon the thoughts of Africans about themselves and the future of their country:

Our deepest fear is not that we are inadequate. Our deepest fear is that were are powerful beyond measure. It is our light, not our darkness, that most frightens us. As we let our own light shine we unconsciously give other people permission to do the same. As we are liberated from our own fears, our presence automatically liberates others.[38]

This position was the final act of bringing apartheid to an end. However, cautioning his fellow South Africans, Mandela warned them not to have too high hopes because the task of rebuilding a country devastated by apartheid was not an easy one. But the transformation of the African continent was now complete.

TUTU AND THE TRUTH AND RECONCILIATION COMMISSION

However, the confession made on January 28, 1997, by five former police officers that they were responsible for deaths on September 12, 1977, added a painful chapter in the annals of those who were determined to go to any length to defend the laager. That these five police officers now asked for amnesty added a tragic twist to the saga of the defense of apartheid. The confessions came as a result of the action that Mandela took in naming Archbishop Desmond Tutu chairman of the Truth and Reconciliation Commission (TRC) to investigate abuses by the apartheid government in order to put the past behind and look to the future.

Writing for *The Christian Science Monitor* of January 30, 1997, Judith Matloff quoted Alex Beraine, vice chairman of the commission, giving the reason for the inquiry as saying, "Our investigative work, combined with the prospects of amnesty, has persuaded those who say they were involved in perpetrating the acts to come forward for the first time" in this national effort to heal the wounds caused by apartheid.[39] The commission made it clear that those who were willing to confess their part in the deaths would be granted amnesty, and those who did not confess would be charged of crimes against humanity.

On February 20, 1997, the author wrote a letter to Bishop Tutu to say:

The emphasis of the investigation should not be forgiveness. Rather, it must be to hold those responsible for those atrocities accountable for their action. If nothing happens to them other than forgiveness, it will perpetuate the pain the Africans have endured and those guilty of these gross offenses will die of laughing. Nothing is more harmful to the future of the country. Further, all levels of the guilty parties should be brought to justice from the lowest rank of the police force and the military to the president. The idea that only those on the front line are guilty can make a mockery of the investigation. It is virtually impossible for those who committed these crimes to do so without support from above.[40]

As a religious leader who was taught the principle that to err is human, to forgive is divine, Bishop Tutu and the commission did not fully understand the implications of focusing on forgiveness in the context of the situation in South Africa. He and members of the commission did not even understand that South Africa needed to hold its own Nuremberg trials in order to begin the real process of healing for the nation.

The line of defense taken by the 1,500 applicants rejected for amnesty is that they were merely following orders in a situation that they saw as a virtual state of war.[41] This was one tragic outcome of the policy of apartheid. The defense of following orders advanced by those accused of crimes against humanity is a familiar one. It was used by the Nazi defendants at the Nuremberg trials from 1945 to 1949 but to no avail. That argument was unacceptable, and it should have been unacceptable to South Africa as well.

Still elusive were applications from many senior cabinet members of Botha and de Klerk governments. Only former law and order minister Adriaan Vlok applied for amnesty. Vlok did this amid reports that General Pierre Steyn, former defense force chief of staff, had submitted a report to de Klerk recommending that some 60 officers, including senior military officials, be investigated for gross abuse of power, and that de Klerk's refusal to do anything about the report constituted a cover-up. But de Klerk denied the charge.[42] Could the national process of healing be initiated in a climate of seeking to preserve memories of apartheid?

On May 19, 1997, the author watched on television in Mutare, Zimbabwe, a parliamentary debate in Cape Town on the activities of the Truth and Reconciliation Commission. A Member of the Inkatha Freedom Party (IFP) severely criticized the TRC and its chair, saying that the

TRC had become an unconventional circus of horrors presided over by a weakly clown craving for the front-page spotlight and that Bishop Tutu was responsible for the failures of the TRC.[43] It would appear that those who were criticizing the commission and Tutu were trying to defend apartheid. Could the national process of healing be initiated in a climate of seeking to preserve memories of apartheid? On June 9, 1997, the author wrote another letter to Bishop Tutu to say:

I have just returned from a research trip to Africa, including southern Africa. On May 19, while I was watching on television a parliamentary debate on the activities of the Truth and Reconciliation Commission in my hotel room in Mutare, Zimbabwe, I was shocked to see a member of the IFP characterize you as "a clown craving for the front-page spotlight." It was sad for me to come to the conclusion that the IFP has been an instrument of Nationalist party policy. I could not have possibly imagined what the IFP would hope to gain by such an attack of a commission whose work is critical to the future of South Africa. I would suggest that the commission's work is so important that it should be expanded to include investigation of other atrocities committed by the Nationalist government in the past. The Sharpeville Massacre, the murder of Steve Biko and others,[44] the death of President Samora Machel, etc., are very important and need to be investigated and the facts put before the people. Unless these facts are fully known and disclosed, South Africa, like many other countries of Africa, will continue to languish in the mire of the past.[45]

Tutu's assistant, Laviana Browne, responded on July 11 to thank the author for his letter, saying "Your comments on the work of the Commission are greatly appreciated."[46]

DODGE PASSES THE BATON TO MUZOREWA IN ZIMBABWE

In discussing Dodge's work in Africa, one needs to understand that his relentless demand for fundamental change emanated from his conviction that the practice for Christianity demands that human beings treat each other as equals. Throughout his years of service in Africa he was motivated by the Christian concept of the brotherhood of man under the fatherhood of God as a religious tenet that sustains the essential elements of society.[47] This is why he argued that the concept of equality must be accepted as a fundamental principle of the development of society itself.

Dodge argued that no society can develop if any of its members remain undeveloped or underdeveloped. He also argued that for society to develop it must experience meaningful change, and he went on to add that change that takes the form of equality in the socioeconomic and political process brings happiness to all members of society. In this way,

Dodge saw human life as "moving from the lower level towards the higher forms"[48] of human interaction to construct and reconstruct society for the benefit all. This is why he concluded that any member of society who oppresses any of its members or denies them an equal opportunity for self-advancement effectively denies society itself an opportunity for its own advancement.

Basing his argument on many years of observation in Africa, Dodge came to believe that because man is the most important object of creation, he is both divine and a social being. He concluded that it is the function of the state to preserve the integrity of society by preserving the sacredness of every member of society.[49] This is why he concluded that because social conditions determine that sacredness, social change must of necessity aim at improving human conditions. From this perspective Dodge, like Huddleston, considered all people in society so important that he refused to accept any other definition of it.

This is the perspective from which he argued that social change determines the nature of human interaction. This is also the perspective from which he launched his crusade to improve the conditions that affected the life of Africans as a manifestation of their sacredness as human beings. This is also the perspective that the Rev. Larry Eisenburg, senior pastor at Old Mutare Methodist Center, accepted when he reacted to Dodge's deportation on July 24, 1964, by stating that Bishop Dodge had become a symbol of African hope and achievement. So many people were stunned by his deportation because this action was a cruel blow to the hopes and aspirations of Africans. Eisenburg concluded that the deportation was not a solution to a national problem because it would be about as easy to hold back the idea of African advancement as to stop the flow of Victoria Falls.[50]

One reaches the conclusion that Dodge made his greatest contribution to the development of Africans by his persistent effort to relate the improvement of human life to the improvement of conditions under which they lived—social, political, economic, and religious conditions. That the colonial government, especially the RF, refused to see things from this angle presented a serious problem that he faced as the leader of the Methodist Church. But unwillingness to accept the status quo is what enabled him to launch and sustain a crusade to change it.

Throughout this study we have furnished evidence to show that the definition of man and his place in society, as understood by religious leaders in Africa, was directly related to their conclusion that the character of the colonial society must be altered completely. The reason for this position was that social change that did not bring about change in the conditions of life of the people was detrimental to their development. Religious leaders did not think it possible to introduce meaningful social change along the lines of their definition without turning over the government to the Africans.

Both Dodge and Huddleston subscribed to this theory as part of their embracing theology of liberation. The Rev. Henry H. Kachidza, vice president of the Rhodesia Christian Conference, who was closely associated with Dodge, spoke for many when he recognized the importance that Dodge attached to this theology. In a letter dated August 1, 1964, addressed to R. W. Scott of the World Council of Churches based in Geneva, Kachidza said that Bishop Dodge was a man and leader who believed in handing over power to the African people, both in church and state, and that his was an idea which most whites found difficult to accept because they still thought that the color of a man's skin determined his place in society. Kachidza concluded that this was why Dodge rejected the attitude among many whites in Africa that suggested that an African was nothing more than a house boy or messenger.[51]

Dodge's positive view of Africans and his confidence in their ability were as clear as his opposition to the colonial government was total and uncompromising. His sensitivity to the fact that the Victorian missionaries sacrificed their blind support of the colonial governments to ensure their security was central to his efforts and was a major factor that influenced his action. He was constantly mindful of the fact that the close cooperation that existed between the colonial governments and the Victorian missionaries became a major instrument that reduced their influence in the life of Africans of the 20th century. He believed that Africans severely criticized the church. Dodge concluded that missionaries who felt the sting of criticism expressed about their work may think it unjust that their mistakes received more attention than did their achievements.[52] This serves as a clear reminder of the indiscretion of the Victorian missionaries which missionaries to 20th-century Africa must learn to avoid.

In arguing that "the close relationship which existed between the Church and the colonial government cannot be ignored,"[53] Dodge knew exactly what he was talking about, and was in fact recognizing the need for fundamental social change in both the thinking and the approach of the 20th-century church to the problems of Africa. To him there was no question that in addition to the colonization of Rhodesia itself as it was known, in 1890, the overthrow of King Lobengula in 1893, the promulgation of the infamous Orders in Council of 1894, the naming of the country "Southern Rhodesia" in 1895, the creation of a legislative council in 1989, all combined to create a set of new social conditions that made the white man an absolute oppressor.

Dodge also concluded that all this happened with the acquiescence of the Christian missionaries. This is why colonialism became stronger with the passage of time and the colonial oppression continued until that gov-

ernment was replaced by an African government in 1980, and Dodge
was there to see it all and to enjoy the fruits of his labor with satisfaction.
The change of government proved the correctness of what he was saying
all along, that meaningful social change can only occur when the government was in the hands of the Africans. Not only was the RF angered
by such a suggestion, it also could not tolerate it. But in its vindictive
action, the RF set in motion a process that finally led to its own demise.

As Dodge saw things, the obsession of the colonial government with
cheap labor as the only form of contribution the Africans were capable
of making, was a political strategy that forced it to design an education
that helped them produce it more abundantly. Nor could the colonial
government perceive the reality that the racist character of both its policy
and society would ultimately lead to a major racial conflict that would
cause its downfall. Dodge's argument that colonialism thrives on racism
helps to explain why the colonial government practiced it in ways that
were intended to make it more effective in sustaining the economic and
political interests of whites at the expense of those of Africans.

Indeed, it is now evident that the economic comfort of colonial entrepreneurs was coming from the educational misery of Africans. As long
as whites retained this form of political power, there was no significant
change likely to take place in the life of Africans. Dodge dedicated his
entire missionary service to seeking an end to this brutal status quo. But
he had no illusion of how difficult his task would be.

As a matter of strategy, Dodge concluded that it was meaningless to
advocate fundamental social change in Zimbabwe without first initiating
fundamental change within the Methodist Church itself. Two years after
he arrived in Zimbabwe, Dodge introduced such changes and began to
appoint Africans to top administrative positions in the church, such as
superintendents, principals of schools, supervisors, board members. This
is what led Kachidza to conclude that Dodge was dedicated to spending
his time and effort building up confidence in the African people.[54] There
is no doubt that in Dodge's mind the desire of the colonial government
to perpetuate the deprived condition of the Africans originated from its
perception and myth of their inferiority and the superiority of the white
man. This is the myth that he unhesitatingly rejected because he believed
strongly that people are what they are due to the nature of the environment in which they grow, and not to inherent inferior intellect.

In stating his belief that the ability of Africans to use the limited education available to them to arouse a nationalistic consciousness showed
the high level and quality of their intellect, Dodge was actually recognizing the positive attributes of the African culture that enabled them to
adjust to new conditions. Therefore, the conditions of their own social
salvation arose when the RF attempted to strengthen the Machiavellian

educational philosophy that the successive colonial administrations had put in place in various forms and had sustained over the years.

Tunisian philosopher Albert Memmi takes this line of conceptual thinking further to conclude that the rise of consciousness among the colonized and the attempt of their colonizers to perpetuate the colonial condition often combine to produce a new social environment for a confrontation between them. Confrontation often leads to an outright struggle, which often ends in the defeat of the colonizer and the victory of the colonized.[55] Dodge had no difficulty throwing the full weight of his influence behind the Africans because he believed that this was the only thing to do to end the oppression and misery to which colonial conditions subjected them.

Dodge's conclusion that it is in the best interest of the Christian Church itself to help in an effort to end colonialism appeared to be close to that of Albert Schweitzer, who served in Africa during the early part of the 20th century but whose values were characteristically Victorian. When he arrived to assume his missionary duties at Lambarene in present-day Gabon in 1913, Schweitzer at first appeared to believe that the white man's presence in Africa was a blessing. But toward the end of his life and career, he was forced to recognize his error of judgment and changed his view about the value of the presence of the white man in Africa. He wrote passionately,

Physical misery is everywhere in Africa. Are we justified in shutting our eyes and ignoring it? Who can describe the injustice and the cruelties that the black people of Africa have suffered at the hands of the Europeans? If a record could be complied, it would make a book containing pages which reader would have to turn over unread because their contents would be too horrible.[56]

Schweitzer sounded like he was talking to his fellow missionaries, not to the colonial governments, for allowing this to happen in their presence.

Unlike Schweitzer, Dodge did not experience the pain of transition of thought from one era to another and of a new Christian experience in Africa. This made his message consistently believable because it was consistent from the beginning of his missionary service to the end. Among the dangers that Dodge wanted to avoid, however, was the knowledge among Africans of the close cooperation that existed between the colonial government and the Victorian missionaries, not because he felt it would be detrimental to his own missionary endeavors, but because he thought it would have an adverse effect on the relationship between him and the Africans. Robert Mugabe, the first prime minister of independent Zimbabwe, put the harmful effect of Victorian missionaries into the context of conditions under which Africans lived, saying that Christian morality and its tenets of justice, brotherhood of man, the love of neighbors, and equality before God were not only ignored, but reversed; but African leaders recognized that Christianity acquiesced to the policies of successive colonial regimes that, contrary to its morality, impoverished the majority in favor of the minority.[57] While Dodge had no difficulty understanding this dimension of Victorian missionaries, some of his fellow missionaries did not comprehend its implications.

The reality of the fact that Dodge had always worked to promote the advent of an African government in all of southern Africa as a manifestation of his Christian witness is demonstrated by his being among the first people to send Mugabe a letter of congratulation on his victory in the elections held in April 1980 for an African government. Dodge was happy to share the joy of the reality of the dream that he had been working toward since he arrived in Zimbabwe in 1956. About Mugabe Dodge observed that the minister was making an excellent beginning and he was doing everything possible to allay the fears of the whites. A personal conversation with both Mugabe and his deputy indicated to Dodge that freedom of expression and thought would be allowed. Dodge said he had written to give Mugabe and his government his full support.[58]

When Henry Kachidza stated in his letter to R. W. Scott that Dodge spent his time and energy building up the confidence in the Africans, he was actually recognizing a quality that made Dodge a unique missionary and a rare religious leader. An examination of some correspondence that he had with various people shows evidence that Africans placed their total confidence in him and that in turn he placed his confidence in them. From this level of relationship emerged a reciprocal trust that was critically important to building an institution designed to serve human needs. Let us briefly discuss five specific examples to see how this mutual trust influenced the conduct of the Methodist Church and of Africans themselves.

The first example: On December 3, 1958, Dodge wrote a letter to Nathan Shamuyariria, who was associate editor of the African Newspapers, to advise him that Samuel Tsopotsa[59] had been appointed principal of Old Mutare Secondary School and Isaac Musamba was appointed superintendent of the Methodist Mutasa-Makoni District and the appointments were made with the knowledge and approval of the Department of African Education.

As an ardent nationalist, Shamuyarira was pleased and impressed with Dodge's effort to promote the advancement of Africans. As a result a warm relationship developed between the two men over the years. This is why in his newsletter of March 14, 1980, Dodge recorded his happiness that Mugabe's government included Nathan Shamuyarira, saying that the inclusion of people like Nathan Shamuyarira in the government was indeed encouraging.[60] He knew that Shamuyarira had an untarnished character he had been developing over the years and Dodge could speak with absolute confidence about that fact.

The second example: On April 18, 1959, Dodge wrote a letter to Lawrence Vambe, veteran African journalist then editor-in-chief of the African Newspapers, to congratulate him on his appointment as information officer in the federal government assigned to Rhodesia House in London. Dodge concluded his letter to Vambe by saying that he and other people in Zimbabwe were confident that he would represent well the total interest of the people of the Federation and wished to extend to him their support and wishes as he was assuming this important assignment.[61] Vambe responded on April 30 to thank him for his thoughtfulness and best wishes, stating that he was indeed encourged to know that he had the best wishes and blessing of people like Dodge and expressed his hope that he would be able to justify the confidence and the trust he was placing in him.[62] Needless to say, among the people who were profoundly disturbed by Dodge's deportation was Vambe. He had grown to respect and admire the strength of his personality and deep commitment to the advancement of the Africans. Throughout the time that he served in the federal government, Vambe remained one of the strongest admirers of Dodge. His own sense of duty, indeed, heavily reflected those of a Christian leader he deeply admired.

The third example: On September 25, 1964, Elisha Mutasa, a Methodist medical doctor Dodge assigned to Nyadiri Methodist Hospital, wrote a letter to the British government with copies to Harold Wilson, the leader of the British Labour Party, Joe Grimmond, the leader of the Liberal Party, Ian Smith, the RF prime minister who was obsessed with independence on his own terms, and to Dodge himself. In the letter Mutasa heavily criticized RF policies and concluded that the African people could not accept the constitution of 1961 because it guaranteed the rule of the country by a white minority government.[63] When Dodge responded on October 19 to offer his support and encouragement, Mutasa felt that he was fighting a worthy cause. When the letter dated October 2 from Harold Wilson and the one dated October 3 from Grimmond assured Mutasa and the Africans that the Labour Party and the Liberal Party would not grant independence to Rhodesia until there was an African government, an already bad situation rapidly deteriorated as Smith began to behave like a bull in a china shop.

Not only did Smith accuse Dodge of complicity in the Mutasa letter, he also arrested Mutasa himself and charged him with action against what Smith called national interests,[64] meaning, of course, RF political interests. But when the court found Mutasa innocent, the Africans throughout Zimbabwe knew exactly the extent of their oppression under the RF. Dodge's reputation and influence among the entire African population suddenly increased as they found him, unlike the Rev. Charles Helm during King Lobengula's struggle against the British in the 19th century, to be an honest and reliable ally in their struggle for self.

The fourth example: In 1965 Dodge appointed Abel Muzorewa, then senior pastor at Old Mutare Methodist Church, coordinator of youth work in an ecumenical effort to reach the young people and bring them into the church structure as part of his effort to think about the future leadership in both the country and the church. Enthusiastic about his new appointment, Muzorewa did everything possible to meet the demands of his position. On June 4 and 17 he wrote to Dodge to express, among other things, his frustration and disappointment over his experiences. Among these was the negative response he received from African political prisoners at Gonakudzingwa and WhaWha Restriction Areas.

Always positive and looking to the bright side of things in situations that are not encouraging, Dodge wrote to Muzorewa on June 23, 1965, to encourage him to continue as a Christian, knowing that full appreciation may come later.[65] When the people knew that Muzorewa had been appointed by Dodge and that he had his support, their attitude changed dramatically for the better. In 1968, when the Methodist Church was looking for someone to succeed Dodge as bishop, Muzorewa was their obvious choice. In 1971, when the Africans were looking for a political leader because all the African nationalists were in detention on orders by Ian Smith, Muzorewa was their obvious choice to play the important role in the birth of independent Zimbabwe in 1980.

The fifth example relates to a young member of the Methodist Church who was suffering under the RF policy of arbitrary arrest of its political foes. In 1964, Obert Mutezo, an ardent and faithful member of the Methodist Church and a dedicated nationalist who did everything to support both his family and his church, was arrested during the state of emergency that followed the banning of ZANU and ZAPU. Along with hundreds of other African political activists, Mutezo never lost his faith in both the Methodist Church and in the rightness of his involvement in the struggle to end the colonial conditions that had oppressed Africans for many years. However, in a state of despair and low spirits, he picked up enough courage to write to Dodge on May 25, 1967, to say that he wanted to thank the Methodist Church and Dodge for the support that he had received. Mutezo stressed the fact that he was a Methodist and was going to remain one for the rest of his life. He also told Dodge that he had enjoyed his work as a steward at Nyanyadzi Methodist Church and that it was an honor for him to represent his district as a delegate to the Annual Conference for several years before he was arrested.[66]

That this was one of the most touching letters Dodge ever received is demonstrated by the tone of his response dated June 28, 1967, saying that he was glad to hear from Mutezo. Dodge observed that undoubtedly

Mutezo had been unable to learn much during the weeks and months of detention. But even so, Dodge said he knew he would be very happy when that period was over.[67] Because Mutezo had discussed his family, Dodge knew that discussing the situation of his own family would comfort him in the knowledge that in life one experiences problems that one does not often anticipate. For Mutezo this was a reassurance that as a concerned fellow Methodist, Dodge was always ready to help and comfort those in need.[68] For Dodge to recognize the agony of a decent African in prison was a restatement of his conviction that the colonial government had to go.

These five examples lead to three conclusions about the effect of the relationships that Dodge had with Africans. The first conclusion is that he regarded his pastoral services far more important than administrator at a time of great national crisis. But to him administrative decisions were not as important as the pastoral service he extended to those who needed it. In spite of all this, this writer found no evidence to suggest that Dodge's administration suffered as a result. Even during the years he was in exile in Zambia, the church's board of finance and coordination functioned as efficiently under his direction outside Zimbabwe as it did during his presence. Dodge knew that the best way to touch and influence people was through personal relationships which the administrative process was not able to do. In each of these five examples one sees Dodge as a truly humble human being whose understanding of the problem of human existence was of a mundane character, real and basic, yet quite touching as it was effective. Nowhere did he write as a bishop of the Methodist Church, but as a friend and pastor ready and willing to help in any way he could. This is why he preferred to be known only as a simple pastor.[69]

The second conclusion is that Dodge's trust of the Africans and his confidence in their ability manifested themselves in the mutuality of respect between him and the people he was in Africa to serve. Without this mutuality of trust, the Methodist Church would not have been able to do what it did. A simple act of writing a letter to Nathan Shamuyarira, Lawrence Vambe, Elisha Mutasa, Obert Mutezo, Abel Muzorewa, Obediah Manjengwa, and others demonstrated the character of a Christian leader whose own sense of humanity furnished a sublime example of the sacredness of human life itself. His deep conviction that everything possible must be done to elevate sacredness to an even higher level as a manifestation of its greatness in all of creation was an operative principle underlying everything that he did. Is it really surprising that he had such a tremendous influence among Africans?

The third conclusion is that in the nature of the relationship that Dodge had with Africans, whether it was over an afternoon cup of tea, or a lavish dinner, those who came to know him readily recognized his humility and desire to know and love people and serve them to the best of his ability. With a possible exception of one case,[70] Dodge always took a positive view of the problem that the Africans were experiencing. His ability to encourage, to advise, and to counsel indeed made him a trustworthy friend in a time of need.

Of course one could say that he had no choice because as a pastor that is what he was expected to do as part of his official responsibility, because the conditions of the time demanded it in the same way conditions demanded Father Trevor Huddleston of South Africa in 1958 to condemn apartheid, leading to his deportation. This view is rejected in light of the fact that Father Arthur Lewis of Rusape had openly and strongly supported the RF racist policies and condemned the Africans for demanding equality in society. For Dodge, serving human needs was a sufficient reward in itself.[71]

The charge that Dodge gave Muzorewa on August 28, 1968, soon after he was elected bishop of the Methodist Church, proved to be more than a ceremonial occasion to officially recognize him as head of the Methodist Church. Muzorewa regarded his election as a mission and mandate to carry on the crusade started by a leader whose commitment to the transformation of Zimbabwe was unquestionable. Was he equal to the task? Isaac H. Bevins, assistant general secretary of the Global Ministries of the United Methodist Church based in New York, and who knew Muzorewa well, said of him and the book that Abel Muzorewa presented an anthology of true revolutionary African personality. The story of the struggle for an independent Zimbabwe had to be told now. It must be told by an African who had been intimately involved in the process.[72]

In accepting the baton from Dodge, Muzorewa knew that the race was on and the race must be won. His strength to run part of the race came from the recognition that the African people needed total liberation—liberation of the soul, mind, and body—that was a central target of theology of liberation. He knew that the entire gospel of the whole person had a dynamic message that, when accepted, would lead many from the land of Egypt of colonial conditions to the promised land of self-actualization and independence. Muzorewa, like Tutu, operated by a fundamental theological tenet so often enunciated by leaders with vision and foresight, especially in Africa, that any society must embrace non-racial principles to ensure its progress.

Events began to move rapidly, beginning with the crisis caused by the RF educational policy from 1968 to 1971, leading to the political crisis of Ian Smith and the British government in 1972 when Muzorewa was invited to chair the African National Council, and finally exploding when Muzorewa launched a major campaign to bring change to Zimbabwe when all other efforts failed.

Speaking in London in 1973, Muzorewa gave a clear picture of the situation Africans faced under the policy of the RF government to indicate his determination to change it. He said, "Whether I am in the best hotel of Oxford or London or New York or anywhere in the world, whether I sit on the desk of a graduate school, whether I have 5,000 pounds sterling in my bank, I feel a slave in the country of my birth."[73]

Muzorewa's role in the Geneva conference of 1976, the negotiations that he and Rev. Ndabaningi Sithole and Chief Jeremiah Chirau held with Ian Smith, and the elections that were held in March 1979 from which he emerged as winner and served for six months as interim prime minister, all testify to the degree that he was able to play his role well. When Britain finally worked out a permanent constitution in 1980, Muzorewa accepted the verdict of the people and let Robert Mugabe assume the office of prime minister on April 18, 1980. Muzorewa's role in the transformation of Zimbabwe was complete. He, like Tutu, returned full-time to his pastoral duties.

CONCLUSION

From the preceding discussion, it would seem that the development of politics in South Africa and Zimbabwe after the involvement of Desmond Tutu and Abel Muzorewa took two essential aspects into consideration. The first is the recognition of the vital importance of the individual. Self-awareness is an important principle that both Tutu and Muzorewa tried to develop as an essential tenet of national political development implies engaging in those activities that seek to promote individual advancement as a foundation upon which to build national advancement. Self-awareness demands the availability of equal opportunity for all people.

Without equality of opportunity, the individual cannot engage in self-fulfilling activity. This is the reality that Albert Memmi says enables the recently colonized in any country to assert themselves in relation to the definition of their needs.[74] This results in a political behavior that satisfies the individual and the nation.

The second aspect is that when the government recognizes the importance of individual self-determination, it responds by formulating policies that facilitate individual effort. Memmi concludes that this effort ultimately translates into national development.[75] The relationship that exists between educational development of the individual and fulfilling other needs constitutes an article of faith in developing nations, and has inspired the quest for a new society fully committed to a new political, social, and economic development.

This line of thinking is what Memmi takes into consideration to conclude that for the recently colonized "the important thing to do is to rebuild, to reform, to communicate, and to belong"[76] as a fulfillment of themselves. It is this definition of liberation, both political and mental, that gives birth to a new society, a true symbol and a manifestation of the search for a new social system.

Other considerations are important to take note of. Although Zimbabwe tried to become a one-party state in December 1987, the people opposed it so strongly that is was not implemented. This author is of the opinion that the introduction of this form of government is an action that all nations of Africa must avoid at all costs. As young nations struggling to find paths into the future, South Africa and Zimbabwe must be cautious and fervent in avoiding forms of government that entail political characteristics of the Nationalist Party in South Africa and the RF government in Zimbabwe. Checks and balances are an essential component of any nation that is struggling for advancement, including South Africa and Zimbabwe.

Without checks and balances, corruption and other irregularities by government officials go uncorrected and the citizens pay the ultimate price. In this regard South Africa and Zimbabwe have experienced the agony of oppression by governments that did not care for the conditions of their people. While President Robert Mugabe and President Nelson Mandela are sensitive about the importance of preserving democratic governments that they have helped to develop under difficulty conditions, some members of their administrations may not be able to demonstrate such sensitivity. For example, in 1989 Zimbabwe was rocked by a major scandal that raised questions about the future. Realizing the political damage the scandal had inflicted on his ability to discharge his responsibility to the country as a senior government official, and as one of the six government officials implicated in corruption, Maurice Nyagumbo—veteran politician, dedicated nationalist, and close associate of President Mugabe—took his own life to spare his family further embarrassment and national disgrace.

Mugabe himself was deeply saddened by both the extent of the damage the scandal had done to the country and by the death of a man who had done so much for his people during the struggle for independence. But this national tragedy did not diminish the resolve of the people to resist the introduction of a one-party system of government. On the contrary, it intensified it.

This was not all. When, on August 4, 1989, Minister of Education and Culture Dzingai Mutumbuka, was fined $105,000 for his role in the corruption, events moved much closer to a major national crisis.[77] At that point, a new wave of political tension emerged from an unlikely place, the University of Zimbabwe itself. In August 1989, professors issued a statement criticizing the government for taking action that they said constituted a set of conditions that were calculated to make "it impossible for the institution to discharge its proper constitutional responsibilities and functions as a university."[78]

The arrest and detention of law professor Kempton Makamure appeared to be a culmination of incidents that the faculty members believed constituted harassment by the government, because of their opposition to what was widely reported to be government corruption and degenerating political and economic conditions. That these developments were a sequel to the demonstrations that were staged by students at the university in September 1987 against reports of continued corruption by some government officials suggests the critical nature of the crisis. When the students called for academic freedom and their inalienable rights and demanded that the university administration lift its tacit ban on the student magazine, *Focus*,[79] relations between the university and the government became more seriously strained, even though, by provisions of the national constitution, the national president is also the chancellor of the university.[80]

The conclusion that in 1989 the national political climate in Zimbabwe was deteriorating rapidly is substantiated by a series of events that took place in quick succession. Displeased with the efforts the government was making to restore the confidence of the public, students at the university engaged in a variety of activities that the government concluded hovered on defiance of the law. On August 9 senior government minister Joshua Nkomo and Minister of Education and Culture Faye Chung,[81] went to the university in an effort to defuse the situation. They held a meeting with the students and tried to establish a climate of dialogue. In an impassioned and emotional appeal, Nkomo pleaded with the students, saying that the government did not want a confrontation with students because government leaders were sensitive to the need to preserve a heritage for the future.[82]

A few weeks later the government granted Zimbabwe Unity Movement (ZUM) permission to hold political meetings throughout the country, easing the political tension that was disrupting national programs and sending a clear message that the government must abandon the idea of a one-party state. For a period of time in 1989, the entire country was held in suspense over what the future held politically. The elections held on March 24, 1990, show that the intent of the government to turn the country into a one-party state was not shared by many people. Not only did seven political parties contest the elections, but throughout the country various forms of violence were reported, related to the question of a one-party state.

In a statement issued on the day of the elections, the Catholic Church's Justice and Peace Commission criticized the government's intention to install a one-party system against the wishes of the people, saying that the use of firearms against political opponents was a shocking development. By June, the increasing demands on teachers combined with rapidly rising enrollments, inadequate salaries, and declining conditions of service forced teachers to go on strike, threatening to derail the course of national development that Zimbabwe had charted at the inception of independence.

In 1992 Zimbabwe was facing serious problems in its development. The Zimbabwean dollar had declined to such a low level that, combined with the worst drought since 1896, the economy had been destroyed, putting thousands out of employment and posing serious political implications for the country. These were problems that Zimbabwe never anticipated in the aftermath of the collapse of the RF. But they were created by the government's wish to institute a one-party system which often has a potential for abuse.

Yes, President Mugabe and his government are extremely sensitive to the need to protect the rights of all people. But a future government may not be so sensitive and the precedent that might be established would not serve the needs of the country well. That Mandela has not encountered these problems is the fact that he has not attempted to introduce a one-party system of government. It is hoped that he will not try to do so in the future.

These unfortunate developments do not indicate that democracy is in danger in Zimbabwe; they merely stress the importance of protecting it at all cost. This is what President Mugabe has done. To guard against the possibility of a new social malaise, nations of Africa in general must remember that in such a political ideology as one-party state or president for life, new forms of colonialism may emerge to impose new conditions of oppression, perhaps worse than those the Africans endured under European colonial governments.

This author rejects unreservedly the arguments advanced by many African national leaders that democracy is too costly and is divisive. On the contrary, the practice of democracy ensures that all people express their political views freely. In his study, *Tomorrow Is Another Country: The Inside Story of South Africa's Road to Change*, Allister Sparks, the author of *The Mind of South Africa*,[83] and a South African, concludes that the transformation of South Africa from a minority rule to majority government represents the dawn of a new millennium, a new country with new horizons and divisions.

There will be enormous new challenges, too, but the democratic structures are there to resolve and grow through them. For the graffito says building a new nation is a continuous process. The construction never ends."[84]

That is the ultimate manifestation of national liberation that the combination of education and democracy in any country makes possible. Both

Tutu and Muzorewa struggle to make this a reality of national life in South Africa and Zimbabwe.

IMPLICATIONS

This study suggests three implications about the relationship that exists between the role of the individual development and political development in South Africa and Zimbabwe. The first implication is that the primary intent of both countries must be to ensure the development of the individual in a larger social context. The development of the individual means self-actualization. This includes self-sufficiency, security in one's personhood, and fulfillment of those goals that are unique to the individual. It means the promotion of one's interests consistent with one's talent. It means freedom to set goals and objectives and to establish priorities. It means ability to generate an environment that gives one freedom of choice to pursue study programs of one's interests. It is only when one's educational needs have become fulfilled that one plays a role in helping one's society fulfill its needs.[85] This is how the elements of national development are put in place. The underlying principle in the relationship between these elements is that there must be successful educational innovation to make it possible. This suggests the conclusion that the end of the colonial laager has presented the Africans a new opportunity which they must utilize to ensure their development.

The second implication is that a truly politically independent nation can only arise from a truly independent population. A truly independent population can only emerge from educated individuals. Many nations of Africa, including southern Africa, have yet to realize this truth. Without an educated population, nations will always be oppressed by a combination of forces such as social ills, racial bigotry, tribal or ethnic conflict, and political dissent, all of which southern Africa has experienced. One reaches the conclusion, therefore, that educational innovation is in the best interest of the nations themselves.

The important thing for South Africa and Zimbabwe to keep in mind is that educational development is an important condition of political development. The two cannot be separated. About this important principle in the relationship between the two, Paulo Freire concludes that "ability to communicate ideas of self-consciousness"[86] forms an essential part of an education designed to ensure self-fulfillment as an important step toward creating an environment of national development. This means that cooperative efforts must constitute a viable channel to successful development.

The third implication is that the greatest threat to national development comes from the desire of some governments to institute one-party systems. The possibility of a one-party system has existed in Zimbabwe for quite some time since 1980. Government leaders seem to neglect the fact that in Africa the philosophy of one-party government has shown evidence to prove that it robs the people of a genuine desire to promote ideas of individuality as a condition of national development, and replaces their confidence for the future with an abyss of despair.

What has been discussed about Zimbabwe substantiates the accuracy of this conclusion. In this kind of social and political setting, the educational process has only peripheral meaning because individual incentive and self-motivation, which are important characteristics of human achievement, are rendered meaningless by the government's desire to have its own philosophy and policy prevail at the expense of the goals and objectives of the individual. Since he assumed the office of president on May 9, 1994, Nelson Mandela has maintained the importance of a multiparty democracy. The difference between South Africa and Zimbabwe is the attitude of the people.

In South Africa the introduction of a one-party state is an affront to human freedom and dignity and must be avoided at all costs. While the Nationalist Party ruled South Africa supreme for nearly half a century, both the educational process and human interactions suffered a severe setback. The maintenance of democracy is too important to be tampered with because the survival of any nation and the course of national development depend on it. No matter how government officials see it, a one-party system of government is nothing less than a form of dictatorship.

This is why, for example, massive demonstrations staged against the government of Kenneth Kaunda in Zambia led to an attempted military coup in June 1990. Once he took office in October 1964, Kaunda not only instituted a one-party rule, he also alienated Zambians by creating a political environment that denied them a role in the affairs of their country. That is exactly what Hastings Banda did in Malawi from 1964 to 1994. In 1994 both Kaunda and Banda were voted out of office as a result of being forced to accept the principle of free elections. Both men stood condemned by both their own people and the international community. They left office in disgrace, instead of as national heroes who tried to serve their respective countries.

In August 1989 a leading African educator in Zimbabwe, Edward Mazaiwana, expressed some views that are important to the development of African countries in general. He suggested that initiative for national development is undertaken from the perspective of recognizing the needs of the people. He expressed his view that expansion in education is meaningless unless it is anchored in democratic principles. He added that problems of economic development, transport, and population increase must be approached from the perspective of recognizing the fact that whatever is done must be done in seeking to meet the needs of the people. He concluded that this is how national development can take place.[87] National leaders of any country in Africa must reject defending practices of the colonial systems in the same way the colonial governments themselves did. South Africa and Zimbabwe, be well advised and be wise!

NOTES

1. Trevor Huddleston, *Naught for Your Comfort* (New York: Doubleday, 1956), p. 247.

2. Ibid., p. 247.

3. Ibid., p. 249.

4. Ibid., p. 248.

5. Ibid., p. 249.

6. Ibid., p. 7.

7. David Welsh, "Four Men on the Bridge," in *The Watershed Years* (Johannesburg: Creed Press, 1991), p. 64.

8. Ibid., p. 65.

9. Anti-Apartheid Movement, *Trevor Huddleston, CR: 80th Birthday Tribute* (London: Anti-Apartheid Movement), June 14, 1994.

10. Desmond Tutu, "Deeper into God: The Spirituality of the Struggle," in James Wallis and Joyce Holleyday (eds.), *Crucible of Fire: The Church Confronts Apartheid* (Maryknoll, NY: Orbis Books), 1989, p. 63.

11. Ibid., p. 140.

12. Ibid., p. 142.

13. Ibid., p. 145.

14. Mandela was born on July 18, 1918. This means that when he made the statement on February 11, 1990, he was 71 years old. For details of this fascinating man, see his autobiography, *Long Walk to Freedom: The Autobiography of Nelson Mandela* (Boston: Little, Brown, 1994).

15. Nelson Mandela, Address to the People, who came to greet him on his release from prison on February 11, 1990.

16. Ibid.

17. Nationalist Party and the ANC, in a communiqué issued at the end of the first session of negotiations between the Nationalist government and the ANC, May 4, 1990.

18. The leader of the Black Consciousness Movement who was murdered in 1977 by the South African police.

19. Scott MacLeod, "South Africa: Extremes in Black and Whites", *Time* (March 9, 1992), p. 38.

20. Ibid., p. 39.

21. Alan Pizzey, Reporting for CBS from Johannesburg (March 13, 1992).

22. Alan Pizzey, "South Africa: Day of Decision" CBS broadcast (March 18, 1992).

23. Ibid.

24. Bruce W. Nolan, "South Africa Says Yes," *Time* (March 30, 1992), p. 34.

25. Allister Sparks, South African journalist, during an interview with Ted Koppel, on ABC's *Nightline* (March 18, 1992).

26. Ibid.

27. Ibid.

28. ABC-TV, "South Africa," during *The Evening News* (April 11, 1992).

29. Ibid.

30. Ibid.

31. Alan Pizzey, reporting from South Africa for the CBS-TV News Service (June 12, 1992).

32. *Time* (July 6, 1992), p. 19.

33. *Time* (September 21, 1992), p. 16.

34. *New York Times* (December 12, 1980), p. 11.

35. *Time* (February 21, 1994), p. 35.

36. Nelson Mandela, address to South Africa, May 2, 1994, following the ANC's victory in the elections held April 26–28, 1994, as reported by CNN.

37. Ibid.

38. Nelson Mandela, Inaugural Address, Cape Town, May 9, 1994.

39. Judith Matloff, "In South Africa, to Forgive Is to Find Out," in *The Christian Science Monitor* (January 30, 1997), p. 1.

40. Dickson A. Mungazi, Letter to Desmond Tutu, Chair, Truth and Reconciliation Commission, Pretoria, February 20, 1997.

41. In 1996 Tutu criticized Mandela for what he characterized as moral indiscretion for having a relation with the widow of Somora Machel, president of Mozambique who was killed in a plane crash in 1986. On July 18, 1998, during Mandela's 80th birthday celebration, Tutu said he was happy to see two lonely people come together to formalize their love for each other.

42. In the postapartheid era, it was not easy for anyone to admit anything. The tendency was to deny it to protect oneself. De Klerk was no exception.

43. South Africa Broadcasting Corporation, "Parliamentary Debate on Truth and Reconciliation Commission," May 18, 1997.

44. In his study, *South Africa Belongs to Us: A History of the ANC* (Harare: Zimbabwe Publishing House, 1988) p. 177, Francis Meli lists names of 76 Africans who died while in political detention in South Africa from 1963 to 1985. Certainly the causes of these deaths need investigation if South Africa hopes to put the past behind it.

45. The author, in a letter to Bishop Desmond Tutu regarding debate in the South African Parliament on Truth and Reconciliation Commission, June 9, 1997.

46. Laviana Browne, Assistant to Bishop Tutu, letter dated July 11, 1997 addressed to the author about the Truth and Reconciliation Commission.

47. R. Dodge, "The Church and Man," an unpublished essay, January 3, 1966, p. 2.

48. Ibid.

49. Ibid., p. 3.

50. Larry Eisenberg, an unpublished letter to the editor, *The Rhodesia Herald*, (July 24, 1964). The editor declined to publish the letter and to give reasons for his decision. This suggests that freedom of the press was curtailed in Zimbabwe during the time that the RF was at the height of its power.

51. H. Kachidza, a vice president of the Rhodesia Christian Conference, in a

letter dated August 1, 1964, addressed to R. W. Scott of the World Council of Churches in Geneva.

52. R. Dodge, *The Unpopular Missionary* (Westwood, NJ: Fleming H. Revell, 1964), p. 18.

53. Ibid., p. 19.

54. Kachidza, August 1, 1964.

55. Albert Memmi, *The Colonizer and the Colonized* (Boston: Beacon Press, 1965), p. 29.

56. A. Schweitzer, an excerpt in *The Christian Century*, October 8, 1969, p. 87.

57. R. Mugabe, Foreword to Canaan S. Banana, *Theology of Promise: The Dynamics of Self-reliance* (Harare: The College Press, 1982), p. vi.

58. R. Dodge, a newsletter, written from Harare, Zimbabwe, March 14, 1980. Dodge sent a copy of this newsletter, as well as many others that he wrote over the years, directly to this author.

59. From 1959 to 1962 Tsoposta served as headmaster, but it was not until 1963 that he was promoted to the position of principal. Within the structure of the Methodist schools, and certainly within that of other denominations, the position of principal was higher than that of headmaster.

60. R. Dodge, newsletter, March 14, 1980.

61. R. Dodge, in a letter dated April 18, 1959, addressed to Lawrence Vambe.

62. Lawrence Vambe, in a letter dated April 30, 1959, addressed to Dodge.

63. Elisha Mutasa, in a letter dated September 25, 1964, addressed to the British government.

64. There was absolutely nothing that Mutasa, Dodge, and others did that could be considered against "national interest."

65. R. Dodge, in a letter dated June 23, 1965, addressed to Abel Muzorewa.

66. Obert Mutezo, in a letter dated May 25, 1967, addressed to Dodge.

67. R. Dodge, in a letter dated June 28, 1967, addressed to Obert Mutezo.

68. When the writer was a student at Morningside College, Dodge came to visit the students. On one occasion during the flight to Sioux City, he made the acquaintance of Medgar Evers, the director of the Mississippi chapter of the NAACP, who was coming to Sioux City for an appearance at the local civic center. Dodge and Evers developed a tremendous respect for each other, and when he learned that Evers had been assassinated in an ambush one night in Jackson, Mississippi, Dodge was deeply shaken.

69. Ralph Dodge, Response to a questionnaire, May 20, 1986.

70. From among the Dodge papers that this writer examined, the exception is the correspondence that Dodge had between July 11, 1963, and December 13, 1965, with Chazireni Nkomo (no relation of Joshua Nkomo), who had been expelled from his business operation at Old Mutare because of allegations of improper business practices, forcing him to sustain a financial loss of $540.00. Nkomo accused Dodge of wrongful dismissal and threatened to sue him personally. Dodge responded on July 11, 1963, to say, "You should search your own conscience to see if you dealt fairly with your colleagues at Old Mutare and with your church." This response was uncharacteristic of Dodge's way of resolving issues. While Nkomo subsequently dropped the suit, the relationship between him and the Methodist Church remained seriously strained, posing other possible serious implications at a time of crisis. It is the opinion of the writer that

the misunderstanding between Dodge and Nkomo was a result of a breakdown in communication.

71. Dodge, Response to a Questionnaire.

72. Isaac H. Bevens, "Foreword," in Abel Muzorewa, *Rise Up and Walk: The Autobiography of Abel Tendekai Muzorewa* (Nashville: Abingdon Press, 1978), p. ii.

73. Abel T. Muzorewa, "The Role of the ANC," in E. S. Wilmer (ed.), *Zimbabwe Now* (London: Rex Collins, 1973), p. 116.

74. Memmi, *The Colonizer and the Colonized*, p. 138.

75. Ibid., p. 139.

76. Ibid., p. 135.

77. Zimbabwe, *The Herald* (August 4, 1989).

78. Zimbabwe, *Parade News Magazine* (August 1989), p. 44.

79. Ibid.

80. In his study, *Colonial Policy and Conflict in Zimbabwe: A Study of Cultures in Collision, 1890–1979* (New York: Crane Russak, 1992), this author discusses reasons why this practice must be changed.

81. Faye Chung became minister of education on August 4, 1989, when Dzingai Mutumbuka was forced to resign from his government position following his conviction on charges of corruption.

82. Zimbabwe, *The Herald* (August 11, 1989).

83. For a parallel study, see this author's *The Mind of Black Africa* (Westport, CT: Praeger Publishers, 1996).

84. Allister Sparks, *Tomorrow Is Another Country: The Inside Story of South Africa's Road to Change* (Chicago: University of Chicago Press, 1995), p. 239.

85. Dickson Mungazi, "Educational Innovation in Zimbabwe: Possibilities and Problems," in *The Journal of Negro Education*, Vol. 52, No. 2, 1985.

86. Paulo Freire, *Pedagogy of the Oppressed*, trans. M. B. Ramos (New York: Continuum, 1983), p. 62.

87. Edward Mazaiwana, interview with Dickson A. Mungazi, Harare, Zimbabwe, August 15, 1989.

Selected Bibliography

BOOKS

Anglin, Douglas (ed.). *Conflict and Change in Southern Africa: Papers from a Scandinavian Conference*. Washington, DC: University Press of America, 1978.

Austin, Reginald. *Racism and Apartheid in Southern Rhodesia*. Paris: UNESCO, 1975.

Banana, C. S. *Theology of Promise: The Dynamics of Self-reliance*. Harare: The College Press, 1982.

Barber, James. *Rhodesia: The Road to Rebellion*. London: Oxford University Press, 1967.

Bate, H. M. *Report from Rhodesia*. London: Melrose, 1953.

Berens, Denis, and Albert B. Planger (eds.). *A Concise Encyclopedia of Zimbabwe*. Gweru: Mambo Press, 1988.

Boesak, Allan. *Black and Reformed: Apartheid, Liberation, and the Calvinist Tradition*. Maryknoll, NY: Orbis, 1984.

Brooks, Edgar. *Native Education in South Africa*. Pretoria: Van Schaik, 1930.

Brownlee, Margaret. *The Lives and Work of South African Missionaries: A Bibliography*. Cape Town: The University of Cape Town, 1952.

Buis, Robert. *Religious Beliefs and White Prejudice*. Johannesburg: Raven Press, 1975.

Bull, Theodore. *Rhodesia Crisis of Color*. New York: Quadrangle Books, 1978.

Carter, Gwendolyn, and Patrick O'Meara. *Southern Africa: The Continuing Crisis*. Bloomington: Indiana University Press, 1978.

Cell, John W. *The Highest Stage of White Supremamcy: The Origins of Segregation in South Africa and the American South.* London: Cambgridge University Press, 1962.

Clark, Steve (ed.). *Nelson Mandela Speaks: Forging a Democratic Nonracial South Africa.* New York: Pathfinder, 1993.

Clements, Frank. *Rhodesia: A Study of the Deterioration of a White Society.* New York: Frederick Praeger, 1969.

Cory, Robert, and Dianna Mitchell (eds.). *African Nationalist Leaders in Rhodesia's Who's Who.* Bulawayo: Books of Rhodesia, 1977.

Cox, Courtland. *African Liberation.* New York: Black Education Press, 1972.

Curtin, Philip. *Africa South of the Sahara.* Morristown, NJ: Silver Burdett, 1970.

Davidson, Basil. *The Black Man's Burden: Africa and the Curse of the National State.* New York: Times Books, 1992.

Davidson, Basil. *Modern Africa: A Social and Political History.* London: Longman, 1994.

Davidson, Francis. *South Africa and Central Africa: A Record of Fifteen Years of Missionary Labors Among the Primitive Peoples.* Elgin, IL: Brethren Publishing House, 1915.

De Klerk, F.W. *Address to Parliament of the Republic of South Africa.* Pretoria: Government Printer, 1990.

Diffendorfer, Ralph (ed.). *The World Service of the Methodist Episcopal Church.* Chicago: Council of Board of Benevolences, 1928.

Dodge, Ralph E. *The Church and Politics.* Old Umtali: Rhodesia Mission Press, 1960.

Dodge, Ralph E. *The Revolutionary Bishop Who Saw God at Work in Africa: An Autobiography.* Pasadena, CA: William Carey Library, 1986.

Dodge, Ralph E. *The Unpopular Missionary.* Westwood, NJ: Fleming H. Revell, 1964.

Du Boulay, Shirley. *Tutu: Voice of the Voiceless.* Grand Rapids, MI: William Eerdmans Publishing Company, 1988.

Dubow, Saul. *Racial Segregation and the Origns of Apartheid in South Africa, 1919–36.* New York: St. Martin's Press, 1989.

Fraser, D. *The Future of Africa.* Westport, CT: Negro Universities Press, 1911.

Freire, Paulo. *Pedagogy of the Oppressed.* Trans. M. B. Ramos. New York: Continuum, 1983.

Gelfand, Michael. *Gubulawayo and Beyond: Letters and Journals of Early Missionaries to Zimbabwe, 1870–1887.* London: George Chapman, 1968.

Green, J. S. *Rhodes Goes North.* London: Bell and Sons, 1936.

Gross, Felix. *Rhodes of Africa.* New York: Frederick A. Praeger, 1957.

Grove, G. C. *The Planting of Christianity in Africa.* London: SPCK, 1959.

Grundy, Kenneth. *South Africa: Domestic Crisis and Global Challenge.* Boulder, CO: Westview Press, 1991.

Hapgood, David. *Africa in Today's World Focus.* Boston: Ginn and Company, 1971.

Harden, Blaine. *Africa: Dispatches from the Frigile Continent.* New York: W. W. Norton and Co., 1990.

Hargreaves, J. D. *Decolonization in Africa.* New York: Longman, 1988.

Hassauig, Schioldberg. *The Christian Missions and the British Expansion in Southern Rhodesia, 1888–1923.* Ann Arbor, MI: University of Michigan Microfilms, 1960.

Hendrikz, E. A. "Cross-Cultural Investigation of the Number Concepts and Level of Number Development in Five-Year-Old Urban Shona and European Children in Southern Rhodesia." Master's thesis, University of London, 1965.

Herbstein, Dennis. *White Man, We Want to Talk to You*. London: Oxford University Press, 1979.

Huddleston, Trevor. *Naught for Your Comfort*. New York: Doubleday, 1956.

Jaster, Robert. *The Defence of White Power: South African Foreign Policy under Pressure*. New York: St. Martin's Press, 1989.

Kachingwe, Sarah et al. *Sally Mugabe: A Woman with a Mission*. Harare: ZANU-PF Central Committee. 1994.

Kapenzi, Geoffrey. *The Clash of Cultures: Christian Missionaries and the Shona of Rhodesia*. Washington, DC: University Press of America, 1978.

Kaunda, Kenneth. *Zambia Shall be Free*. New York: Frederick Praeger, 1963.

Kevin, Thomas, and Gwendolen M. Carter (eds.) *From Protest to Challenge: A Documentary History of African Politics in South Africa, 1852–1964*. Stanford, CA: Stanford University Press, 1972.

Knorr, Kenneth. *British Colonial Theories*. Toronto: University of Toronto Press, 1974.

Kraemer, H. *The Christian Message to a Non-Christian World*. New York: Harper and Brothers, 1938.

La Guma, Alex (ed.). *Apartheid: A Collection of Writings on South Africa by South Africans*. New York: International Publishers, 1971.

Lardner-Burke, Desmond. *Rhodesia: The Story of Crisis*. London: Albourne, 1966.

Lovejoy, Paul (ed.). *African Modernization and Development*. Boulder, CO: Westview Press, 1991.

Lyons, Charles. *To Wash and Aethiop White: British Ideas About Black African Educability, 1530–1960*. New York: Teachers College Press, 1975.

Mandela, Nelson. *Long Walk to Freedom: The Autobiography of Nelson Mandela*. Boston: Little, Brown, 1994.

Marquard, Leo. *The People and Policies of South Africa*. London: Oxford University Press, 1969.

Martin, David, and Phyllis Johnson. *The Struggle for Zimbabwe*. Harare: Zimbabwe Publishing House, 1981.

Maxey, Kees. *The Fight for Zimbabwe: The Armed Struggle in Southern Rhodesia*. London: Rex Collins, 1975.

Meli, Francis. *South Africa Belongs to Us: The History of the ANC*. Harare: Zimbabwe Publishing House, 1988.

Memmi, Albert. *The Colonizer and the Colonized*. Boston: Beacon Press, 1965.

Mlambo, Eshmael. *Rhodesia: The Struggle for a Birthright*. London: Hurst and Company, 1972.

Mugomba, Agrippah, and Mougo Nyaggah. *Independence Without Freedom: The Political Economy of Colonial Education in Southern Africa*. Santa Barbara, CA: ABC—Clio, 1980.

Mungazi, Dickson A. *Colonial Education for Africans: George Stark's Policy in Zimbabwe*. New York: Praeger Publishers, 1991.

Mungazi, Dickson A. *Colonial Policy and Conflict in Zimbabwe: A Study of Cultures in Collision, 1890–1979*. New York: Crane Russak, 1992.

Mungazi, Dickson A. *The Cross Between Rhodesia and Zimbabwe: Racial Conflict in Zimbabwe, 1962–1979.* New York: Vantage Press, 1981.

Mungazi, Dickson A. *Education and Government Control in Zimbabwe: A Study of the Commissions of Inquiry, 1908–1974.* New York: Praeger Publishers, 1990.

Mungazi, Dickson A. *The Honored Crusade: Ralph E. Dodge's Theology of Liberation and Initiative for Social Change in Zimbabwe.* Gweru: Mambo Press, 1991.

Mungazi, Dickson A. *The Last British Liberals in Africa: Michael Blundell and Garfield Todd.* Westport, CT: Praeger Publishers, 1999.

Mungazi, Dickson A. *The Last Defenders of the Laager: Ian D. Smith and F. W. de Klerk.* Westport, CT: Praeger Publishers, 1998.

Mungazi, Dickson A. *The Mind of Black Africa.* Westport, CT: Praeger Publishers, 1996.

Mungazi, Dickson A. *The Struggle for Social Change in Southern Africa: Visions of Liberty.* New York: Crane Russak, 1989.

Mungazi, Dickson A. *To Honor the Sacred Trust of Civilization: History, Politics, and Education in Southern Africa.* Cambridge, MA: Schenkman, 1983.

Mungazi, Dickson A., and L. Kay Walker. *Educational Reform and the Transformation of Southern Africa.* Westport, CT: Praeger Publishers, 1997.

Muzorewa, Abel T. *Rise Up and Walk: The Autobiography of Abel Tendekai Muzorewa.* Nashville: Abingdon Press, 1978.

Muzorewa, Abel T. "The Role of the ANC," in E.T. Wilmer (ed). *Zimbabwe Now.* London: Rex Collins, 1973.

Naylor, W. S. *Daybreak in the Dark Continent.* New York: The Young Peoples' Missionary Movement, 1905.

O'Callaghan, Marion. *Rhodesia: The Effects of Apartheid on Culture and Education.* Paris: UNESCO, 1979.

Oldham, James. *White and Black in Africa.* New York: Green and Company, 1930.

Parker, Franklin. "Early Church-State Relationship in African Education in Rhodesia and Zambia." In *World Yearbook of Education, 1966.*

Paton, Alan. *Cry, the Beloved Country.* New York: Charles Scribner's Sons, 1948.

Paton, Alan. *The Land and People of South Africa.* New York: J. B. Lippincott, 1964.

Peck, A. J. *Rhodesia Accuses.* Boston: Western Islands Press, 1966.

Ranger, Terence. *The African Voice in Southern Rhodesia, 1898–1930.* Evanston, IL: Northwestern University Press, 1970.

Ranger, Terence. *Revolt in Southern Rhodesia, 1896–1897.* Evanston, IL: Northwestern University Press, 1967.

Rasmussen, R. Kent. *Historical Dictionary of Rhodesia/Zimbabwe.* London: Scarecrow Press, 1979.

Raynor, William. *Tribe and its Successors: An Account of African Traditional Life after European Settlement in Southern Rhodesia.* New York: Frederick Praeger, 1962.

Rea, Frederick. *Missionary Factor in Southern Rhodesia.* Salisbury: Historical Association of Rhodesia and Nyasaland, 1962.

Riddell, Roger. *From Rhodesia to Zimbabwe: Education for Employment.* Gweru: Mambo Press, 1980.

Rogers, C. A., and C. Franz. *Racial Themes in Southern Rhodesia: Attitudes of the White Population.* New Haven, CT: Yale University Press, 1967.

Rolin, Henri. *Les Los at l'Administration de la Rhodesie*. Brussels: l'Etablissment Emil Bruylant.

Samkange, Stanlake. *Origins of Rhodesia*. New York: Frederick Praeger, 1964.

Samkange, Stanlake. *What Rhodes Really Said About Africans*. Harare: Harare Publishing House, 1982.

Schweitzer, Albert. *Our Task in Colonial Africa*. New York: Harper Brothers, 1948.

Shamuyarira, Nathan. *Crisis in Rhodesia*. London: Deutsche, 1964.

Shelton, Kenneth. *Bishop in Smith's Rhodesia*. Gweru: Mambo Press, 1985.

Sparks, Allister. *The Mind of South Africa*. New York: Alfred A. Knopf, 1989.

Sparks, Allister. *Tomorrow Is Another Country: The Inside Story of South Africa's Road to Change*. Chicago: University of Chicago Press, 1995.

Sparrow, G. *The Rhodesian Rebellion*. London: Brighton, 1966.

Stack, Louise, and Donald Morton. *Torment to Triumph in Southern Africa*. New York: Friendship Press, 1976.

Todd, Judith. *The Right to Say No: Rhodesia 1972*. Harare: Longman, 1987.

Tutu, Desmond M. *Crying in the Wilderness: The Struggle for Justice in South Africa*. Grand Rapids, MI: William B. Eerdmans, 1982.

Tutu, Desmond M. *Hope and Suffering*. Grand Rapid, MI: William B. Eerdmans, 1984.

Tutu, Desmond M. *The Rainbow People of God*. New York: Bantam Books, 1995.

Tutu, Desmond M. Preface to Steve Biko, *I Write What I Like*. London: Boweidmer, 1996.

Tutu, Naomi. *The Words of Desmond Tutu*. New York: Newmarket Press, 1989.

Walker, L. Kay, and Dickson A. Mungazi. *Colonial Agriculture for Africans: Emory Alvord's Policy in Zimbabwe*. New York: Peter Lang Publishing, 1998.

Wallis, Jim, and Joyce Holleyday (eds). *Crucible of Fire: The Church Confronts Apartheid*. Maryknoll, NY: Orbis Books, 1989.

Welsh, David. "Four Men on the Bridge." In *The Watershed Years*. Johannesburg: Creed Press, 1991.

Williams, M. G. *Africa for Africans*. Grand Rapids, MI: William B. Eerdmans, 1969.

Willis, A. J. *An Introduction to the History of Central Africa*. London: Oxford University Press, 1964.

Wilmer, E. T. (ed.). *Zimbabwe Now*. London: Rex Collins, 1973.

World Almanac and Book of Facts. Mahwah, NJ: Funk and Wagnalls, 1996.

World Alamanac. *Current Biography Yearbook*. New York: Funk and Wagnalls, 1985.

MATERIALS BY RALPH E. DODGE

"The African Church Now and in the Future," an essay, August 1966.

A Brief Biographical Sketch: Ralph Edward Dodge, Eunice Elvira (nee Davis) Dodge, Ralph Edward Dodge, Jr., Lois Ann Dodge Stewart, Clifford Russell Dodge, Margaret Jean Dodge, February 1964.

"Christianity Falls Short in Southern Africa," an essay, August 1966.

"The Church in Africa," an episcopal address in *The Official Journal of the Methodist Church*. Old Mutare: Rhodesia Mission Press, 1963.

"The Church and Culture," an essay, January 1961.

"The Church and Freedom," an essay, 1963.
"The Church as the Giver of Abundant Life," an essay, May 1959.
"The Church and Law and Order," an essay, February 1964.
"The Church and Man," an essay, January 1966.
"The Church and Political Community," an essay, 1963.
"Churches and the Color Bar," *The Presbyterian Outlook*, Vol. 146, No. 9, March
    2, 1964.
Devotional Address delivered at the General Conference of the Methodist
    Church, Denver, April 29, 1960.
"Edwardo Chavambo Modlane (1920–1969): A Tribute to an African Nationalist,"
    October 1979.
Letter to William Harper, FR Minister of Internal Affairs, July 17, 1964.
Letter to Obert Mutezo, June 28, 1967; in reply to a letter from Mutezo to Dodge,
    May 25, 1967.
Letter to Abel Muzorewa, June 23, 1965.
Letter to Garfield Todd, March 19, 1959.
Letter to Lawrence Vambe, April 18, 1959; with reply from Vambe, April 30,
    1959.
"The Liberation of Southern Africa," an essay, December 1965.
A Newsletter addressed to Methodist missionaries, February 24, 1964.
Newsletter, March 14, 1980.
"On Being Declared Prohibited Immigrant," July 28, 1964.
"Our Christian Witness in Rhodesia Today," an essay, 1965.
"Our Ministry in a Changing World," an audiotape. Pitts Theological Library,
    Emory University, Atlanta, December 1965.
"O Zimbabwe, Zimbabwe," Farewell address delivered at Harare Methodist
    Church, July 31, 1964.
"A Political Community," an essay, May 1964.
Presidential Address: Southern Rhodesia Christian Conference, March 1964.
"A Program of Anthropological Research for Missionaries," dissertation, Hart-
    ford (CT) Seminary, 1944.
"Some Thoughts on Christian Action in Rhodesia Today," an essay, June 1965.
Statement on Deportation Order, July 19, 1964.

MATERIALS BY OTHER PEOPLE ABOUT DODGE

Dodge, Ralph E., Jr., Response to a questionnaire from the Author, June 15, 1986.
Mungazi, Dickson A. An Introduction of Bishop Dodge to St. Paul United Meth-
    odist Church, Lincoln, Nebraska, September 14, 1975.
Mutasa, Elisha, Medical Doctor, Nyadiri Methodist Hospital. Letter to the British
    government with copies to Sir Alex Douglas-Home, British Foreign and
    Commonwealth Secretary; Harold Wilson, leader of the British Labour
    party; Joe Grimmond, leader of the British Liberal Party; Ian Smith, Rho-
    desian Prime Minister; Edgar Whitehead, former Prime Minister of
    Rhodesia; British High Commissioner to Rhodesia, and to Dodge, October
    2, 1964.
Lawrence, Jesse, General Secretary of the British Methodist Church in Rhodesia.
    A statement on Bishop Dodge's deportation, July 17, 1964.

Shepard, D. E. Private Secretary to the Minister of Internal Affairs, Rhodesia, Letter to Mrs. E. Griffin, Methodist Official, About Bishop Dodge's Deportation, August 13, 1964.

GOVERNMENT DOCUMENTS IN ZIMBABWE

Annual Reports of the Director of Education in Zimbabwe

Various years, 1924–1957.

Parliamentary Debates (Rhodesia)

Various years, 1955–1983.

Reports of the Director of Native Education in Zimbabwe

Various years, 1926–1978.

Reports of Commissions of Inquiry in Zimbabwe

Commission of Inquiry into Native Education (F. L. Hadfield, chairman), 1927
Commission of Inquiry into White Education (Alexander Russell, Chairman), Ref. A/2/17, 1916.
Report of the Commission of Inquiry into African Primary Education (L. J. Lewis, Chairman), 1974.
Report of the Commission of Inquiry into Discontent in the Mangwende Reserve (James Brown, Chairman), 1961.
Report of the Commission on Higher Education in the Colonies (Justice Asquith, Chairman), the British Colonial Office, Ref. Cmd.6647, 1945.
Report of the Commission of Inquiry into Native Education (A. V. Judges, Chairman), 1962.
Report of the Land Commission (Morris Carter, Chairman), Ref. CSR/3/26, 1925.

OTHER GOVERNMENT DOCUMENTS AND MATERIALS

Chabala, R. M. (administrative secretary to President Nelson Mandela), letter to Dickson A. Mungazi, January 28, 1997.
Huggins Godfrey. *Education Policy in Southern Rhodesia: Notes on Certain Features* (Salisbury: Government Printer, 1939.)
Huggins, Godfrey. "Education in Southern Rhodesia: Notes on Certain Features," 1939. Zimbabwe National Archives.

Huggins, Godfrey. "Partnership in Building a Country," a political speech, December 21, 1950.

Rhodesia. *Report of the Commission of Inquiry into Racial Discrimination* (Vincent Quenet, Chairman), Ref. 27015/36050, April 23, 1976.

Rhodesia. *Education: An Act*, No. 8, 1979.

Smith, Ian D. "Rhodesia's Finest Hour: Unilateral Declaration of Independence," November 11, 1965. Zimbabwe National Archives.

South Africa: "President F. W. de Klerk: First Year in Office." Pretoria: Government Printer, 1990.

South Africa. *Official Yearbook*. Pretoria: Government Printer, 1981–1982.

South Africa: "The Birth of the New South Africa." Pretoria, Government Printer, 1990.

South Africa: "The National Economy of South Africa, 1989–90." Pretoria: Government Printer, 1990.

Southern Rhodesia. *Annual Reports of the Secretary for African Education, 1957–1979.*

Southern Rhodesia: *Legislative Debates*, 1923–1961.

Zimbabwe-Rhodesia. *Report of of the Constitutional Conference*, Ref. R2R3. London. Lancaster House, December 21, 1979.

Zimbabwe: "Not in a Thousand Years: From Rhodesia to Zimbabwe," a documentary film, PBS, 1981.

CHURCH PUBLICATIONS AND DOCUMENTS

Catholic Church. *The Land Tenure Act and the Church*. Gweru: Mambo Press, 1970.

Catholic Church. *Moto*. Gweru: Mambo Press, May 1983.

Catholic Church. *Pastoral Letter: Violence in Southern Africa*. London: S.C.M. Press, 1970.

Christian Century Foundation. *Christian Century*. October 8, 1969.

Christian Council of Rhodesia. "Agricultural Missions of Churches in Rhodesia and the Role of the Church in Rural Development." Mutare: Old Mutare, 1972.

Christian Council of Rhodesia. *Annual Reports*. Salisbury, 1969, 1970.

Christian Council of Rhodesia. "The Church and Human Relations: A Consultation." Old Mutare, August 1964.

Christian Council of Rhodesia. *The Church and Human Rights*. Annual Report, 1965.

Christian Council of Rhodesia. *Resolution to the Ministry of Education*, Salisbury, April, 28, 1970.

Christian Council of Rhodesia. "Response to Unilateral Declaration of Independence," November 26, 1965. Zimbabwe National Archives.

Conference of Missionary Society. "Violence in Southern Africa: A Christian Assessment." Harare: Conference of Missionary Society, October 28, 1970.

Executive Committee of the Methodist Church. "Statement on the Banning of Bishop Abel Muzorewa." Geneva, August 21, 1970.

Heads of Denominations. "Memorandum to the Ministry of African Education." Harare: Heads of Denominations Council, February 26, 1970.

Heads of Denominations. "Resolution on the Government Policy on African Education." Harare: Heads of Denominations Council, April 28, 1970.

Lamont, Donal. *An Open Letter to the Prime Minister.* Old Mutare: Old Mutare Methodist Archives, October 26, 1976.

Methodist Annual Conference. Resolution Warning Rhodesia Against Unilateral Declaration of Independence, press release May 17, 1964.

Methodist Church. *Official Journal of the Rhodesia Annual Conference.* Old Umtali: Rhodesia Mission Press, 1971.

Methodist Church. "Resolution Condemning the Government Policy of Five Percent Cut in Salary Grants for African Primary Teachers." Harare: The Methodist Church, June 13, 1970.

Methodist Church. "Resolution Warning the Government Against Unilateral Declaration of Independence." Murwewa: Methodist Annual Conference, May 1963.

Methodist Church. *Umbowo.* Old Mutare: Rhodesia Mission Press, 1963–1976.

Methodist Episcopal Church. *The Christian Advance,* Vol. 2, No. 1. New York: Methodist Church, 1918.

Methodist Episcopal Church of Rhodesia. *Official Journal of the Methodist Church.* Old Mutare: Rhodesia Mission Press, 1901–1976.

National Council of Churches. *Africa Is Here.* New York: Board of Foreign Missions, 1952.

United Methodist Church. *Southern Africa.* New York: Board of Global Ministries, 1986.

NEWSPAPERS AND MAGAZINES

African Daily News, The, January 16, 1961, February 20, 1964.

Bantu Mirror, The, February 19, 1947, July 20, 1948, March 3, 1949.

Christian Science Monitor, The, March 21, 1990.

Globe and Mail, Toronto, December 16, 1978.

Herald, The, July 10, 1989, August 4, 1989, August 11, 1989.

Journal of Social Change and Development in Southern Africa, The, No. 38/39. Harare, January 1996.

Lincoln Evening Journal, The, September 25, 1976, October 4, 1976, October 21, 1976, October 28, 1976, October 29, 1976, November 6, 1976, December 19, 1976, November 25, 1977, January 27, 1978, February 7, 1978, March 3, 1978, February 16, 1978, January 31, 1979, June 21, 1979, August 7, 1979, September 10, 1979, February 8, 1980.

London Observor, May 8, 1982.

Moto, July, 1963, September, 1963, April, 1964, December, 1965, September, 1966, February, 1967, May, 1983.

New York Times, October 13, 1989, December 12, 1980.

Newsweek, July 2, 1979.

Omaha World Herald, April 18, 1979.

Rhodesia Herald, The, August 24, 1902, September 7, 1917, November 12, 1965, April 5, 1967, November 12, 1968, August 15, 1970.

Washington Post, The, November 3, 1988, August 27, 1989.

Time, October 12, 1976, October 11, 1976, November 16, 1976, March 6, 1978, July
    7, 1979, August 13, 1979, March 30, 1992, July 6, 1992, September 21, 1980,
    February 21, 1994.
Times of London, October 12, 1976, November 6, 1976.

UNPUBLISHED MATERIALS

British Methodist Church. "The Waddilove Manifesto: The Education Policy of
    the Methodist Church." Waddilove, February 8–9, 1946 (Mimeographed).
Browne, Laviana, Assistant to Bishop Desmond Tutu. Letter to Dickson A. Mun-
    gazi about Truth and Reconciliation Commission, July 11, 1997.
Chimbadzwa, Josiah. "The Seed Is Planted," a tape Recording made by Rev. E.
    Sells, 1968. Old Mutare Methodist Archives.
Floyd, Jean. "A Kraal School in Uzumba Reserve," an essay on African Educa-
    tion. Old Mutare Methodist Archives, 1956 (mimeographed)
Harper, William. Letter dated July 22, 1964, addressed to Dodge.
Jowitt, Harold. "The Reconstruction of African Education." Unpublished Masters
    Thesis, The University of Cape Town, 1927. Zimbabwe National Archives.
Kachidza, Henry. Letter dated August 1, 1964, addressed to the World Council
    of Churches in Geneva.
Mandela, Nelson. Address to South Africa, May 2, 1994, following ANC's elec-
    tion victory April 26–28, 1994.
Mandela, Nelson Inaugural Address, Cape Town, May 9, 1994.
Mungazi, Dickson A. Interview with Abel T. Muzorewa, Harare, July 28, 1983.
Mungazi, Dickson A. Interview with Ian D. Smith, Harare, July 20, 1983.
Mungazi, Dickson A. Interview with Ndabaningi Sithole, Harare, July 20, 1983.
Mungazi, Dickson A. Letter to F. W. De Klerk on the effect of apartheid on
    Southern Africa, February 15, 1990.
Mungazi, Dickson A. Letters to Bishop Desmond Tutu, Chair, Truth and Rec-
    onciliation Commission, Pretoria, South Africa, February 20, 1997, June 9,
    1997.
Nkomo, Joshua. Letter dated July 18, 1964, addressed to Dodge.
Pizzey, Alan. "South Africa: Day of Decision," CBS broadcast, March 18, 1992.
Shephard, D. E. (private secretary to the Minister of Internal Affairs). Letter dated
    July 22, 1964, addressed to Dodge.
Rhodesia Socialist Party. "The Policy of the Rhodesia Socialist Party." Mutare,
    1970 (mimeographed).
Todd, Garfield. Telegram dated July 17, 1964, sent to Dodge.
Tutu, Desmond M. "Apartheid in South Africa," appearance on Phil Donahue
    Show. New York, January 7, 1986.
ZANU-PF. *The Election Manifesto of the ZANU-PF: A Statement of Goals and Prin-
    ciples*: Harare: ZANU-PF Office, 1979.

MATERIALS AND DOCUMENTS ON SOUTHERN
AFRICA IN GENERAL

Africa Action Committee. *Uhuru for Southern Africa.* Kinshasa, December 15, 1984.
Anad, Mohamed. *Apartheid: A Form of Slavery.* New York: United Nations, No.
    37/71, 1971.

Anglo-Rhodesian Relations: Proposals for a Settlement, Ref. Cmd/RR/46/71, November 25, 1971.

Anti-Apartheid Movement. *Trevor Huddleston CR: 80th Birthday Tribute*. London: Anti-Apartheid Movement, June 14, 1994.

Ayittey, George. "In Africa Independence Is a Far Cry from Freedom," *The Wall Street Journal*, March 28, 1990.

Davidson, Basil. *Africa: New Nations and Problems*, a documentary film. Arts and Entertainment Network, 1988.

Evans, M. *The Front-line State, South Africa and Southern African Security: Military Prospects and Perspectives*. Harare: University of Zimbabwe, 1989.

Gordimer, Nadine. *Gold and the Gun: Crisis in Mozambique and South Africa*, a documentary film. Arts and Entertainment, Network, 1990.

Lagon, David. "Results of the Crisis in Rhodesia," *The Globe and Mail* (Toronto), December 16, 1978, p. 1.

Landis, Elizabeth. "Apartheid and the Disabilities of Women in South Africa." New York: United Nations Unit on Apartheid, 1975.

Macmillan, Harold. "Commonwealth Independence and Interdependence." An address to the Joint Session of the South African Parliament, Cape Town, February 3, 1960.

Malianga, Morton (a spokesman for ZANU). "We Shall Wage an All Out War to Liberate Ourselves." Statement issued on April 30, 1966, following a battle between the colonial forces and the African nationalist guerrillas on April 29.

Mandela, Nelson. "A statement made in Cape Town soon after his release from Victor Verster Prison," SABC, February 11, 1990.

Mandela, Nelson. "Speech given in Soweto during a reception held in his honor," February 12, 1990.

Mazaiwana, Edward. Interview with Dickson A. Mungazi, Harare, Zimbabwe, August 15, 1989.

McHarg, James. "Influences Contributing to Education and Culture of Native People in Southern Rhodesia," dissertation, Duke University, 1962.

McNamara, Robert. "The Challenge of Sub-Sahara Africa," in John Crawford Lectures Washington, DC, November 1, 1985.

Morton, Donald. "Partners in Apartheid." New York: Center for Social Action, United Church of Christ, 1973.

Mungazi, Dickson A. "Educational Innovation in Zimbabwe: Possibilities and Problems," in *The Journal of Negro Education*, Vol. 52, No. 2. Washington DC: Howard University, 1985.

PBS. "Not in a Thousand Years: From Rhodesia to Zimbabwe," a documentary film, 1982.

"Prospects of a Settlement in Angola and Namibia," a statement by the Parties [Representatives of the United States, Angola, SWAPO, Cuba].

Rhodesia Front Government. *The Dynamic Expansion in African Education*, a policy statement. Ref. INF/NE/Acc.40/2710, April 20, 1966.

Riddell, Roger. *From Rhodesia to Zimbabwe: Alternatives to Poverty*. A position paper. Gweru: Mambo Press, 1978.

Rubin, Leslie. "Bantustan Policy: A Fantasy and a Fraud." New York: United Nations, Unit on Apartheid, Number 12/71, 1971.

Snitowsky, Michael. "Rhodesia Talks: Fiery Black Nationalists versus Hardcore

White Segregationists," *Lincoln* (NE) *Evening Journal*, October 27, 1976, p. 20.

Thompson Publications, *Parade*. Harare, August 1989.

TransAfrica. *Namibia: The Crisis in U.S. Policy Toward Southern Africa.* Washington, D.C., 1983.

United Nations. *A Crime Against Humanity: Questions and Answers on Apartheid.* New York, 1984.

United Nations. *Program of Action Against Apartheid.* New York, October 25, 1983.

World Bank. *Accelerate Development in Sub-Sahara Africa: An Agenda for Action.* Washington, DC: World Bank, 1983.

World Council of Churches. "Involvement in the Struggles Against Oppression in Southern Africa, 1966–1980."

ZANU. *Liberation Through Participation: Women in the Zimbabwean Revolution.* Harare: ZANU, 1981.

ZANU. *Zimbabwe: Election Manifesto,* 1979.

Zimbabwe Conference of Catholic Bishops. *Our Mission to Teach: A Pastoral Statement on Education.* Gweru: Mambo Press, 1987.

Index

About the Author

DICKSON A. MUNGAZI is Regents Professor of Education and History at Northern Arizona University. His numerous publications include *The Last British Liberals in Africa* (Praeger, 1999), *The Last Defenders of the Laager* (Praeger, 1998), *The Mind of Black Africa* (Praeger, 1996), and *Educational Policy and National Character* (Praeger, 1993).

CPSIA information can be obtained at www.ICGtesting.com
Printed in the USA
LVOW041107141211

259278LV00005B/3/P

9 780275 966805